CLASSICAL
GREEK AND ROMAN
DRAMA

THE
MAGILL
BIBLIOGRAPHIES

Other Magill Bibliographies:

The American Presidents—Norman S. Cohen
Black American Women Novelists—Craig Werner
Contemporary Latin American Fiction—Keith H. Brower
Masters of Mystery and Detective Fiction—J. Randolph Cox
Nineteenth Century American Poetry—Philip K. Jason
Restoration Drama—Thomas J. Taylor
Twentieth Century European Short Story—Charles E. May
The Victorian Novel—Laurence W. Mazzeno
Women's Issues—Laura Stempel Mumford

CLASSICAL GREEK AND ROMAN DRAMA

An Annotated Bibliography

ROBERT J. FORMAN
Professor of English
St. John's University

SALEM PRESS

Pasadena, California   Englewood Cliffs, New Jersey

Library of Congress Cataloging-in-Publication Data

Forman, Robert J.
  Classical Greek and Roman drama / Robert J.
  Forman.
      p.   cm. — (Magill bibliographies)
    ISBN 0-89356-659-4
    1. Classical drama—History and criticism—Bibli-
ography. 2. Classical   drama—bibliography.   I.
Title.   II. Series.
Z7018.D7F67   1989
[PA3024]
016.882 ' 01—dc20   89-10805
                                                    CIP

In Memory of My Mother

CONTENTS

CONTENTS

CONTENTS

EDITORIAL STAFF

ACKNOWLEDGMENTS

Not to thank the members of the St. John's University community who contributed to the production of this book would be a shoddy oversight. Dean Catherine J. Ruggieri of the university's St. Vincent's College was enthusiastic about this project from its inception and smoothed the way repeatedly toward its completion. Dr. Jack P. Franzetti, chair of the college's literature division, served as mentor, confidant, and friend to the writer. Mrs. Pat Sena, Mrs. Millie DiGregorio, and the admirable staff of the university's Word Processing Center treated the manuscript as carefully as if it were their own. Ellen C. Reinig, Jo-Ellen Lipman Boon, and their colleagues at Salem Press were, as in the past, valued editors.

INTRODUCTION
The Evolution of Classical Drama

Origins (c. 600 B.C.)

A major paradox of literary history is that classical drama, the noble genre that shaped the Western world's understanding of theater, itself had a modest beginning: the lyric dithyramb, a choral song of rustic origin sung at festivals in honor of Dionysus, the Greek fertility god who came to be associated with the wine grape. Dithyrambic choruses were unpretentious. Appropriate to the ecstatic worship of Dionysus, each ran the gamut of moods from intense joy to unremitting sorrow. The earliest dealt with one or another of the many legends that sprang up around this colorful deity.

By tradition, it was Arion (fl. c. 625 B.C.), a poet born in Methymna on Lesbos, who first shaped these rustic songs into the definite patterns of strophe and answering antistrophe during his residence at the court of Periander, tyrant of Corinth. Thus it was that Arion was credited as the inventor of the dithyrambic chorus, and legends grew up about him as well. The most famous describes his rescue by dolphins, charmed by his songs, from Corinthian sailors who had determined to kill him at sea for his possessions. The Augustan grammarian Gaius Iulius Hyginus tells the story in his *Liber Fabularum*, 94 (*Book of Fables*), and the Greek historian Herodotus (1.24) mentions that a bronze statue of a man riding a dolphin was erected by Arion atop Mount Taenarum in the southern Peloponnesus as thanksgiving for his safe return.

Legends notwithstanding, choreographed dithyrambs, with subject matter broadened to include other mythic themes, were regularly performed at Athens by mid-sixth century, at the Greater Dionysia in spring, and the Lenaea in early winter. Fifty persons, standing in a circle around an altar, danced from right to left as half the group sang the strophe, then from left to right as the other half answered with the antistrophe. The need for a leader to mark the rhythm became evident as the choreography became more intricate and stylized. Originally, it was his job to mark the metrical stress of the poetry as the chorus moved round the *orchestra* (the circular dancing floor). There was, additionally, some slight musical accompaniment, usually provided by one or two flutes and tambourines played by musicians stationed outside the dancing circle. Such audiences as there were looked down at the *orchestra* from surrounding hills and elevations; these rises provided a natural means of transmitting sound.

By the end of the sixth century, Lasos of Hermione (fl. c. 520 B.C.) a poet and musician resident at Athens under the Pisistratids, had introduced greater variety of rhythm and more complex instrumentation; he also originated prize competitions for the best dithyramb. Thespis, also an Athenian and a contemporary of Pisistratus, introduced the *hypocrites* (answerer), whose role was to answer the choral leader.

Contests would become the principal means of introducing new works and would increasingly become a means of display, for wealthy individuals vied for the most sumptuous outfitting of the separate choruses that performed the works entered in competition. Solo roles began to appear, primarily as a means of relieving the tedium of initiating verse and response. Unfortunately, this innovation also opened the way to bombast, for there is evidence that much inferior dithyrambic verse soon appeared and that it was produced with heavy emphasis on spectacle.

Fortunately, there were also excellent dithyrambists, and some of their work survives. These include Pindar (c. 522-c. 438 B.C.), whose dithyrambic verse is the largest in amount extant, as well as Simonides of Ceos (c. 556-c. 468 B.C.), best known for his epitaph to the Spartans who died at Thermopylae, and Bacchylides of Ceos (fl.c. 500 B.C.), the nephew of Simonides. Bacchylides wrote famous surviving dithyrambs on Theseus as well as numerous panegyric odes for Olympian victors.

Development of Greek Tragedy—Aeschylus (c. 525-456 B.C.)

Incredible as it may seem, tragic drama achieves its full development in the Greek world within the hundred years of the fifth century B.C. Several factors hastened its development, among them the increasing mediocrity of the dithyramb, which often degenerated into operatic pageants without real substance. Aeschylus, a young man at the turn of the century, knew at first hand the struggles of the Greek world against barbarian invasions. He fought the Persians at Marathon, Salamis, and Plataea, and the language of his plays, often overtly patriotic, may well reflect the feelings of a soldier who served gallantly.

It is clear that Athenians considered Aeschylus their patriot-playwright and that a basic conservatism, which harmonized with their own instincts, pervades his dramas. This conservatism appears most obviously in Athenian poetry, which retains the beauty and pathos of lyric even as it introduces a grandeur of thought and theme never reached by the dithyramb. The chorus retains an important role, but Aeschylus heightens dramatic effect through the *deuteragonistes* (second actor), who supplemented the *protagonistes* (first actor), first introduced in late dithyramb. This innovation portrayed dramatic conflict in immediate, visible terms; drama became a struggle of individuals representing larger ideas rather than two sections of a chorus, each part collectively arguing its position. Aeschylus also appears to have supervised every aspect of production, including the training of the chorus. Only Richard Wagner (1813-1883), the nineteenth century German composer of music dramas, appears to have been as committed to the fusion of poetry, music, and spectacle as Aeschylus.

Both Aeschylus and Wagner lived on the brink of startling innovations in the theater, but Aeschylus, unlike Wagner, changed conventions without becoming an iconoclast or the focus of his own *mythos*. In short, the subject matter of Aeschylus' plays complements the conservatism of the verse in which they were written. Right-minded law, harsh as it may be, repeatedly asserts itself over disordered passion.

This is as true in the *Suppliants* (the story of the Danaids), generally considered the oldest of the extant plays, as it is in the *Eumenides*, in which Orestes, murderer of his mother Clytemnestra, must obtain vindication from the ancient Athenian murder court of the Areopagus. Though only seven of as many as ninety of Aeschylus' tragedies remain, each of the seven asserts the primacy of law and provides an often severe, but by Greek tradition appropriate, correction to an intolerable condition.

Oddly, for Aeschylus appears to have had quite orthodox views on religion, these corrections originate from natural rightness rather than divine intervention. Persian conquerors, despite the overwhelming might that they possess, can never be at peace with the unlawfulness of their conquests and must inevitably lose (the *Persae*); the same holds true for insurrectionists—witness the fate of Polyneices (*Seven Against Thebes*). The will to withstand injustice is similarly limitless (*Prometheus Bound*), even when such ruthlessness stems from Zeus himself.

The *Oresteia*, the only surviving trilogy of Greek drama, illustrates this pattern in its cycle of plays. Clytemnestra and Aegisthus are no more secure in their illicit love for having murdered Agamemnon. The *Agamemnon* ends at this point, but the lovers know that Orestes will return, even as they try to convince themselves that he will not. Their own murder in the *Choephoroe* (*Libation Bearers*), the result of a conspiracy by Orestes and his sister Electra, is a necessary but extralegal response which spreads the miasma to the succeeding generation, an intolerable imbalance resolved only in the *Eumenides*.

That next to nothing is known of Aeschylus' personal life is one indication of the degree to which the themes of his works became identified with him, even in ancient times. He appears to have resided at Hiero's court at Syracuse, Sicily, about 470 B.C. Hiero gave similar patronage to Simonides and Pindar, and it is likely that the three poets were resident there simultaneously. It is wrong to trust the legend that Aeschylus was forced to make this journey because of expulsion from Athens for having profaned the Eleusinian Mysteries of Demeter. There is no evidence of this, and the very charge is at odds with what is known about Aeschylus. It is clear that Aeschylus died on Sicily, during a second visit made in 456 B.C.

Further Refinements in Greek Tragedy—Sophocles (c. 495-405 B.C.)

Even as Aeschylus was shaping tragic drama, his younger contemporary Sophocles was introducing his own innovations, and these were almost immediately favorably received by Greek audiences. Sophocles' first tetralogy was produced at the Greater Dionysia in 468 B.C. when he was only twenty-seven, and won the competition over Aeschylus' entry. This victory secured the younger playwright's place as reigning dramatist of Athens, and the fact that he had a greater inclination than Aeschylus to involve himself with the life of the city appears to have made Sophocles a more personally popular figure than his senior colleague.

More is known about Sophocles' life than about that of Aeschylus. Sophocles was born in Colonus, the deme of Attica a little more than a mile northwest of Athens, and came from an upper-middle-class family. His father, Sophilus, made his fortune in the manufacture of arms and armor and provided Sophocles with the best education available at the time. This included training in music, gymnastics, and dancing. Athenaeus (1.20 e-f) records that the fifteen-year-old Sophocles led a chorus of boys who sang the paean composed to celebrate the victory at Salamis, that he played the lyre accompaniment in the production of his own no longer extant *Thamyris*, and that he played the role of the Phaeacian princess Nausicaä in his lost play that name. He had an impressive military record as well, serving as general with Pericles in the expedition against Samos and again with Nicias during the Peloponnesian War. In 435 B.C., he was appointed chief manager of the allied treasury, which was stored on the Acropolis, and in 413 B.C. was on the commission that investigated the proposed oligarchic constitution.

These considerable involvements evidently did not limit Sophocles' activities in the theater. He wrote at least one hundred plays, though all but seven survive merely as fragments or titles. The seven complete extant works are the *Trachinae* (*Women of Trachis*, named for the chorus and treating the death of Heracles), the *Ajax*, the *Philoctetes*, the *Electra*, and the three plays dealing with the Oedipus legends but not written as a trilogy: *Oedipus Tyrannus*, *Oedipus at Colonus*, and *Antigone*. His plays won twenty first prizes in the Greater Dionysia and an even larger number of second prizes, indicating that Sophocles was the most popular of the tragedians in his own time.

Sophocles continued to refine the form developed by Aeschylus, first by adding a *tritagonistes* (third actor) to supplement the Aeschylean second actor. He also modified the role of the chorus, reducing its role in advancing plot even as he increased its numbers from twelve to fifteen. Sophocles also emphasized spectacle more than Aeschylus, providing more elaborate choral odes and costuming as well as rejecting the Aeschylean idea that each trilogy need present a single story. Each of Sophocles' plays presented a discrete action, and unity came from consistency of characterization within the work itself. These innovations irrevocably moved the tragic form beyond the dithyramb.

Internal elements also distinguish Sophocles' plays from those of Aeschylus. First of all, whether mythic royalty or heroes, Sophocles' characters always have a plausibility that makes them human. One can imagine an Antigone in real life, but it is considerably harder to envision an Aeschylean Prometheus. That Sophocles maintains Aeschylean loftiness and reverence for traditional religion, even as he introduces humanism, is a further tribute to his skill.

Innovation and Tragicomedy—Euripides (480-406 B.C.)

Euripides shattered nearly every convention of theater so carefully set by Aeschylus and Sophocles and did this even as Sophocles was at the height of his fame. His unconcern for tradition, or, more positively, his determination to introduce unconventional subject matter in equally eccentric ways, makes him an intriguing and vexing figure in theater history. He clearly provoked similar contradictory feelings among his contemporaries, reflected by the obvious delight

Aristophanes takes in impugning Euripides' maternal origins (as, for example, in *Thesmophoriazusae* 386, 455; *Acharnians* 478; *Knights* 17; and *Frogs* 840).

Whether or not of the lowest social class, there is undoubted patriotism in the etymology of Euripides' name, coined like a patronymic from "Euripus," scene of the first Greek victory over the Persian navy. It is also clear that he had the finest possible education; he was a student of Anaxagoras, Protagoras, and Prodicus. Prodicus was also the rhetorician who taught Pericles, so it is not surprising that Euripides' plays were often praised for their graceful diction. Euripides was a contemporary of Socrates, and some have concluded (dubiously) that Socrates actually contributed to his plays.

Like many Greek boys, Euripides loved athletics, but he turned early to drama and supposedly wrote his first play while still in his teens. His debut at twenty-five (455 B.C.) with a play called *Pleiades* was inauspicious and resulted in only a third prize. There is no way for the contemporary reader to judge how this poor showing reflects on the quality of this no longer extant play, though it is worth noting that Euripides' masterpiece, *Medea*, also was judged third when it first appeared in 431 B.C., while his equally excellent *Hippolytus* received first place in 428 B.C. It is entirely possible that by this later date the instinctively conservative Athenian audience had accustomed itself to the unconventional nature of Euripides' works. One can support this conjecture by the anecdote that appears in Plutarch's *Nicias* (29.4-5) on the disastrous naval expedition to Syracuse, Sicily, in 413 B.C. Tradition holds that Athenian captives were spared, treated well, and even released based on their ability to quote from Euripides' works. At any rate, Euripides' works were generally known and considered worthwhile enough to be remembered.

Euripides never visited Sicily, so far as is known, but it does appear that it was a combination of his unhappy personal life (indicated in his having divorced both his first and second wives, Melito and Choerile, for adultery) and the general disarray of civic life at Athens which caused him to accept residence at the court of Archelaos, King of Macedonia, soon after 408 B.C. It is certain that Euripides' enemies at Athens cited what amounts to the agnosticism of his plays to engineer a suit for impiety against him. Aristotle, in his *Rhetoric* 3.15, claims that this charge of irreligion was largely based on elements of the *Hippolytus*, while Aristophanes, in his *Wasps* 1045, notes Euripides' domestic problems.

It is known that Euripides wrote his strange and wonderful play the *Bacchae* while in exile in Macedonia. This final play is his parodic view of the worship of Dionysus, told through the myth of Pentheus' death at the hands of Dionysian maenads. Likely, Pentheus' *sparágmos* (tearing to pieces), combined with the myth of Actaeon, who was torn apart by his own hounds, gave currency to the story that Euripides himself was mortally wounded by a pack of wild dogs. Whatever the cause, Euripides did die while in Macedonia in 406 B.C., and Archelaos, well aware that Athens had treated Euripides less than kindly in his final years, refused to return the body for burial, sending it instead to Pella, a town in Macedonia on the river Lydias.

The Rise of Greek Comedy (c. 550 B.C.)

As tragedy evolves from the *trágus ode* (goat-song) of Dionysus, so comedy derives from the *kommoí* (laments), the ribald and bawdy poems that were also a part of the Dionysian festivals. Often its origins are localized at Megara, a small region between the Corinthian and Saronic gulfs, south of Boeotia and west-northwest of Attica. Epicharmus of Ceos (c. 540-c. 450 B.C.) supposedly transferred the form to Sicily and broadened its mythic subject matter to include contemporary personalities and situations drawn from real life. The same Thespis who is credited with creating the *hypocrites* of early tragedy is also said to have shaped rustic comedy to the more urbane taste of Attica, and in this task had the aid of his contemporaries Chionides and Magnes. Unfortunately, these three are merely important names in the history of theater, as nothing survives of their work. It was not until sometime after 480 B.C., when comedy was structured along the same narrative lines as tragedy, that it received equal recognition with this slightly older, complementary dramatic form.

The first works that one could call comic dramas were actually political parodies and were filled with every variety of personal abuse. These were the plays of Crates (fl. c. 449 B.C.) and Cratinus (519-422 B.C.); the wicked humor of these works made them instant popular successes and encouraged other comic playwrights to become even more outrageous. By mid-fifth century, then, what came to be called "Old Comedy" was born, filled with political allusions and peculiarly Athenian in its grotesque portrayal of actual personalities and events. Hyperbole is the essential ingredient of Old Comedy, and exaggerated views of controversial elements in Athenian life made these plays devastating political weapons, but the fall of Athenian democracy in 404 B.C. after the Peloponnesian War doomed this uninhibited form of comic drama. It became illegal after 416 B.C. to portray living persons onstage and, because of straitened finances, prohibitively expensive to outfit a chorus of twenty-five members. For a brief time, approximately 400-338 B.C., Greek comedy entered its "Middle Comedy" period, so called because it marks the phase after Aristophanes and before Menander.

No complete Middle Comedy plays survive, but it is known that they were considerably less political and less spectacular than those of Old Comedy. Writers of Middle Comedy faced the challenge of presenting drama that was socially meaningful while avoiding attacks on specific individuals. Apparently, they resolved this problem by writing burlesques that focused on types and general human foibles. They also parodied the Athenian obsession with philosophizing and tragic drama. If the ancient testimonies are correct, there were a great many Middle Comedy plays, and more than eight hundred of them survived to the second century A.D. It is questionable, though, whether Athenian audiences found them completely satisfying, for it was precisely during the period of Middle Comedy that the plays of Euripides achieved their greatest popular acceptance.

Middle Comedy first presented the character types that would receive their full development in New Comedy: wise slaves, foolish masters, courtesans, ardent lovers, and parasites. The major difference is that New Comedy moved away from social questions and recognizable settings to introduce stock plots and develop characterization. Fathers are well-intentioned but ridiculously stern; young lovers are hopelessly ardent in seemingly impossible love affairs; old men care more for their pots of gold than the few remaining years of their lives; sycophants and parasites mastermind incredible swindles. In every sense, New Comedy is "situation comedy." Its foremost practitioner is Menander, and its stock plots appear, often in conflated form, in the Latin adaptations of Plautus and Terence.

Consistent in all three periods of its development is comedy's general adherence to the form of tragic drama. The plays of Aristophanes (all examples of Old Comedy) best illustrate tragedy's division of dialogue as *prologos*, *episodion*, and *exodos* (prologue, episode, and exit, respectively, as marked by choral interludes) translated into comedic form. The choruses of Aristophanes' plays (for example, *Wasps*, *Birds*, *Frogs*) are often central elements. Comedy in all of its phases, however, is necessarily more loosely structured than tragedy, with greater reliance on language and less on plot. This change, as much as political and financial necessity, doomed the chorus in New Comedy, in which it either disappears completely or becomes vestigial.

Old Comedy — Aristophanes (444-388 B.C.)

One measure of Aristophanes' success as comic playwright is the ire that he seems to have aroused among the Athenian authorities. The demagogue Cleon, supposedly because he recognized the unflattering portrait of himself in *Knights* (424 B.C.), challenged Aristophanes' right to citizenship based on the dubious argument that Aristophanes' father Philippus, a native of either Rhodes or Egypt, was merely a resident alien of the city. *Knights* caused the kind of minor scandal in which Athenian audiences delighted. The whole affair gave the play and its author instant notoriety. The historian Thucydides (3.36.6) provides a portrait of Cleon's political machinations, corruption, and bravado that is as unflattering as that in *Knights*, though both Aristophanes and Thucydides were probably influenced as much by their own political prejudices as the undeniable corruption of their subject.

Socrates, on the other hand, accepted the parody of himself that appears in *Clouds* with good grace and amusement, supposedly rising from his place to bow before the audience when his comic persona appeared onstage. *Clouds* came to be Aristophanes' most celebrated play, though it won only a third prize when it first appeared; it satirized the Sophists, who taught the populace to think in a *phronisterion* (thinking-factory). That Socrates was not a Sophist (for he did not accept money to teach) was unimportant to Aristophanes. Socrates still represented to him the pernicious influence Sophist dialectic could have on a citizenry that was unprepared to use it judiciously, and Socrates clearly was the most recognizable of the teachers then practicing in Athens.

Other works of Aristophanes treat particularly sensitive contemporary issues. His early comedy *Acharnians* (425 B.C.) was written during the Peloponnesian War as a plea for peace with Sparta. An old farmer, Dicaeopolis, has made a private treaty with the Spartans while all the rest of Attica remains at war. He enjoys a private marketplace, in which only he may trade; others would like to join him, but they have been bound by their leaders to continue the war. The play begins with the chorus of Acharnians addressing the audience on behalf of the playwright, contending that he has Athens' best interests at heart. The deme of Acharnae, located to the north of Athens, had actually been keen supporters of the war, having provided three thousand hoplites (heavy-armed soldiers), more than ten percent of the whole allied infantry, so there is considerable irony in the play's setting. *Peace* (421 B.C.) continues the theme by describing an expedition to Olympus to rescue Peace from War, who has imprisoned her in a pit and has Zeus' blessing to do so.

Birds (414 B.C.) relates the grandiose plans of birds to build *Nephelococcygía* (Cloudcuckooland) midway between Olympus and earth to intercept communications from on high and gift-offerings to the gods from below. This story line is a brilliant thrust at the disastrous expedition to Sicily masterminded by Alcibiades in 415 B.C. *Lysistrata* (411 B.C.) presents a conspiracy of women, run with military efficiency, to withhold sex from men until they conclude a lasting peace, while the *Thesmophoriazusae* (c. 410 B.C.) describes another women's conspiracy, among those attending the Thesmophoria (a winter farm festival in honor of Demeter), to bring the tragedian Euripides to justice for his hatred of women. In *Ecclusiazusae* (*Assembly of Women*, 392 B.C.), women take both their husbands' clothes and their places in the *Ecclesía* (popular assembly) in order to propose abolition of wealth and class distinctions, as well as marriage and homes, and to begin a state with common ownership of land and state rearing of children. This is a parodic criticism of the theoretical state outlined in Plato's *Republic*.

Aristophanes' comedies also parody Athenian love of litigation. *Wasps* (422 B.C.) describes the incredibly complex judgment procedures of the Athenian courts, its chorus of wasps representing the massive juries Athenian trials required. Cleon appears peripherally through the names of the play's primary characters: Philocleon (love-Cleon) and his son Bdelycleon (despise-Cleon). All business and responsibilities forsaken, these ordinary citizens slave away for a juror's fee of three obels while ruthless power brokers hold the real reins of government. *Frogs* (405 B.C.), though later, is similar in that it presents a contest between the tragedians Aeschylus and Euripides, held in the Underworld, to determine the more excellent playwright. Euripides' death in 406 B.C. probably inspired this play, but classic tragedy was also dead, and this play metaphorically notes its demise.

Plutus (408 B.C.; revised, 388 B.C.) derives its title from the god Wealth, who is suddenly given his sight by Asclepius, god of medicine, so that he will not continue to grant prosperity to those who should not have it. The result is, essentially, that the gods are thrown out of work. There is no need for Hermes, god of merchants and thieves, and no need to petition Zeus for relief from distress. The world, by contrast, enjoys unparalleled happiness. Aristophanes rewrote *Plutus* without a chorus, reflecting changed production styles and the advent of Middle Comedy.

Aristophanes wrote at least forty plays, though only the eleven discussed above survive complete. There are fragments of twenty-six others and four additional fragmentary works attributed to him. Though he provides the only substantive examples of Greek Old Comedy, there is enough to imagine the devastating effects this variety of comic drama must have had in the hands of a master playwright.

New Comedy—Menander (c. 342-c. 291 B.C.)

The modern world can have only an incomplete appreciation of Menander's greatness. He wrote more than a hundred plays, but what remains is seventy-three titles and numerous, often sizable fragments. Clearly, Menander was a master of plot and characterization. The episodic nature of New Comedy allowed his plays to be excerpted for ancient school anthologies. Essentially, these collections form the body of Menander's works that exists today. These excerpts caused the original dismembering of Menander's works, and this dismemberment was completed by the Latin adaptations of Plautus and Terence. It has been the continuing task of Menander scholars to reconstruct elements of Menander's originals based on Plautus' and Terence's texts, though this task is often frustrated by *contaminatio* (contamination), the combining of several Greek plots into a single Latin comedy. The *Andria* of Terence, for example, combines Menander's *Andria* and *Perinthia*; Terence's *Eunuchus* derives from Menander's *Eunuchus* and *Kolax*.

It may well be that the aristocratic background of Menander predisposed him to the absurd situations of New Comedy, so dependent on their keen portraits of lower-class types. He was a friend of Epicurus and received a genteel education through support of his uncle Alexis. Menander's early death, by drowning in the Piraeus, ended a life otherwise without misfortune and a career absolutely without reversal.

Origins of Roman Drama (c. 300 B.C.)

Roman drama was founded upon the Greek, though it required a certain period for its gestation. What first appears in Italy, around 200 B.C., is extemporaneous poetry that has rustic origins similar to its counterpart in sixth century Greece. The Fescennine verses were rude and mocking pieces written as satires or recited extempore at local festivals, harvest celebrations, and even weddings. They were essentially popular amusements, in their later versions planned to appear unplanned. That they were usually bawdy can be inferred from the most often-cited etymology of their name: *fascinum* (phallus). Only snatches of this doggerel remain, through the citations of classical authors (for example, Catullus 61.126; Tibullus 2.1.55; Vergil, *Georgics* 2.385). Fescennine verse was soon broadened to include various subjects in a variety of meters (in contrast to the standard Saturnians or trochaics of the Fescennines), and so arose the *saturae* (singular, *satura*). These were not satires in the modern sense but "medleys," a number of themes loosely joined, snatches of prose mixed with an assortment of verse. Their etymology likely derives from the *satura lanx*—or fruit bowl—because of their varied elements.

Livius Andronicus (fl. c. 250 B.C.) first brought plot to the Roman stage around 240 B.C. Essentially his plays were translations of Greek originals, but Livius is important for his application of Latin, still in its infancy as a literary language, to the sophisticated Greek dramatic repertory. This move could not have been an easy task, but because Livius was born in Magna Graecia (the Greek-settled areas of southern Italy) and brought as a slave to Rome after the fall of Tarentum, he had perfect command of both tongues. Only fragments of Livius' work remain, but he apparently translated both comedies and tragedies. Livius was acclaimed in antiquity for his translation of Homer's *Odyssey* into Saturnian verse; he also treated the same subjects as the Greek tragedians, though he used no presently extant originals for his translations.

Livius' contemporary Gnaeus Naevius (c. 270-c. 199 B.C.) also produced epic poetry, writing his own account of the First Punic War, but his contribution to Roman drama is the introduction of the historical play, the *praetexta*, so called because its heroes wore the *toga praetexta* (purple-hemmed toga) of Roman magistrates. The *praetextae* were also imitations of Greek originals, but their costumes made them popular fare for Roman audiences. Naevius, as well as his successors Quintus Ennius (239-169 B.C.), Marcus Pacuvius (c. 220-c. 130 B.C.), and Lucius Accius (c. 170-c. 86 B.C.) all produced *praetextae* as well as tragedies. Of these, Ennius was the most prolific and the most versatile, writing as well a massive epic history of Rome, the *Annales* (*Annals*), a chronicle of events from Rome's founding to his own day. All tried, in varying degrees, to introduce Italianate elements into their plays, but there can be little doubt (even from the scant fragments which remain) that none produced plays comparable with those of the fifth century Greeks.

Masters of Roman Comedy—Plautus (254-184 B.C.) and Terence (c. 190-c. 159 B.C.)

Roman drama found its most fertile ground in New Comedy. Stock characters, contrived plots, and timeless situations provided the ingredients savored by audiences, and Rome was blessed in having two comic playwrights, Titus Maccius Plautus and Publius Terentius Afer, who fearlessly adapted Greek originals and freely conflated them when they chose, to create delightful complications of plot. The whim of history has left a legacy of ancient comedy precisely the opposite from that of tragedy: complete plays of Plautus and Terence against substantive fragments only of Menander and much less of the other playwrights from whom they borrowed.

Plautus and Terence are very different in their approaches to comedy. Terence, by contrast with his older contemporary, evidently preferred the more refined plays of Greek New Comedy as his sources. One result of this preference is that his plays show a Hellenism largely absent in Plautus. There is, correspondingly, relatively little allusion to Roman customs in Terence's works, and not one of the plays whose titles is extant bears a wholly Latin name. There is little attempt to reproduce dialect or differing social levels among the characters of Terence's plays and less of the outrageous punning, bawdy talk, or obscene innuendo that one finds in Plautus.

Twenty of Plautus' plays survive, only six of Terence, but it is clear that Terence saw his mission as purifying the language he inherited from Plautus, making it more in the tone of Menander's Greek, less like the farces of Rome's infant theater. All Plautus' and Terence's plays use Greek dress (*pallium*) as opposed to Roman costume. Terence's plays appealed to the literati, but they did not escape censure. The historian Suetonius reports that Julius Caesar referred to Terence as "dimidiate Menander" (a Menander cut in half), and Terence has often been accused of moralizing in his comedies. Still, both Plautus and Terence influenced a wide variety of successors. Saint Jerome sheepishly admits he slept with a copy of Terence's works under his pillow; the young Saint Augustine knew Plautus' and Terence's plays from performances at Carthage; William Shakespeare adapted Terence's *Adelphoe* (*Brothers*) for his *The Two Gentlemen of Verona*; and both Plautus and Terence have been praised by generations of writers as different as Petrarch and Montaigne.

Imperial Drama—Seneca (c. 4 B.C.-A.D. 65)

Despite Terence's attempts to sophisticate Roman drama, it always retained a certain rustic quality. Atella, an Oscan town in Campania (the region just south of Rome), produced a species of farce that survived as a half-literary, half-improvised form to the end of the first century A.D. Gaius Petronius Arbiter (first century A.D.), in his spoof of Neronian Rome, the *Satyricon* (53), has the grotesque, wealthy freedman Trimalchio proclaim that he allows only these *fabulae Atellanae* to be performed in his home. The remark implies a lack of good taste, equivalent to preferring a burlesque routine to a Shakespeare comedy.

Lucius Annaeus Seneca, son of a rhetorician and a Spanish provincial born at Corduba, emerges amid this continuing comic tradition, writing tragedies that are free adaptions of Greek plays. His works are filled with rhetorical flourishes, aphorisms, and brilliant declamations and were probably "closet dramas" intended for reading before small audiences rather than for stage performance. Central to each of his plays is some element of philosophizing, as one might expect from the fact that Seneca was primarily a philosopher. Indeed, Seneca's philosophic output was so considerable, even that part of it which remains extant, that for a time his tragedies were thought to have been written by some other playwright, though few contemporary critics hold this position.

Seneca occupied the not entirely enviable role of writer at the imperial courts of Gaius (Caligula), Claudius, and Nero. As one might expect, he suffered the usual rises and falls in imperial favor. Gaius, the most incontestably mad of the emperors, had plotted his death, but Seneca was spared because it was thought that Seneca's frail health would eliminate him naturally. Claudius liked him and made him tutor to the imperial family, but this situation ended when his involvement with Julia Livilla, daughter of Germanicus, aroused the ire of Messalina, Claudius' third wife.

Seneca was then exiled to Corsica, where he stayed eight years until Messalina's death. He subsequently became tutor of the eleven-year-old Nero. Seneca remained bound to Nero's caprices until that emperor accused him, in 65 A.D., of entering into conspiracy with Calpurnius Piso and ordered him to commit suicide. The historian Tacitus reports that Seneca obeyed Nero's order by opening his veins and ultimately hastening a slow death by inhaling the vapors of a stove. All the while, he discoursed with his friends on the happiness he would enjoy in his next life. Eight tragedies definitely by Seneca survive. A ninth play, *Octavia*, is a *praetexta*, and some critics believe that it was written by a different author.

The Focus and Use of This Bibliography

This volume, like the others in the Magill Bibliography series, is intended for high school students, college undergraduates, and general readers as a guide to reading and research. It aims at providing translations, commentaries, and criticism that are basic as well as accessible in most college and public libraries. For this reason, the emphasis remains throughout on book-length works that are introductory in character, rather than dissertations or more esoteric articles from scholarly journals. Where such items do appear, this writer has made a judgment that they are in some way appropriate; the annotations accompanying them always specify in what way or which parts are suitable.

The first section of the bibliography, "General Studies," provides an extensive annotated list of books and articles pertaining to the study of classical Greek and Roman drama. This general section is followed by individual annotated listings for nine playwrights, treated in alphabetical order. Each chapter includes entries under the headings "Recommended Translations and Commentaries" and "Recommended Criticism," followed by entries keyed to specific plays. There then follows a general criticism section. For the general play and dramatist headings, the best-known transliteration and/or its English title has been used. Within each annotation, the names and titles appear as they do in the source cited.

A peculiarity of book-length criticism in classical drama is that most introductory volumes treat the genre as a whole or groups of plays rather than individual works. One challenge in compiling this bibliography has been to make access to this welter of excellent material easy. For this reason, criticism appears cross-listed wherever possible both under the individual plays it treats and under the general entries that conclude each section. The sections themselves appear alphabetically by playwright, again with a view toward ease of use.

Many writers of introductory criticism arrange their material discursively, treating several plays at once and considering a playwright's entire output over the length of an entire volume. Since it is impossible to cross-list such scattered, even though excellent, discussions, these items appear with general entries, paired with annotations that explain as clearly as possible which plays they treat and what the author's thesis is. Such volumes often contain indexes of passages cited, and readers should refer to these when they have the volumes in hand. This bibliography contains a number of critical studies on each extant drama. Even if a given title should not appear in the individual listings, readers will find this criticism specified in the annotations of the general listings.

Those unable to read Greek or Latin should not hesitate to use those portions of the commentaries specified in the recommended translations and commentaries lists. The annotations always specify in what ways and to what degree this material is suitable for such readers. Similarly, since all the materials in this volume are obtainable, the age of a cited work should not deter readers from consulting it. Regardless of whatever else they may have been, the Victorians were often superb teachers, and they were also brilliant classicists.

It should be obvious, therefore, that this bibliography has a focus fundamentally different from those published for scholars and teachers. Citations to scholarly bibliographies appear under general criticism, but to reproduce their content here would create a huge but considerably less useful work for general readers.

General Studies

Adrados, Francisco R. *Festival, Comedy, and Tragedy: The Greek Origins of Theatre*. Translated by Christopher Holme. Leiden, Netherlands: E. J. Brill, 1975.
A handbook suitable for undergraduates that considers the origins of drama more in depth than comparable texts. It provides chapters on the elements and history of the theatrical genres, examines connections of theater and ritual, the major tragedians and comic playwrights, and ancient theater outside the Greek world but as influenced by Greek theater conventions.

Arnott, Peter D. *The Ancient Greek and Roman Theatre*. New York: Random House, 1971.
This general introduction to ancient theater provides a good survey of major areas such as Greek and Roman theater buildings, origins, actors, discussions of the major playwrights, though strongest on Euripides. Roughly half the book deals with aspects of the Roman theater (rare in an introductory text that also considers the Greek theater), and there is a welcome final chapter on entertainment of the later Roman world: mime, pantomime and dance, gladiatorial contests and beast hunts.

_____ . *Greek Scenic Conventions in the Fifth Century B.C.* Oxford, England: Clarendon Press, 1962.
An excellent complement to the Bieber and Pickard-Cambridge volumes cited below. Arnott concentrates on debated or open questions concerning the *scaenae* (all that which is on the stage, not just "settings"). He avoids matters on which general agreement exists, and those that do not materially affect

movement onstage or within the theatre. There are introductory chapters on the arena and platform and subsequent chapters on stage furnishings, stage scenery, rural theatre settings, and creating spectacle and illusion. Three intriguing appendices conclude the volume; these deal with staging the final scene of Aeschylus' *Prometheus Bound*, the suicide of Ajax, and portraying death on the stage.

Aylen, Leo. *The Greek Theater*. Rutherford, N.J.: Fairleigh Dickinson University Press, 1985.
Aylen writes this complete but nontechnical survey from the viewpoint of a theater director contemplating the production of a Greek play. The book assumes no previous background in classics and is likely to appeal equally to undergraduate students and readers interested in theater history. All Greek quotations are translated. The book begins with a brief examination of ancient theater logistics and how best use could be made of its space. A historical summary and discussion of the theater festivals follow in successive chapters. There are separate chapters on production (settings, actors, masks and costumes, and music), choral dance, fifth century drama, and the four major Greek playwrights, as well as basic discussions of Aeschylus' *Prometheus Bound*, Sophocles' *Antigone*, and Aristophanes' *Frogs*. There is a good chapter on the satyr play (the final play of a tetralogy), one on decline of the theater, and one on folk theater and mime. Appendices on chronology, a fragment of Euripides' *Orestes*, and women in the fifth century audience are especially useful.

_____ . *Greek Tragedy and the Modern World*. London: Methuen, 1964.
This study begins with the assumption that all literature in some way mirrors the period in which it was written. Classical drama, however, though it deals with highly particularized situations, has a timeless appeal no less strong in the modern than in the ancient world. Its strength arises primarily through its timeless themes of human weakness and nobility. Aylen examines these elements in the context of discussions designed for general readers.

Bacon, Helen H. *Barbarians in Greek Tragedy*. New Haven, Conn.: Yale University Press, 1961.
Bacon focuses on the historical aversion Greeks felt for non-Greeks and on the term *barbaroi* (literally, "barbarians"), which described all non-Greeks, though not necessarily pejoratively. She uses illustrations from tragic drama, which best reflects popular taste, to describe how foreigners appear in dramatized myth and to analyze what the reactions of the Greek characters are to them. See the parallel study by Timothy Long, *Barbarians in Greek Comedy*, cited with general entries on Menander, below.

Bain, David. *Actors and Audience: A Study of Asides and Related Conventions in Greek Drama.* Oxford Classical and Philosophical Monographs. Oxford, England: Oxford University Press, 1977.

Bain argues that the value of asides in both tragic and comic drama is their ability to involve members of the audience intimately with the action of the play. This technique, as well as monologues, can also clarify motivation and explain states of mind. Bain illustrates with a variety of selections, noting how the words of the speaking actor produce sympathy with or alienation from the stage character. Sometimes, sympathy shifts during the course of a single play, and Bain shows how the chorus of tragic drama, as a basically neutral single personality, can function to bring about this change. A portion of his book, containing the most important elements of his thesis, appears under the title "Audience Address in Greek Tragedy" in *Classical Quarterly* 25 (1975): 13-25; here he dwells on the importance of Greek Old Comedy in the developing of audience address techniques.

Baldry, H. C. *The Greek Tragic Theatre.* New York: W. W. Norton, 1971.

Designed as an introduction with chapters on reconstructing the nature of ancient tragedy; the material and textual evidence; the relationship of the city to the drama festivals; the festivals themselves; theater buildings; performances; the character of Orestes as treated by Aeschylus, Sophocles, and Euripides; and the decline of Greek tragedy. There is a short bibliography on theater history and performance, playwrights and plays, texts and translations. The companion volume on comedy by F. H. Sandbach is cited below.

Beare, W. *The Roman Stage.* 3d ed. London: Methuen, 1964.

The classic volume on Roman theater history. Beare traces the origins of Roman drama and devotes separate, brief chapters to Livius Andronicus, Gnaeus Naevius, Marcus Pacuvius, and Lucius Accius. He provides longer, general studies of Plautus and Terence in separate chapters. The second half of the book discusses native comedy (*fabulae togatae*) and popular farce (*fabulae Atellanae*). Especially worthwhile are the chapters on mime, organization of the Roman theater, masks, costumes, and stage settings. Fifteen short appendices deal with interesting related questions such as seating, entrances, the *angiportum* (alley-way) and its use in comedy, stage curtain and doors, meters, the chorus and its omission, a triple comparison of Plautus, Terence, and Seneca, and vase paintings as evidence for staging. There are eight plates of theater buildings and related art as well as a good bibliography.

Bieber, Marguerite. *History of the Greek and Roman Theatre.* Princeton, N.J.: Princeton University Press, 1939.

This profusely illustrated volume traces the development of ancient theater

with hundreds of photographs, diagrams, drawings, and lucid, eminently readable text. There are chapters on every phase of ancient theater, beginning with
the satyr play and early tragedy, the best-known tragedians; Old and Middle
Comedy; then continuing with the Dionysia and development of the theater
building, scenery, and acting. There are discussions of New Comedy and
Menander and the Hellenistic theater building as well. Half the volume is
devoted to an equally well illustrated discussion of Roman theater: the phlyax
farces (Italian popular comedy), Republican drama, the art of acting at Rome,
the Roman theater building, and the plays of Seneca. There is a good final
chapter on the influence of the ancient on the modern theater, as well as a
selected bibliography and a useful list of illustrations and sources.

Brooke, Iris. *Costume in Classic Greek Drama*. New York: Theatre Arts, 1962.
This small but important volume, whose author has written extensively on
nearly all periods of English street and theater dress, is a generously illustrated
introduction to materials used in Greek theater costumes, armor, insignia of
gods and goddesses, jewelry, footwear, masks, headdresses, and the process of
equipping a chorus. Though without scholarly apparatus, the book is quite
sound and most readable as an introduction.

Buxton, R. G. A. *Persuasion in Greek Tragedy: A Study of Peitho*. New York: Cambridge University Press, 1982.
Considers that *peitho* (persuasion) is an element central to the liberal and
creative arts and explores the levels on which this element appears in Greek
tragic drama. Buxton notes persuasion's close ties to rhetoric and holds that its
application to tragic drama reflects the social character of the drama festivals
themselves. Because the Greeks saw persuasion in moral terms, *peitho* often
appears in tragedy with implications of contrasting modes of behavior: virtue
as opposed to deceit or violence, with emphasis on the political and social
implications of immoral conduct. The first chapter analyzes persuasion as it
was understood in archaic Greece, Athens, the "barbarian" territories immediately beyond Greece, and in the contacts between the Greek world and the
Near East. The second chapter considers the goddess Peitho, her cult and how
she is represented in literature and the arts; how she assumes secular forms in
political thought; and how she is contrasted with *bia* (violence) and *dolos*
(grief or suffering). Three final chapters consider Aeschylus' *Suppliants*,
Prometheus, and *Oresteia*; Sophocles' *Philoctetes* and *Oedipus at Colonus*;
and Euripides' *Medea* and *Hecuba*.

Cornford, Francis Macdonald. *The Origins of Attic Comedy*. London: Edward Arnold, 1914. Reprint. Garden City, N.Y.: Doubleday, 1961.
This study follows the anthropological approach to literature that was originally developed by J. G. Frazer. Use of anthropological archetypes has largely

ef, solid discussions of each of the major works or the most important
gments. Plautus and Terence figure prominently in Duff's discussion of
ly theater history. There are also good discussions of the earliest play-
ights (Livius Andronicus, Gnaeus Naevius, and Quintus Ennius), about
om information written for general readers is difficult to obtain.

erald F. *The Origin and Early Form of Greek Tragedy*. Martin Classical
ctures 20. Cambridge, Mass.: Harvard University Press, 1965.
se argues that Greek tragedy is the result of two successive "creative acts,"
first by the shadowy figure known as Thespis (sixth century B.C.), who is
nventionally credited with having introduced the protagonist (first actor)
d, as a result, the dialogue that ensued. The second of these innovations,
ltiple characters, each with a distinct personality, is the work of Aeschylus
d his successors. Else's arguments do not so much reject as ignore the more
nventional explanations of tragedy's origin from choral dithyramb and re-
ious ritual. They also avoid consideration of the Aristotelian *Poetics*, which,
Else rightly observes, contains problems of its own that argue against
qualified acceptance. In part, Else's book is a reaction to the Cambridge
hool, classicist-anthropologists such as J. G. Frazer and Gilbert Murray,
ose explanations of tragedy's origins were tied to ancient religious and tribal
actices.

J. Peter, ed. *Greek Tragedy and Political Theory*. Berkeley: University of
lifornia Press, 1986.
series of essays by various authors, each of whom juxtaposes a topic relating
classical tragedy to an element of contemporary politics, thereby arguing for
e timeless nature of Greek drama. Charles Segal discusses the relationship
tween Greek tragedy and society; Anthony J. Podlecki, the relationship
tween city and ruler; Froma Zeitlin, Thebes as setting for Athenian drama-
ts; Michael Davis, political themes and madness; Ann M. Lane, the politics
Antigone; Joel D. Schwartz, human and political action in *Oedipus Ty-*
nnos; Laura Slatkin, exile and integration themes in the *Oedipus at Colonus*;
ben, political corruption in Euripides' *Orestes*; Arlene W. Saxenhouse, the
igins of cities and their myths in Euripides' *Ion*; and Stephen G. Salkever,
agedy and the education of the common people through Aristotle's thought as
sponse to Plato.

on, John. *A Companion to Greek Tragedy*. Austin: University of Texas Press,
72.
his volume is useful for readers new to the Greek tragedies. Essentially, it is a
ok of plot summaries that treats all the extant plays of Aeschylus, Sophocles,
nd Euripides, including the pseudo-Euripidean *Rhesus*. It includes a short

fallen out of favor with the advent of structural and ser
Cornford's study, primarily of ritual in Aristophanic co
cited. Cornford discusses death and resurrection motif
pearance of new kings and deities in new forms, the chor
elements, types of comic masks and characters, and th
between comedy and tragedy. His illustrations come prim
dies of Aristophanes, but his discussion is general and far
except the first contain an afterword and appendix summa
comedies by Theodor H. Gaster, known for *The New Go*
one-volume condensation of Frazer's ten-volume opus.

Devereux, George. *Dreams in Greek Tragedy: An Ethno-P*
Berkeley: University of California Press, 1976.
An unusual work in the tradition of Claude Lévi-Str
structuralists. It begins with the premise of all structurali
ogy (essentially that literature reflects an unchanging an
ness). It examines the motif of the dream in Aeschylus' *I*
Suppliants, and *Oresteia*; in Sophocles' *Electra*; and i
Hecuba, and *Iphigeneia*. It then establishes the varieties
narrative, sleeping behavior, dream- narratives, implausi
is primarily interested in establishing links between
Aeschylus and the plays of Euripides. He holds that th
ilarities among the ways dreams are described and portr
continuity in Greek drama which is often overlooked.

Duckworth, George E. *The Nature of Roman Comedy: A Stu*
tainment. Princeton, N.J.: Princeton University Press, 195
The most definitive study of Roman comedy availabl
Duckworth concentrates on Plautus and Terence. He a
characters of each of their plays and discusses stage con
Roman humor, and popular entertainment. To a less
discusses the influence of Greek New Comedy. Particula
discussions of Plautine and Terentian influence on Englis
adaptations in Spain, Germany, Holland, and France;
Jonson; seventeenth and eighteenth century comedy; a
There is an appendix on manuscripts and editions of I
good but somewhat dated bibliography, and a complete i

Duff, J. Wight. *A Literary History of Rome*. Edited by A.
York: Barnes & Noble, 1953, rev. ed. 1959.
Outstanding readable yet scholarly treatments of early t
(volume 1, chapter 4); Roman tragedy after Ennius (vol
Seneca (volume 2, part 2, chapter 3). Capsule biogra

essay on the origins of Greek drama, a glossary of technical terms, and a bibliography.

Fifty Years (and Twelve) of Classical Scholarship. New York: Barnes & Noble Books, 1968.
This superb book of essays on the history of scholarship in all areas of classical studies contains excellent chapters on Greek tragedy by T. B. L. Webster, Greek comedy by K. J. Dover, and Roman drama by W. A. Laidlaw. Each chapter contains sections on available school texts, editions, and commentaries; trends in scholarship to the mid-1960's; works on production, dramatic technique, origin, and meter; available general works; and material on the individual authors. Brief appendices to each chapter deal with more specialized works on various aspects of ancient drama.

Flickinger, Roy C. *The Greek Theatre and Its Drama*. 4th ed. Chicago: University of Chicago Press, 1973.
This volume is useful as a handbook for those new to the Greek drama. It contains no new interpretations or special insights, but it does organize a large mass of material coherently. There are essays on the origin of tragedy and of comedy, the influence of religion, the early use of the chorus, actors, the festivals, physical conditions of the theater, and theater conventions and records.

Garton, Bruno. *Personal Aspects of the Roman Theatre*. Toronto: University of Toronto Press, 1972.
Garton's analysis springs from the observation that much associated with Roman comedy is apparently impersonal and depends upon type. The plays themselves are translations, sometimes conflations as well, of Greek New Comedies. Even Terence's prologues, though they mention circumstances attending a play's production, never allude specifically by name to the individuals involved. Nevertheless, Garton contends that one can learn much of Roman tastes and something of the playwrights themselves from Romanizing elements within the plays.

Goldhill, Simon. *Reading Greek Tragedy*. Cambridge, England: Cambridge University Press, 1986.
A good introduction to Greek tragedy for those readers who have not studied the ancient language. The author closely examines and translates relevant sections of the surviving plays to illustrate how the tragedies illustrate the Greek awareness of language, of relations and family relationships, of sexuality, of tradition, of madness, of blindness and insight, and of sophistry, philosophy, and rhetoric. He analyzes how Euripides transgresses the boundaries of tragedy as established by Aeschylus and Sophocles as well as specific questions of

performance and performability. There is a good bibliography of works cited; particularly worthwhile are the specialized articles dealing with difficulties within the plays.

Haigh, A. E. *The Tragic Drama of the Greeks*. Oxford, England: Clarendon Press, 1896. Reprint. New York: Dover, 1968.
Despite its age, this volume remains a useful handbook. It contains a good section on early tragic drama, chapters on Aeschylus, Sophocles, and Euripides with summary discussions of the extant plays, and two chapters of observations on the form and character of Greek tragedy and its later history.

Harsh, Philip Whaley. *A Handbook of Classical Drama*. Stanford, Calif.: Stanford University Press, 1944.
This older study, essentially a student text, is often cited and remains readily available. It contains basic information on the origins of Greek and Roman drama, theaters, production procedures, festivals, actors, and costumes. There are short lives of the playwrights and capsule summaries of the plays.

Henderson, Jeffrey. *The Maculate Muse: Obscene Language in Attic Comedy*. New Haven, Conn.: Yale University Press, 1975.
An entirely scholarly treatment of obscenity in Attic comedy generally and in Aristophanes' plays, and of scatological references in specific works. Such references are discussed by varieties as classified by the author, assuming the reader's familiarity with Greek and by number as in a commentary. Though not specifically intended for general readers, this book could well be useful to those puzzled by the cryptic humor sometimes found in Aristophanes' bawdy passages.

Herington, John. *Poetry into Drama: Early Tragedy and the Greek Poetic Tradition*. Sather Classical Lectures 49. Berkeley: University of California Press, 1985.
A good history of Greek drama that considers pretragic poetry in Greece, the confluence of poetry and myth to create drama, and the nature of the resulting tragic poetry. There are good appendices on professional reciters, religious festivals, musicians, choruses, and nontragic, nondramatic poetry given as performance.

Jones, John. *On Aristotle and Greek Tragedy*. London: Chatto & Windus, 1962. 2d ed. 1967.
Essentially, this volume aims to discover exactly what Aristotle actually says about Greek drama in his *Poetics*. It then reads these principles against Aeschylus, Sophocles, and Euripides as a test of the author's reading of Aristotle's ideas. There is no evidence, Jones believes, that Aristotle entertained the concept of the tragic hero. Jones also examines the implications of Aristo-

tle's dictum that dramatic characters must serve the plot and discusses key terms such as *mimesis* (imitation) and *hamartía* (tragic flaw).

Kitto, H. D. F. *Form and Meaning in Drama: A Study of Six Greek Plays and of Hamlet*. London: Methuen, 1956, 2d ed. 1964.
Excellent discussions for students and general readers of the plays of Aeschylus' *Oresteia* (*Agamemnon*, *Choephori*, and *Eumenides*) and of Sophocles' *Philoctetes*, *Antigone*, and *Ajax*. A transitional chapter on Greek and Elizabethan tragedy is followed by a substantial discussion of Shakespeare's *Hamlet*. Kitto holds that each of these plays makes its own standards for the dramatic effect it produces, that each constituted an important phase in the history of tragic drama.

_____ . *Greek Tragedy: A Literary Study*. New York: Doubleday 1939, 1950, 1954.
This relatively short volume is valuable as a historical introduction to tragedy for the general reader. A chapter on pre-Aeschylean tragedy makes contrasts with Aeschylus' *Suppliants* and notes lyric elements in that play. A second chapter considers the early plays of Aeschylus (*Persae*, *Septem*, *Prometheus*); still another examines the *Oresteia*, followed by some general remarks on Aeschylus' technique. Chapters 5 through 7 use a similar approach on the plays of Sophocles, 8 through 13 on the distinctive nature of Euripidean drama.

Knox, Bernard. *Word and Action: Essays on the Ancient Theater*. Baltimore: Johns Hopkins University Press, 1979.
This collection of essays and reviews was written during a twenty-five-year period. All items except Knox's prologue, "Myth and Attic Tragedy," have previously appeared. Knox concentrates on Aeschylus, Sophocles, and Euripides and deals with such matters as the third actor in Aeschylus' plays, the implications of the word *tyrannos* in reference to the *Oedipus* of Sophocles, the dating of the *Oedipus Tyrannos*, thoughts on Euripidean tragicomedy, and a "coda" on Shakespeare's *The Tempest* and the ancient comic tradition. The remainder of the volume contains insightful reviews of important works on ancient drama.

Konstan, David. *Roman Comedy*. Ithaca, N.Y.: Cornell University Press, 1983.
An excellent introduction to Roman comedy, particularly strong on its relationship to the family and Roman society. Unlike other treatments of the subject, Konstan's work does not consider Roman comedy as a mere translation from Greek originals. He emphasizes, through discussion of selected plays by Plautus and Terence, that these playwrights chose originals with immediate application to audiences of Republican Rome. Each play appears in its own chapter-length discussion: Plautus' *Aulularia* (*Pot of Gold*) as describing the

relationship of city-state and individual; his *Asinaria* (*Comedy of Asses*) as caricature of the family; the *Captivi* (*The Captives*) as mirroring the conflict between city-state and nation; *Rudens* (*The Rope*) as utopian city-state; *Cistellaria* (*Casket Comedy*) as a comedy of social classes; Terence's *Phormio* and caste questions; his *Hecyra* (*The Mother-in-Law*) as comedy of morals; Plautus' *Truculentus* as moral satire.

Kott, Jan. *The Eating of the Gods: An Interpretation of Greek Tragedy*. Translated by Edward J. Czerwinski. New York: Random House, 1973.

This unusual and occasionally eccentric book makes striking comparisons and offers unusual juxtapositions. Kott compares the Greek worldview to Jacques Monod's *Chance and Necessity*, Aeschylus and Claude Lévi-Strauss, the Greek chorus and the Peking opera. He traces Greek tragedy as used by later writers such as Joseph Conrad, Franz Kafka, Antonin Artaud, Albert Camus, and Jean-Paul Sartre. There are intriguing discussions of *Ajax*, *Alcestis*, *Heracles Furens*, *Philoctetes*, the *Bacchae*, *Medea*, the *Oresteia*, and the *Electra*. There are also extended comments on Shakespeare's *Hamlet* and *Cymbeline*. The title of the book is an oblique reference to *omophagia* (eating of flesh), part of the orgiastic worship of Dionysus, patron deity of Greek theater.

Lattimore, Richmond. *Story Patterns in Greek Tragedy*. Ann Arbor: University of Michigan Press, 1965.

Reduces the action of the extant Greek tragedies to several recurring patterns. Beginning with the observation that tradition required the ancient playwright to adhere to the basic narrative lines of the myths dramatized, Lattimore notes how it allowed emphasis on characterization, recurring imagery, language, and spectacle. As a result, Greek tragedy presents variations of patterns that involve *hamartía* (the tragic "flaw"), in which a character makes a wrong moral decision based on pride, or variations on the revenge theme (in which discovery and reversal follow a wrong moral choice). The author draws upon a wide range of classical literature, moving far beyond the ancient tragedies, to illustrate his arguments.

Lesky, Albin. *Greek Tragedy*. Translated by H. A. Frankfort. London: Ernest Benn, 1965.

One of the best general surveys of Greek tragedy. Lesky deals with fundamental questions of special interest to those approaching the genre for the first time. The first chapter seeks a definition of tragedy; the second traces tragedy's beginnings. In a third, Lesky discusses the predecessors of Aeschylus, then follows it with separate chapters on Aeschylus, Sophocles, and Euripides. There is a final section on postclassical tragedy, a short bibliography (almost entirely of basic works in German), and short lists of scholarly works, editions, and translations of Aeschylus, Sophocles, and Euripides.

_____ . *Greek Tragic Poetry*. Translated by Matthew Dillon. New Haven, Conn.: Yale University Press, 1972.

Lesky's larger, more detailed, more scholarly study of Greek tragedy. There are three separate chapters on origins; Thespis (and what can be deduced about this shadowy originator of tragic poet); and Choirilos, Phrynichos, and Pratinas (little-known predecessors of Aeschylus). The three largest chapters treat Aeschylus, Sophocles, and Euripides; each of these begins with biographical notes, then discusses manuscript tradition and editions, and follows with discussions of the extant tragedies of each, the fragments, and the distinctive approach of each to drama. There is a very short chapter on the fragments of Ion, Agathon, and Kritias, and a longer final chapter on tragedy's decline.

Lever, Katherine. *The Art of Greek Comedy*. London: Methuen, 1956.

Traces development of Greek comedy from its archaic stages (600-470 B.C.), assembling what evidence exists concerning legendary figures such as Susarion, Epicharmus, and Thespis. An outline of the fertility rituals of Dionysus leads to a discussion of Old Comedy at Athens followed by three chapters on Aristophanes: as inheritor of the traditions of Dionysian ritual, as comic dramatist who found his themes in the political and social life of Athens, as poet forced to turn from sensitive political and social issues and to generate new comic forms. Final chapters survey Athenian Middle and New Comedy.

Lucas, D. W. *The Greek Tragic Poets*. 2d ed. London: Cohen & West, 1959.

A standard introduction to Greek tragedy. The first chapter provides a good survey of its political, social, and religious background; the second discusses the nature of Greek tragedy: its origins, the lyric and dithyrambic precursors, the rise of drama festivals and theaters. Three separate chapters treat Aeschylus, Sophocles, and Euripides, discussing who and what influenced each and providing brief outlines of each extant play. A useful chronology of literary and political events keyed to the lives of the three major dramatists concludes the volume.

Norwood, Gilbert. *Greek Comedy*. London: Methuen, 1931.

The great virtue of this dated study is that it gives rather more information on the early comedians than one can otherwise readily find. There are substantial essays on Epicharmus, Cratinus, the school of Crates, Eupolis, as well as Aristophanes, Menander, and comic meters. There is some scholarly apparatus, though its secondary sources are dated and so not always readily available.

Pickard-Cambridge, A. W. *Dithyramb, Tragedy, and Comedy*. Revised by T. B. L. Webster. 2d ed. Oxford, England: Clarendon Press, 1962.

The standard work on the origins of Greek tragedy, satyric drama, and comedy. Pickard-Cambridge provides the most information on the dithyramb available in a single source to English readers. He follows it with an equally impressive chapter on the origins of Greek tragedy, a subsequent chapter on the beginnings of Greek comedy, a long appendix on the form of Old Comedy, and a shorter one on F. M. Cornford's seminal study, *The Origins of Attic Comedy* (1914). Most interesting is the substantial final chapter, on Epicharmus, who wrote comedies in Greek at Syracuse, Sicily, during the reigns of Gelo (485-478 B.C.) and Hiero (478-467 B.C.). Pickard-Cambridge cites all the available testimonia to reconstruct the nature of these plays. There are forty-nine plates, all works of art related to the development of ancient drama.

_____ . *Dramatic Festivals of Athens*. Revised by John Gould and D. M. Lewis. 2d ed. Oxford, England: Clarendon Press, 1968.
The most important work on the Greek drama festivals available in English. The first part of the book considers the Anthesteria (most ancient of the rural festivals of Dionysus), the Lenaia, the rural Dionysia, and the Panathenaia. Pickard-Cambridge then discusses the Great, or City, Dionysia, considering its origins, procession, events, and the trilogies and tetralogies of plays offered. He examines the procedures for appointing *choregoi* (those who financed the equipping of a chorus), selection of actors and judges, revivals and revision of plays. A third section discusses actors: their numbers, methods of delivery; the next considers costumes and masks, the satyr play, and Old and New Comedy. There are informative sections on the nature of the chorus, the audience, and the relative professionalism of those concerned with production of drama. This latter section emphasizes the increasing importance of regional guilds. A substantial bibliography and complete index conclude the volume.

_____ . *The Theatre of Dionysus in Athens*. Oxford, England: Clarendon Press, 1946, reprints 1956, 1966.
Pickard-Cambridge uses the best preserved theater, the theater of Dionysus at the foot of the Acropolis (less restored than that at Epidaurus) in order to deduce several important conclusions about the nature of Greek drama. He describes the precinct in the earliest times (before the Spartan lawgiver Lycurgus, c. 800 B.C.), notes evidence in the major playwrights on the Lycurgean precinct, then considers iconography on surviving pottery and the Hellenistic and Roman structures. The study makes basic assumptions: that variations in structure are logical and that chronology can be inferred from logic; that careless work reflects later additions; that the stone structure was preceded by one in wood; that every artist's or architect's ideas must have been derived from some other source. One can debate the merit of these premises though not the scholarship of this impressive work, which is profusely illustrated with photographs, diagrams, and foldout plans.

Poole, Adrian. *Tragedy: Shakespeare and the Greek Example*. New York: Basil Blackwell, 1987.

An excellent and unusual book in an area of continuing interest: Shakespeare's use of Greek tragic drama as inspiration for his own plays. Poole's volume presents more detailed and specific discussion than one usually finds in comparable books. He compares specific Shakespeare plays with specific Greek antecedents. Some of the comparisons, such as discussion of *King Lear* against the *Oedipus at Colonus* and the *Bacchae*, are striking, and all are well argued. Other chapters compare *Macbeth* and the *Oresteia*, *Hamlet* and the *Oedipus Tyrannus*, and there are insightful references to the ways in which a number of other authors, among them Robert Browning, George Eliot, T. S. Eliot, and Samuel Beckett, have used Greek tragic drama. Primarily though, this work is about Greek drama, read with and against later works.

Sandbach, F. H. *The Comic Theatre of Greece and Rome*. New York: W. W. Norton, 1977.

This small volume is a general study with chapters on Athenian comedy, Aristophanes, Old and New Comedy, Menander, drama at Rome, Plautus, Terence, and an appendix that discusses frequently asked questions, such as whether there was painted scenery, what kinds of costumes were employed, whether there were three doors or one for entrances and exits, to what extent women comprised the audience, and whether portrait masks were used. There is a glossary of technical terms as well as a selected bibliography of texts, translations, and general works for each playwright. The companion volume on tragedy by H. C. Baldry is cited above.

Segal, Charles. *Interpreting Greek Tragedy: Myth, Poetry, Text*. Ithaca, N.Y.: Cornell University Press, 1987.

This series of essays, all by Segal and published separately in other contexts, presents a logically connected view on what Greek tragedy means for modern readers. Segal considers that Greek tragedy is most meaningful when tied to modern principles of psychoanalytic interpretation, and he uses Sigmund Freud's theories, the structuralism of Claude Lévi-Strauss, the semiotics of Jacques Lacan, and selections from the Greek tragedians (primarily Sophocles) to illustrate how one may read ancient drama in this way. The study assumes no previous knowledge of psychoanalytic, structural, or semiotic theory, and it is intended as an introduction to these ideas.

Segal, Erich, ed. *Greek Tragedy: Modern Essays in Criticism*. New York: Harper & Row, 1983.

A collection of excellent essays on topics related to Greek tragic drama. Each is written by a distinguished scholar. Some of the best are "Emotion and Meaning in Greek Tragedy" by Oliver Taplin; "The Shield of Eteocles" (on

Aeschylus' *Seven Against Thebes*) by Helen H. Bacon; "Salamis Symphony: The *Persae* of Aeschylus" by S. M. Adams: "The *Suppliants* of Aeschylus" and "The Guilt of Agamemnon," both by Hugh Lloyd-Jones; "Imagery and Action in the *Oresteia*" by Ann Lebeck; "Clytemnestra and the Vote of Athena" (on the *Eumenides* of Aeschylus) by R. P. Winnington-Ingram; "Character in Sophocles" by P. E. Easterling; "Ajax" by Karl Reinhardt; "Antigone: Death and Love, Hades and Dionysus" by Charles Segal; "On Misunderstanding the *Oedipus Rex*" by E. R. Dodds; "Euripides: Poet of Paradox" by Erich Segal; "The *Medea* of Euripides" by Bernard M. W. Knox; "Tragedy and Religion: The *Bacchae*" by Thomas G. Rosenmeyer; and "From Tragedy to Philosophy: *Iphigenia in Aulis*" by Bruno Snell.

Sinclair, T. A. "Part Four: Drama." In his *A History of Classical Greek Literature from Homer to Aristotle*. London: Macmillan, 1934. Reprint. New York: Collier Books, 1962.

A substantial section of this handbook provides basic information on origins, productions, festivals, actors, and costumes, as well as summary discussions of the lives and works of Aeschylus, Sophocles, Euripides, and Aristophanes. Discussions are necessarily brief, sometimes insufficient to comprehend complete plot lines, and there is little or no interpretation. Even so, the book gives valuable direction to the beginning reader and provides a good survey of Greek drama before Menander.

Stanford, W. B. *Greek Tragedy and the Emotions: An Introductory Study*. London: Routledge & Kegan Paul, 1983.

An analysis of the techniques by which the Greek tragedians moved their audiences. Stanford considers that emotion is a central constituent of all tragic drama, though the emotions tragic authors evoke vary widely. There are two chapters on aural elements (song, music, noises, cries, silences, and the spoken word), one on the visual element and use of spectacle, and still others on vocabulary, style, and imagery.

Taplin, Oliver. *Greek Tragedy in Action*. London: Methuen, 1978.

Three introductory chapters discuss the evolution of the Greek theater, emphasizing its ambience and the importance of understanding in what environment the plays were performed. A second section is essentially a handbook giving detailed expositions of Aeschylus' *Oresteia*, the Oedipus plays of Sophocles, and the *Medea*, *Trojan Women*, and *Bacchae* of Euripides. The final section explores the consequences of appreciating classical drama in modern performances: one chapter on the experience of a modern audience, another on the role of the modern director.

Trendall, A. D., and T. B. L. Webster. *Illustrations of Greek Drama*. New York: Praeger, 1971.

Illustrates, by means of photographs and explanatory text, situations from the tragedies of Aeschylus, Sophocles, and Euripides. The pottery shown dates from as early as the eighth and as late as the third century B.C. Aristophanes' and Menander's subjects appear, though these illustrations are fewer, reflecting the smaller pictorial tradition of comedy.

Vernant, Jean-Pierre, and Pierre Vidal-Naquet. *Tragedy and Myth in Ancient Greece*. Translated by Janet Lloyd. Atlantic Highlands, N.J.: Humanities Press, 1981.
A structuralist study that analyzes how the ancient dramatists transformed the preexisting myths to give them a tragic character lacking in the myths themselves. The book consists of eight essays, five by Vernant (on how the social and psychological conditions of fifth century Greece favored development of classical tragedy; on how Greek tragedy depends on opposed tensions and ambiguities; on the place of the will; on Oedipus as a social and psychological symbol; on ambiguity and reversal in Sophocles' *Oedipus*), and three by Vidal-Naquet (on the tragic hero, on the hunting and sacrifice motifs in Aeschylus' *Oresteia*, and on the relationship between Sophocles' *Philoctetes* and the military training required in the fifth century of all male Athenians). The authors intend their study for general readers, but such readers should understand that this and similar structuralist studies often draw conclusions that are radical when set against traditional criticism.

Walcot, Peter. *Greek Drama in Its Theatrical and Social Context*. Cardiff: University of Wales Press, 1976.
What began as a religious festival of Dionysus became, relatively quickly, a secular and social occasion, cosmopolitan in that the drama festivals brought together Greeks from the entire Peloponnesus, but also socially unifying in that drama audiences included members of every social class. Walcot's study examines interrelationships of class in chapters concerned with production, actors, audiences, and plots.

Walton, J. Michael. *Greek Theatre Practice*. Westport, Conn.: Greenwood Press, 1980.
A readable, nontechnical introduction to ancient Greek theater. The organization is chronological with chapters on how history influenced productions at Athens, on the drama before Aeschylus, the festivals, and theater buildings. Unusual and worthwhile is a substantial discussion on how both Sophocles' and Euripides' *Electra* would have been staged, masked acting in the two plays, and recognition and conclusion in the two *Electras*. A final chapter considers drama in the fourth century and after.

_____ . *Living Greek Theatre: A Handbook of Classical Performance and Modern Production*. Westport, Conn.: Greenwood Press, 1987.

Unusual, both from its perspective and insight, and written with theater students and general readers in mind. Part 1 highlights the basic features of Greek tragedy and comedy and examines how and under what conditions the plays were first performed. Short analyses of all thirty-three extant Greek tragedies follow in part 2; these include dates of composition (when known), characters, plot summaries, staging problems, and the theatrical and dramatic qualities of each. This part concludes with a brief discussion of tragedy in the Roman world. The same format is used for examining each of the comedies of Aristophanes and Menander with a brief consideration of how Plautus and Terence adapted Greek New Comedy. Part 4 discusses selections from the drama criticism of Plato, Aristotle, Horace, Vitruvius, Lucian, Athenaeus, and Pollux, while the final section discusses major revivals of classical dramas in Greece, continental Europe, England, and North America. There is a good glossary of technical terms and a selected biography that emphasizes translations and works on theater history.

Webster, T. B. L. *Greek Theatre Production*. London: Methuen, 1956, 2d ed. 1970.
The three areas Webster focuses upon are scenery, staging, and costumes. Each is treated chronologically within geographical areas (Athens, Sicily and Italy, mainland Greece, the Greek islands, Asia and Africa) with emphasis on local productions from the sixth century through the time of the Roman Empire. There is discussion of the predramatic performances and how local performance affected costume. The last chapter traces the history of staging, scenery, and costumes in chronological narrative and considers why Athens continued to exert a profound influence in these areas throughout the fifth and fourth centuries B.C. Most unusual and worthwhile is a list of over 250 theater-related monuments (with approximately forty of these illustrated in plates).

AESCHYLUS

Recommended Translations and Commentaries

Oresteia (Agamemnon, Libation Bearers, Eumenides)
Denniston, J. D., and Denys Page, eds. *Agamemnon*. Oxford, England: Oxford University Press, 1957.
   A Greek text with English commentary and introductory essay. The commentary stresses textual difficulties but also treats staging and technical questions. The introductory essay provides basic information on the life of Aeschylus, the times and social atmosphere in which he wrote, production history of the *Oresteia* trilogy, and the manuscript tradition. A selected bibliography lists major editions of the *Agamemnon* and scholarship from the period of 1945 to 1955.

Fagles, Robert, trans., with W. B. Stanford. *The Oresteia: Agamemnon, The Libation Bearers, The Eumenides.* New York: Penguin Books, 1984.
   Supersedes the translation by Philip Vellacott, originally published by Penguin in 1956. Fagles translates the *Oresteia* with considerable depth and power and introduces a modernity that generally retains a faithfulness to the Greek text. This edition has the advantage of considerably more notes than one usually finds in Penguin editions; these are detailed and insightful and, along with an accompanying glossary, were prepared with the collaboration of W. B. Stanford. There is also a critical introduction to Aeschylus that traces the history, ideas, and symbolism of the *Oresteia*.

Fraenkel, Eduard, ed. *Commentary on Agamemnon*. 3 vols. Oxford, England: Clarendon Press, 1950.
   Volume 1 will probably be of greatest use to the general reader, for it contains background on Aeschylus, the Greek theater, and the important position of the *Agamemnon* in the development of Greek drama. The commentary is a standard work, impressive, scholarly, and too technical for the generalist. It, nevertheless, remains an important and often cited work.

Garvie, A. F. ed. *Aeschylus' Choephori*. Oxford, England: Clarendon Press, 1986.
   Garvie's substantial commentary accompanies the Greek text of Sir Denys Page. Of greatest interest to the general reader is Garvie's excellent introduction, which contrasts the lack of personal information Homer's the *Iliad* provides about the house of Agamemnon with the revealing portrait Aeschylus offers. Garvie also places the *Choephori (Libation Bearers)* in context as the second play of the *Oresteia* and contrasts the relatively simple plots of

Aeschylus' plays with those by Sophocles. Though textual matters predominate in the line-by-line commentary, Garvie allots a generous amount of space to problems of staging and to important imagery and motif. There is a solid bibliography, an index of Greek words, and a general index.

Lloyd-Jones, Hugh, ed., trans. *The Agamemnon by Aeschylus*. Greek Drama Series. Englewood Cliffs, N.J.: Prentice-Hall, 1970.
A volume in the Prentice-Hall Greek Drama series, it presents a running commentary on the same page as the portions of the text to which the commentary refers and contains the introduction to Greek drama reproduced in all the volumes in the series. Lloyd-Jones' own introduction summarizes the stage action of the *Agamemnon* and discusses its characters. His commentary assumes no knowledge of Greek and is consistent with his translations of the remaining plays of the trilogy, cited below.

——————— . *The Libation Bearers by Aeschylus*. Greek Drama Series. Englewood Cliffs, N.J.: Prentice-Hall, 1970.
The second volume of Lloyd-Jones' translation of the *Oresteia* trilogy, published in the same format as that of the *Agamemnon*, cited above.

——————— . *The Eumenides by Aeschylus*. Greek Drama Series. Englewood Cliffs, N.J.: Prentice-Hall, 1970.
The third volume of Lloyd-Jones' translation of the *Oresteia*. It follows the format of the *Agamemnon*, cited above.

Lowell, Robert, trans. *The Oresteia*. London: Faber & Faber, 1979.
A translation of Aeschylus' trilogy in the style of the eminent American poet Robert Lowell. Lowell notes in his preface that he aimed not so much at a literal rendering as at reproducing with direct simplicity the effect Aeschylus' poetry might have had upon the ancient audience. Lowell's is primarily a reader's translation rather than an actor's edition. It is suitable for use by those primarily interested in grasping the contemporary poet's conception of the ancient playwright.

Raphael, F., and Kenneth McLeish, trans. *The Serpent Son: A Translation of the Oresteia*. Cambridge, England: Cambridge University Press, 1979.
A contemporary English version designed for acting and prepared originally for the British Broadcasting Corporation's television production of 1979. What the translation loses in fidelity to the Greek it gains in modernity and drive. There is no complete apparatus, though brief notes do elucidate the text. A short introduction discusses the background of the myth, the trilogy as a whole, and provides plot summaries of its three plays.

The Persians

Broadhead, H. D., ed. *Aeschylus: Persae*. Oxford, England: Oxford University Press, 1950.

An edition of the play with critical notes, apparatus, and commentary but without English translation. The commentary is designed for undergraduate students of Greek, although it can be read with a reasonably literal translation to elucidate content and stage action. Broadhead includes a very good introductory essay on the historical background implicit in the play and on its production history.

Lembke, Janet, and C. J. Herington, eds., trans. *Aeschylus: Persae*. New York: Oxford University Press, 1981.

This readable modern translation of the *Persians* remains surprisingly faithful to the Greek and has the additional virtue of a historical introduction, essential for an adequate understanding of the play. It is intended for general readers and, certainly, is one of the best nontechnical versions available.

Podlecki, Anthony J., ed., trans. *The Persians by Aeschylus*. Greek Drama Series. Englewood Cliffs, N.J.: Prentice-Hall, 1970.

An excellent English translation with a commentary designed specifically for those unable to read Greek. The format is particularly convenient, for notes appear immediately below the portions of the text to which they refer. Podlecki avoids most textual and language problems, except where these relate to clarifying stage action. There are also excellent introductory essays, designed for general readers, on modern understanding of Greek tragedy, on the Greek dramatists, on the times in which they wrote, on performance, and on meter. These essays appear verbatim in the other volumes of the series, all cited herein. Podlecki's own introduction discusses the action of the play against its historical setting.

Sidgwick, A., ed. *Aeschylus: Persae*. Oxford, England: Oxford University Press, 1903, reprint 1980.

This school edition of the Greek text, with English commentary and brief introduction to the historical background the play assumes, has become a standard for those reading the play in the original. It remains available through regular reprintings, and the commentary can be used by all readers to elucidate stage action, symbolism, and historical illusions.

Vellacott, Philip, trans. *Prometheus Bound and Other Plays*. New York: Penguin Books, 1961.

Also contains the *Suppliants*, *Seven Against Thebes*, and *Persians* as well as an introduction and essential notes. See entry below under *"Prometheus Bound."*

Prometheus Bound

Conacher, D. J., ed. *Aeschylus' Prometheus Bound: A Literary Commentary.* Toronto: University of Toronto Press, 1980.

This commentary is intended for students, with or without a knowledge of Greek. It considers how Aeschylus adapted the mythological tradition of Prometheus and discusses the fragmentary evidence for *Prometheus* as one play of a trilogy whose other plays are not extant. The largest part of the commentary presents an overview of the play and close discussions of its various sections. The author concentrates on the role of the human race, whose position in the cosmos is at the heart of the conflict between Zeus and Prometheus. Appendices summarize the principal critical positions on the question of Aeschylean authorship and discuss problems of staging. There is a short bibliography designed for undergraduate and general readers.

Griffith, Mark. *Aeschylus' Prometheus Bound.* New York: Cambridge University Press, 1983.

Primarily designed as a student's edition of the play. Griffith presents an excellent introduction to the Prometheus myth, provides a cleverly drawn map that charts the wanderings of Io, and then turns to the plot, characters, and technique of Aeschylus' play. Griffith touches on the authenticity question as well. The bulk of the work is its Greek text and English commentary. Readers without Greek will, nevertheless, find the commentary useful for its introductory paragraphs on each of the play's scenes, as well as for its cross-references to other classical authors.

Havelock, Eric A., ed., trans. *Prometheus Bound by Aeschylus.* Greek Drama Series. Englewood Cliffs, N.J.: Prentice-Hall, 1970.

This excellent translation is designed for non-Greek readers, with the convenience of a nontechnical running commentary printed on the same page as those portions of the text to which it refers. The standard introduction to Greek drama, which appears in all volumes of the series, deals primarily with origins and early production. Havelock's own introduction, to the *Prometheus*, deals with the figure of human conscience and free will enslaved by unreasoning force; it is particularly insightful.

Scully, James, and C. J. Herington, trans. *Prometheus Bound.* New York: Oxford University Press, 1975.

A good translation with a brief introduction and a short set of notes following the text. The introduction considers the mythic background of Prometheus' conflict with Zeus and the symbolism of Prometheus enchained. There is also some commentary on Io as another of Zeus' victims, discussion of the plot, and observations on its static nature.

Thomson, George, ed., trans. *The Prometheus Bound*. Cambridge, England: Cambridge University Press, 1932. Reprint. Salem, N.H.: Ayer, 1988.
The English commentary can be used to accompany the English translation this edition includes with its Greek text. Thomson's edition, long out of print in its original edition, contains much of interest to both students of Greek and general readers, especially concerning the figure of Prometheus, the role of Zeus, and the play's meaning in view of its enigmatic final scene.

Vellacott, Philip, trans. *Prometheus Bound and Other Plays*. New York: Penguin Books, 1961.
Originally designed as the companion volume to Vellacott's translation of the *Oresteia*, this volume is kept in print as a volume in the Penguin Classics series. It also contains the *Suppliants*, the *Seven Against Thebes*, and the *Persians*, as well as a brief introduction and some essential notes.

Seven Against Thebes
Dawson, Christopher M., ed., trans. *The Seven Against Thebes by Aeschylus*. Greek Drama Series. Englewood Cliffs, N.J.: Prentice-Hall, 1970.
A good translation with the advantage of a nontechnical commentary printed on the same page as those portions of the text to which the commentary refers. The volume begins with a good introduction to Greek drama, reproduced in all volumes of the series. Dawson's own introduction discusses stage action and characters.

Hecht, Anthony, and Helen H. Bacon, trans. *Aeschylus: Seven Against Thebes*. New York: Oxford University Press, 1973.
The translation reflects the creative gifts of the British poet Anthony Hecht and the scholarly insight of the American classicist Helen Bacon. There are notes, though these are relatively few and rather slight. The notes avoid all textual matters except where there are questions essential to meaning. A glossary of names is helpful for readers unacquainted with the mythic background the play assumes. A short introduction outlines the play scene by scene.

Hutchinson, G. O., ed. *Aeschylus: Septem contra Thebas*. Oxford Classical Text Series. New York: Oxford University Press, 1985.
Provides a Greek text with commentary in English and an introductory essay that discusses the myths attending the House of Oedipus and the Theban Civil War, Aeschylus' dramatization of these, a production history of the *Seven Against Thebes*, and the manuscript tradition. The commentary elucidates important stage action and may be used with relative ease by readers without a knowledge of Greek. There is a selected bibliography that focuses on scholarly articles about Aeschylus and this play.

Page, Denys, ed. *Septem quae supersunt*. Oxford, England: Oxford University
    Press, 1972.
    A Greek text of the *Seven Against Thebes* without translation but accompanied
    by an excellent English commentary that contains much useful information on
    stage action, production history, and interpretation in addition to more techni-
    cal questions of language, text, and meter of interest to readers of Greek. The
    commentary is divided by scene and contains a synopsis of stage action at each
    division. An introductory essay includes information on the life of Aeschylus,
    an overview of the play, and notes on meter and manuscript tradition.

Vellacott, Philip, trans. *Prometheus Bound and Other Plays*. New York: Penguin
    Books, 1961.
    This volume also contains the *Suppliants*, *Seven Against Thebes*, and *Persians*,
    as well as an introduction and essential notes. See entry above under *Prome-
    theus Bound*.

The Suppliants

Lembke, Janet, ed., trans. *Aeschylus: The Suppliants*. New York: Oxford University
    Press, 1975.
    The virtues of this translation are considerable; it is literal, yet readable and
    nonidiomatic. It is readily available and pleasing in its design. Even so, it lacks
    the more thorough commentary this play requires, providing only a few pages
    of notes following the text and a general introductory essay on stage action and
    a note on production.

Vellacott, Philip, trans. *Prometheus Bound and Other Plays*. New York: Penguin
    Books, 1961.
    Contains the *Suppliants*, *Seven Against Thebes*, and *Persians* in addition to the
    Prometheus. There is a brief introduction and some essential notes. See entry
    above under *"Prometheus Bound."*

Complete Collections

Grene, David, and Richmond Lattimore, eds. *Aeschylus*. Vols. 1 and 2. The Com-
    plete Greek Tragedies. Chicago: University of Chicago Press, 1969.
    Various translators have produced a series of excellent translations of all the
    extant Greek tragedies, remarkably literal and available in relatively inexpen-
    sive editions. There are two Aeschylus volumes; the first contains translations
    of the *Oresteia* trilogy and an excellent introductory essay, all by Lattimore.
    Volume 2 includes S. G. Benardete's translations of the *Suppliants* and the
    Persians and Grene's translations of *Seven Against Thebes* and *Prometheus
    Bound*. The second volume lacks satisfactory introductions to these plays,
    though the translations are of uniformly high quality. The remaining volumes
    in this collection appear below, listed by playwright.

Rose, Herbert. *A Commentary on the Surviving Plays of Aeschylus*. 2 vols. Amsterdam: Hollandsche Vitgevers Maatschappis, 1958.

This text is primarily a scholar's commentary, and it is difficult for those without access to a university or research library to obtain. It also assumes knowledge of classical Greek. Nevertheless, it is valuable to all readers of Aeschylus because it offers insights on the plays lacking suitable complete commentaries: *Persians*, *Seven Against Thebes*, and *Prometheus Bound*.

Smyth, H. Weir, and Hugh Lloyd-Jones, trans. *Aeschylus*. 2 vols. Loeb Classical Library. Cambridge, Mass.: Harvard University Press, 1922, rev. ed. 1963.

These two volumes remain in print as part of the Loeb Classical Library and follow the regular format of that series: a Greek text of all the extant plays with English on facing pages. The convenience for a reader with some Greek is clear; nevertheless, the translation is markedly nonliteral and stiff, not recommended for a first reading of Aeschylus' plays. The second volume contains the major fragments published from 1930 to 1960 with translations. This unusual feature is a decided asset for the general reader without knowledge of Greek. Also worthwhile and otherwise difficult for general readers to locate is the complete list of printed editions of Aeschylus' plays, dating from the earliest Aldine printing of 1518 to the first quarter of the twentieth century. This list appears at the beginning of volume 1, following a brief essay on the life and times of Aeschylus. Volume 1 contains all the extant plays except the *Oresteia* trilogy; the latter appears in volume 2 with the fragments.

Recommended Criticism on Aeschylus

Oresteia (Agamemnon, Libation Bearers, Eumenides)
Buxton, R. G. A. "Aischylos: *Oresteia* and Conclusion." In his *Greek Tragedy: A Study of Peitho*, 105-114. New York: Cambridge University Press, 1982.

Agamemnon presents a series of acts of *bia* (violence), though no healing *peitho* (persuasion). References to *peitho* appear, but it is either ruinous *peitho* or pure deception. Healing *peitho* remains absent in the *Choephoroe* (*Libation Bearers*) and emerges only in the *Eumenides*, when Apollo first encourages Orestes and, ultimately, when Orestes is acquitted by Athena's court.

Caldwell, Richard S. "The Pattern of Aeschylean Tragedy." *Transactions of the American Philological Association* 101 (1970): 77-94.

Caldwell, as Garvie (cited below), notes the apparent simplicity of Aeschylus' plots, how the characters derive from the chorus and serve as its extension. There is always the pattern of introduction, followed by development of the tragic situation and its outcome, but this plan is inevitably supplemented by some element not directly related to the primary subject. The best illustrations of this are drawn from the *Oresteia*.

Dodds, E. R. *The Ancient Concept of Progress and Other Essays on Greek Literature and Belief.* Oxford, England: Clarendon Press, 1973.

Dodds considers the *Oresteia* and *Prometheus* and argues for a pattern that moves from chaos and disorder (in both the religious and political realms) to order that is externally imposed from necessity. Thus both the *Eumenides* and *Prometheus* have outcomes that are unsatisfying but required. That of the *Eumenides* is both political and religious, while the *Prometheus* outlines human limitations as placed against divine will.

Fontenrose, Joseph. "Gods and Men in the *Oresteia.*" *Transactions of the American Philological Association* 102 (1971): 71-109.

Fontenrose is primarily interested in the role prophecy (such as that of Cassandra in the *Agamemnon*) and divine intervention (such as that of Apollo and Athena in the *Eumenides*) play in advancing the action of the trilogy. That Aeschylus manages to introduce such interventions without creating a *deus ex machina* that blatantly interrupts the course of the trilogy is a measure of his skill as a playwright.

Gagarin, Michael. "The Ethical Pattern in the *Oresteia*" and "Sexual and Political Conflict in the *Oresteia.*" In his *Aeschylean Drama.* Berkeley: University of California Press, 1976, pp. 57-86; 87-118.

Chapter 3 of Gagarin's book discusses ethical patterns in the *Oresteia*, noting that the family is the trilogy's center of focus. He notes that the overall tone of the trilogy aims at establishing balance, one play resolving the preceding, one part of a play answered by another part of the same play. He shows, through illustrations, that the concept of *diké* (justice) emerges on personal, family, and societal levels. Chapter 4 continues this discussion, noting that two varieties of antagonisms that the trilogy resolves are sexual conflicts (such as between Agamemnon and Clytemnestra, Orestes and the Furies) and political conflicts (in the tension among Agamemnon, Clytemnestra, Aegisthus, and Cassandra) and between Athena and the Furies).

Goheen, Robert F. "Aspects of Dramatic Symbolism: Three Studies in the *Oresteia.*" In *Aeschylus: A Collection of Critical Essays,* edited by Marsh McCall, Jr. Englewood Cliffs, N.J.: Prentice-Hall, 1972, pp. 106-123.

Notes that three main types of imagery operate in Greek drama: that keyed to language, to action of agents; and to setting. He illustrates all three types in the *Oresteia*, discussing color (related to the tapestry on which Agamemnon walks), persuasion (in Clytemnestra's ensnarement of Agamemnon), and love-hate (illustrated through the kindly Nurse and her having filled Clytemnestra's place in Orestes' childhood).

Goldhill, Simon. *Language, Sexuality, Narrative: The Oresteia.* New York: Cambridge University Press, 1984.

In a structuralist analysis of the trilogy, Goldhill concentrates on the meaning of text as text. He discusses questions of intertextual meanings and motifs and thus concentrates on the recurrence of words, phrases, and constructions. For example, his analysis of the *Agamemnon* examines communication and exchange: the instances of saying, showing, and implying; hesitation and clarity; metaphorical and literal (the net, the tapestry which ensnares Agamemnon). A second part, on the *Choephoroi*, treats paradox, inversion, and the *logos*; what seems and is seen; signs and dreams; meals, raw and cooked. A third deals with the word and the law in the *Eumenides*.

Goldman, Hetty. "The *Oresteia* of Aeschylus as Illustrated by Greek Vase-Painting." *Harvard Studies in Classical Philology* 21 (1910): 111-159.
This article is a pioneering effort in what has subsequently become a fertile area of investigation. Goldman examines specific vase paintings against corresponding scenes in the trilogy in order to determine to what degree earlier iconography of the Orestes myths influenced their presentation onstage, and, more important, how the Aeschylus plays influenced subsequent artists. The fifth century, considered the highest period of attainment both for drama and vase painting in the Greek world, provides an unparalleled opportunity for investigating this interplay of the arts. A. J. N. Prag has pursued this topic in a study noted below.

Hammond, N. G. L. "Personal Freedom and Its Limitations in the *Oresteia*." In *Aeschylus: A Collection of Critical Essays*, edited by Marsh McCall, Jr. Englewood Cliffs, N.J.: Prentice-Hall, 1972, pp. 90-150.
Answers the argument that Agamemnon's death comes about inevitably, as the result of an inherited curse and the grand design of Zeus. Hammond notes that Aeschylus does not mention the curse until the *Agamemnon* is two-thirds complete, which allows Agamemnon and Clytemnestra remarkable freedom of choice; Clytemnestra to plan the murder or not, Agamemnon to succumb to Clytemnestra's plan. Aeschylus likewise maintains the maximum amount of freedom of action in the *Libation Bearers* and the *Eumenides*. The limitations Orestes faces arise from within, primarily from his own personality: the will to avenge the murder of Agamemnon and the will to endure the consequences of his vengeance. Reprinted from an article with the same title in the *Journal of Hellenic Studies* 85 (1965): 42-55.

Herington, John. "No-Man's-Land of Dark and Light: *Oresteia*." In his *Aeschylus*. New Haven, Conn.: Yale University Press, 1986, pp. 111-156.
Considers that the trilogy displays the coherence of its themes best when analyzed as a unity. The *Agamemnon* is unsettling and confusing by itself, but logically so because it describes a world in moral chaos. That there remain fixed moral standards begins to become clear in *The Libation Bearers*, though

elements of hopelessness persist into *The Eumenides*. Herington follows this
thesis with illustrations from the *Agamemnon*, *The Libation Bearers*, and *The
Eumenides*.

Ireland, S. "The *Oresteia*." In his *Aeschylus*. *Greece and Rome*. New Surveys in the
Classics 18. Oxford, England: Clarendon Press, 1986, pp. 23-33.
Identifies the central theme of the trilogy as retribution and, by extension to the
Eumenides, its consequences. Ireland begins by offering ways to interpret the
actions of Agamemnon and by noting the conflict between his roles as leader
of his army and head of his family. He notes that the *Choephoroe* (*Libation
Bearers*) has been undervalued, primarily because the *Agamemnon* and *Eumenides* are so compelling, then briefly summarizes stage action. Ireland's
discussion of the *Eumenides* focuses on the moral pollution theme and considers the roles of Apollo and Athena.

Kitto, H. D. F. "How Intelligent Was Aeschylus?" and "How Intelligent Were the
Athenians?" In his *Poiesis: Structure and Thought*. Sather Classical Lectures
36. Berkeley: University of California Press, 1966, pp. 33-74.
In this two-part, popular lecture from his volume of Sather Classical Lectures,
Kitto deals with the contention that Aeschylus wrote essentially primitive
narrative poetry suited to the unsophisticated audiences who attended his
plays. The first part of the lecture deals with the sophisticated view of the
major and abstract deities Aeschylus presents. This section deals extensively
with the *Oresteia* trilogy. The second part demonstrates the intricate nature of
the *Persae*.

Kuhns, Richard Francis. *The House, the City, and the Judge: The Growth of Moral
Awareness in the Oresteia*. Indianapolis: Bobbs-Merrill, 1962.
Kuhns considers what philosophical and moral lessons the Athenian audience
would likely have drawn from the *Oresteia*. He examines its plays as a philosopher rather than as a classicist and contends that the trilogy is marked by the
increasing appearance of a moral sense within the characters. Orestes is
haunted by the Erinyes (Furies) for the murder of Clytemnestra, though
Clytemnestra suffers no external torment for her having murdered Agamemnon. The moral issues divide between gods and human beings, but also turn on
the differences between the motivations of male and female mortals. There are
also separate chapters on law and the polis and morality's relationship to
catharsis.

Lattimore, Richmond. "Introduction to the *Oresteia*." In *Aeschylus: A Collection of
Critical Essays*, edited by Marsh McCall, Jr. Englewood Cliffs, N.J.: Prentice-
Hall, 1972, pp. 72-89.
Reprinted here is Lattimore's excellent introduction to the trilogy, published

originally in his translation of the *Oresteia*, cited above. He examines each play, discussing at length the relationship between idea and symbol (yoke, snare, bit, net, snake). He then considers the structure of each play and how the three plays are consistent.

Lucas, D. W. "The *Oresteia*." In his *The Greek Tragic Poets*, 2d ed. London: Cohen and West, 1950, rev. ed. 1959, pp. 85-102.
Notes Aeschylus' ability to sustain his themes throughout the trilogy and considers how the three plays successfully reach outside the immediate stage action. The sacrifice of Iphigeneia and Agamemnon's obsession with the Trojan War appear as a dramatic backdrop to his homecoming and help to explain Clytemnestra's vengeance. Then, the events of the *Agamemnon* cause those of the *Libation Bearers* and those of the latter play cause the action of the *Eumenides*. Lucas provides good summaries and discussion, noting these connections.

Murray, Gilbert. "The *Oresteia*" In his *Aeschylus: The Creator of Tragedy*. Oxford, England: Clarendon Press, 1940, reprints 1951, 1958, pp. 177-206.
Murray's analysis extends the length of chapter 6 and notes the increasing dramatic tension of the trilogy, within each play and building within the series. He observes the careful preparation for Agamemnon's arrival, relatively late in the course of the play; this is in contrast with Orestes' immediate arrival in the *Choephore* (*Libation Bearers*) and the plot against Clytemnestra and Aegisthus, which takes the entire play to unfold. Finally, there is the judgment of Orestes in the *Eumenides*, prolonged and in doubt to the play's end.

Otis, Brooks. *Cosmos and Tragedy: An Essay on the Meaning of Aeschylus*. Edited by E. Christian Kopff. Chapel Hill: University of North Carolina Press, 1981.
This volume is the final work of the late Brooks Otis, a classicist best known for his distinguished studies of Virgil and Ovid. It deals primarily with the moral and theological issues raised by the *Oresteia* and relates these to certain stylistic and structural qualities of the trilogy. Otis then relates these to elements in Aeschylus' world and to the development of the playwright's thought. The central questions of guilt, retribution, and divine and human justice appear against the argument that the trilogy shows an evolution from a primitive to a more civilized form of justice. The contrast between Clytemnestra's vengeance killing of Agamemnon and the Eumenides' tormenting of Orestes' conscience is masterfully argued. A final chapter relates the *Oresteia* to Aeschylus' other plays.

Podlecki, Anthony J. "*Oresteia*." In his *The Political Background of Aeschylean Tragedy*. Ann Arbor: University of Michigan Press, 1966, pp. 63-100.
Begins by noting that *diké* (justice) is the major theme of the trilogy and that

Aeschylus was able to turn his plot upon the ambiguity of the Greek word since its plural refers to the proceedings-at-law needed to secure justice. Podlecki then discusses each of the plays and argues that Aeschylus' trilogy would have called to the mind of its audience the Ephialtic Reforms of 462-461 B.C. which marked the victory of the radical element, headed by Ephialtes and Pericles, over the conservative faction of Athenian politics, represented by Cimon.

Prag, A. J. N. *The Oresteia: Iconographic and Narrative Tradition.* London: Aris and Phillips, 1985.
This study, richly illustrated, is a more thorough and systematic investigation of the interplay of iconographic and dramatic representations of the Orestes myths than the more accessible Goldman article cited above. It follows much the same format but introduces pictorial and philological unavailable to her. Prag, like Goldman, considers that the fifth century provides an unparalleled opportunity for investigating these influences: a substantial amount of art and an extant trilogy considered important from its first appearance.

Sheppard, J. T. *Aeschylus, the Prophet of Greek Freedom: An Essay on the Oresteian Trilogy.* The Interpreter Series IV. London: T. Murby, 1943. Reprint. New York: Haskell House, 1974.
This small volume does not present any startling new thesis on the *Oresteia*, but it has the virtue of a scene-by-scene narrative commentary on each of the three plays. What it lacks in scholarly apparatus it supplies in vivid interpretation, and so it is ideal for an introduction to the trilogy. The first chapter summarizes Aeschylus' life and work, while three succeeding chapters discuss the *Agamemnon*, *Libation Bearers*, and *Eumenides*, each in turn. A short epilogue contains general conclusions about the trilogy.

Smyth, Herbert Weir. "*The Oresteia.*" In his *Aeschylean Tragedy.* Berkeley: University of California Press, 1924. Reprint. New York: Biblo and Tannen, 1969, pp. 151-234.
Argues that the plays of the trilogy are so tightly interwoven that they might almost be read as one separate play. Even so, Smyth notes internal differences of rhythm and situation that distinguish the trilogy's constituents. He remarks as well that there are no subordinate plots: Every part of the narrative is devoted to the main action.

Spatz, Lois. "*Oresteia*: Trilogy Preserved." In her *Aeschylus.* Twayne's World Authors Series 675. Boston: Twayne, 1982, pp. 85-137.
Notes the polished completeness of the trilogy, recounts its production history and the background of the myth. Spatz then analyzes the component plays,

noting the internal confusion of the *Agamemnon* and illustrating this theme with passages from the play. Disorder in Agamemnon's household reflects a larger disorder in the cosmos. Spatz then turns to entrapment and animal imagery, which predominate in the *Agamemnon*. She considers the plot of the *Libation Bearers*, noting its similarities with the *Agamemnon*, then that of the *Eumenides*, its straightforward connection with the plot of the *Libation Bearers* and its movement toward resolution.

Taplin, Oliver. *Greek Tragedy in Action*. London: Methuen, 1978.
This work, intended for general readers, presents good general analyses of the *Oresteia* plays, analyzing motifs and dialogue and concluding that verbal activity compensates for the physical stasis of the plays. Taplin also considers Sophocles and Euripides, though his comments on Aeschylus are particularly valuable as an introduction to that playwright. There is some apparatus and a selected bibliography.

Thomson, George. "*Oresteia*." In his *Aeschylus and Athens: A Study in the Social Origins of Drama*. Cambridge, England: Cambridge University Press, 1940. Reprint. New York: Haskell House, 1967, pp. 245-297.
Having explained that what he argues is the connection between the evolution of a society and the survival of tribalism and totemic rituals in its institutions, Thomson notes basic information on the life of Aeschylus, then emphasizes the mythic background of Agamemnon, specifically Agamemnon's father Atreus' slaughter of the sons of his brother Thyestes and his serving of their cooked flesh to the unknowing father. Thomson observes that ritual sacrifice regularly signals the inauguration of a campaign and cites Agamemnon's sacrifice of Iphigeneia, tracing this motif throughout the *Oresteia* and notes its resolution, marking the evolution of a society, in Orestes' judgment at the court of the Areopagus.

Vellacott, Philip. *The Logic of Tragedy: Morals and Integrity in Aeschylus' Oresteia*. Durham, N.C.: Duke University Press, 1984.
This work uses the plays of the *Oresteia* principally, and the *Suppliants* and the *Seven Against Thebes* to a lesser extent, to argue that the themes of "reconciliation" and "a new combination of justice" figure importantly as motifs but that these appear in the context of judicial forms marked by corruption and false logic. Rationalizations justify the murders of Agamemnon, Clytemnestra, and Aegisthus; the acquittal of Orestes follows from suspect arguments and corruption. This deliberate dissembling reflects the political atmosphere of Aeschylus' Athens. Vellacott believes Euripides understood these political connotations in Aeschylus' work and wrote *Electra*, *Iphigenia in Tauris*, and *Orestes* as his own more explicit treatment of these themes.

Vernant, Jean-Pierre, and Pierre Vidal-Naquet. "Hunting and Sacrifice in Aeschylus' *Oresteia.*" In their *Tragedy and Myth in Ancient Greece*, translated by
Janet Lloyd. Atlantic Highlands, N.J.: Humanities Press, 1981, pp. 150-174.
A structuralist study that aims at discerning sociological implications in the
play's recurring imagery. The use of light and dark, of hunting images, and of
animals as metaphors for the primary characters (indeed as primary characters
in the *Eumenides*) contrast and blend the wild and the civilized and eventually
yield a reconciled universe, though not one that is free of tensions.

Wallon, William. *Problem and Spectacle: Studies in the Oresteia*. Heidelberg, West
Germany: Carl Winter, 1980.
Wallon's study on Aeschylean spectacle in the *Oresteia* develops the thesis that
Aeschylus heightens dramatic interest by using certain scenic conventions and
resources as they had never been used before. He concentrates on four elements: language (by using words in almost but not quite the same ways they
had been used before); history (specifically the myths and personalities associated with the house of Agamemnon); costumes (and how Aeschylus modified
and directed attention to these in the text of the trilogy); and actors (particularly the use of men in women's roles). Though designed for the scholar-
specialist, the study is worthwhile for any reader familiar with the *Oresteia*.
There is a bibliography and subject index, and all quotations appear in Greek
with parallel English translations.

Winnington-Ingram, R. P. "*Oresteia.*" In his *Studies in Aeschylus*. New York:
Cambridge University Press, 1983, pp. 73-174.
Observes that Clytemnestra, not Agamemnon, is the dominant force in the
Agamemnon, despite its title. The first part of this analysis of the trilogy is,
accordingly, a study of the impact of each of the plays, given the length of
Clytemnestra's role and the brevity of that of Agamemnon. There follows a
recounting of the mythic background and how Agamemnon's sacrifice of
Iphigeneia is related indirectly in the play. Winnington-Ingram then turns to
Aeschylus' portrayal of Clytemnestra, the relative "masculinity" of her personality, and concludes that Clytemnestra kills Agamemnon not from jealousy
of Chryseis or Cassandra, not from his sacrifice of their daughter, or because
of her love for Aegisthus, but because the dominance of a man is abhorrent to
her. The analysis notes continuation of this theme to the end of the trilogy in
the relative weakness of Orestes and Apollo and the relative strength of the
Furies and Athena.

The Persians

Gagarin, Michael. "*Persae.*" In his *Aeschylean Drama*. Berkeley: University of
California Press, 1976, pp. 29-56.
Gagarin contends that the *Persians* is an unusual play, not so much because it

presents a veiled literary treatment of a historical event (Xerxes' invasion) as because it is written with a dual perspective, both Athenian and Persian. Chapter 2 deals first with what is known about Phrynichus' earlier efforts at historical drama, then analyzes sections of the play against what is known concerning the Second Persian War.

Herington, John. "The Ancient Universe: *The Persians.*" In his *Aeschylus*. New Haven, Conn.: Yale University Press, 1986, pp. 66-77.
The first half of chapter 6 contains Herington's analysis of *The Persians*. He believes that it is actually Aeschylus' easiest play to follow. He notes that, as Aeschylean drama generally does, it moves from verbal to visual elements; from ambiguity to clarity; from human level to divine, thus describing the ancient order of the universe as the Greeks perceived it. He illustrates this thesis through discussion of the play by sections.

Ireland, S. "*Persae, Septem, Supplices.*" In his *Aeschylus. Greece and Rome*. New Surveys in the Classics 18. Oxford, England: Clarendon Press, 1986, pp. 14-22.
This section of Ireland's text provides a capsule summary of the three plays and directs readers to a variety of critical approaches. For the *Persians*, Ireland cites the views of Kitto, Gagarin, and Taplin, all noted herein.

Kitto, H. D. F. "How Intelligent Was Aeschylus?" and "How Intelligent Were the Athenians?" In his *Poiesis: Structure and Thought*. Sather Classical Lectures 36. Berkeley: University of California Press, 1966, pp. 33-74.
Having established that Aeschylus was capable of writing theologically sophisticated poetry in the *Oresteia*, Kitto turns to an analysis of Aeschylus' *Persians* to demonstrate that Aeschylus credited his audience with the ability to recognize the historical implications of the play, despite the fact that he took great liberties in his portrayal of events related to the Second Persian War (480-479 B.C.) in which many who attended the play were either directly or indirectly involved.

Lucas, D. W. "The *Persae.*" In his *The Greek Tragic Poets*, 2d ed. London: Cohen and West, 1950, rev. ed. 1959, pp. 65-73.
Considers the *Persians* was a discretely written play and not part of a trilogy, then reviews the historical background of Xerxes' defeat. Lucas argues that Aeschylus dramatizes the Persian invasion by focusing on the blindness of judgment that causes individuals to make decisions they would not otherwise have made. Success causes this blindness, and prosperity produces insolent pride. The play implicitly contrasts the prudence of Darius, which raised Persia to its greatness, with the rashness of Xerxes, this most apparent in the prayer that Darius appear from his tomb to give the Persians counsel in their hour of need.

Murray, Gilbert. "The *Persae.*" In his *Aeschylus: A Collection of Critical Essays*, edited by Marsh McCall, Jr. Englewood Cliffs, N.J.: Prentice-Hall, 1972, pp. 29-39.

Murray notes that the *Persae* describes historical fact in literary form, specifically the repulse of Xerxes' invasion of Greece. He notes that Aeschylus' version is more compelling than the purely historical account of Herodotus. The article contains a brief production history, Murray arguing that the *Persae* need not have been part of a thematically related trilogy. He then notes the relatively short period between the events the play describes and the play's production, following this with an analysis that illustrates its simple construction.

_____ . "The War Plays: *Persae* and *The Seven Against Thebes.*" In his *Aeschylus: The Creator of Tragedy*. Oxford, England: Clarendon Press, 1940, reprints 1951, 1958, pp. 111-143.

The first half of chapter 4 is a discussion of the historicity of the *Persians*. Murray argues that Aeschylus' account of the Battle of Salamis is more compelling than that of Herodotus, though Herodotus, writing forty years later, had considerably more technical information. The balance of Murray's discussion considers what is known concerning the lost plays with which the *Persians* appeared, then examines the structure of the *Persians*. He follows it with an analysis of the *Seven Against Thebes*, starting at p. 130 (cited below).

Podlecki, Anthony J. "*Persians.*" In his *The Political Background of Aeschylean Tragedy*. Ann Arbor: University of Michigan Press, 1966, pp. 8-26.

Chapter 2 of this study considers the special place of the *Persians* as the only surviving example of historical tragedy. Podlecki notes that it was impossible for Aeschylus to depart in any major way from the historical facts of the Second Persian War, an event familiar to many in his audience. He then shows how Aeschylus gave dramatic coloring to his characters and plot that did not violate historical details, then compares these details to the drama. The first appendix, "Aeschylus on Salamis," analyzes specific sections of the play against Herodotus' account of the battle. The third appendix, "Fragments, Titles, and Theories," discusses the lost play *Glaucus*, the third play of the trilogy that originally included the lost *Phineus* and the *Persians*.

Smyth, Herbert Weir. "*The Persians.*" In his *Aeschylean Tragedy*. Berkeley: University of California Press, 1924. Reprint. New York: Biblo and Tannen, 1969, pp. 64-91.

Notes the distinctive approach to history that Aeschylus uses, different from the sweeping historical dramas of Shakespeare. Smyth then considers the relationship of the play to the Battle of Salamis. He compares the account of Herodotus and cites the dramatic tension inherent in the contest of wills:

Xerxes against Artabanus. The balance of his analysis concerns narrative and descriptive techniques and scene placement for dramatic effect.

Spatz, Lois. "*Persians*: Monodrama." In her *Aeschylus*. Twayne's World Authors Series 675. Boston: Twayne, 1982, pp. 17-35.
Opens with a straightforward plot summary and production history, accepting the *Persians* as the second play of a trilogy which included the *Phineus* and the *Glaucus* and which concluded with a satyr play called *Prometheus*. Spatz notes that the tragedy concentrates its action on the figure of Xerxes; his tragedy becomes that of Persia and by extension that of all who act with rash pride.

Thomson, George. "Athens and Persia" and "Earlier Plays." In his *Aeschylus and Athens: A Study in the Social Origins of Drama*. Cambridge, England: Cambridge University Press, 1940. Reprint. New York: Haskell House, 1967, pp. 220-231; 298-316.
In part 4, chapter 13, Thomson discusses Athens, Persia, and the Second Persian War, culminating in the revolt of the Spartan serfs, the fall of Cimon, and the rise of Athenian imperialism. This section should be read as background to Thomson's understanding of the *Persians*, which he discusses in part 4, chapter 16. He considers the play Aeschylus' least effective drama, interpreting it as an appeal to patriotic sentiment and a variation on the theme that wealth breeds pride, a fault the gods eventually punish.

Winnington-Ingram, R. P. "Zeus in *Persae*." In his *Studies in Aeschylus*. New York: Cambridge University Press, 1983, pp. 1-15.
Through an analysis of religious ideas in the *Persians*, Winnington-Ingram traces the evolution of Aeschylus' theology. Zeus is obviously important in the play, though his name occurs only five times. Three of these references occur in Darius' own words. Winnington-Ingram holds that the religious utterances of the chorus were commonly held by the average Greek, though they do not reflect the views of the chorus in the later *Agamemnon*. In the *Persians*, there is a correspondence between wealth and disaster. In *Agamemnon*, the chorus rejects the notion that prosperity and good fortune cause misery.

Prometheus Bound
Buxton, R. G. A. "Aischylos: *Prometheus Bound*." In his *Persuasion in Greek Tragedy: A Study of Peitho*. New York: Cambridge University Press, 1982, pp. 90-104.
Cites the scholarship that opposes Aeschylean authorship, but also notes that much about the play is Aeschylean. *Peitho* (persuasion) appears as political, erotic, and moral. Zeus' role is *bia* (force) dominated; he operates on the play's political (or cosmic) level. Erotic *peitho* emerges in the character of Io through her eventual reconciliation with Zeus. Moral *peitho* appears in Prometheus' total deafness to all who attempt to deflect his challenge to Zeus.

Dodds, E. R. *The Ancient Concept of Progress and Other Essays on Greek Literature and Belief*. Oxford, England: Clarendon Press, 1973.

Dodds compares the *Prometheus* and the *Oresteia* trilogy to show similarities in works considered so unalike internally that some critics have argued against Aeschylus' authorship of the *Prometheus*. The pattern of action is similar in both cases, moving from disorder to tentative, though not wholly satisfying, resolution; external forces, focused in divine will, dictate the action in both instances, and progress, at least its prospect, emerges amid chaos.

Gagarin, Michael. "*Septem, Supplices, Prometheus*." In his *Aeschylean Drama*. Berkeley: University of California Press, 1976, pp. 119-138.

The last third of chapter 5 is a discussion of *Prometheus*. Gagarin notes the relatively static nature of the play, its lack of dramatic action, then considers the unfavorable portrait of Zeus, Zeus' power, and its ugly extensions in the personifications Kratos (Power) and Bia (Violence). Gagarin notes that some critics, though not he, condemn Prometheus and side with Zeus and that the language and construction of the play allow choice.

Golden, Leon. *In Praise of Prometheus: Humanism and Reason in Aeschylean Thought*. Chapel Hill: University of North Carolina Press, 1966.

The figure of Prometheus represents the blending of human achievement and self-doubt, audacity and tormented conscience. Golden argues that this conception of Prometheus, though often considered specifically modern, was actually realized in Aeschylus' representation of the myth. There is some, though not extensive, consideration of the much-discussed problems of authorship and corrupt text, much more analysis of what Prometheus represents in the context of fifth century Athenian history.

Griffith, Mark. *The Authenticity of Prometheus Bound*. New York: Cambridge University Press, 1977.

One of the best discussions of the undeniable differences between the *Prometheus Bound* and Aeschylus' other plays. Griffith has collected considerable evidence against Aeschylean authorship, though many account for differences in style and subject matter, and language as a reflection of the poet's mature style and his increasing concern with overtly philosophical subjects. There is also a discussion of date, with a later composition favored.

Herington, John. "No-Man's-Land of Dark and Light: *Prometheus Bound*." In his *Aeschylus*. New Haven, Conn.: Yale University Press, 1986, pp. 157-177.

Herington believes that the *Prometheus Bound* is, in its own way, as profound as the *Oresteia* for it too proceeds from chaos: intellectual, political, and religious. He notes the universality of the theme, the rebel opposing higher authority, and remarks that the political and intellectual questions of the play are markedly different from earlier Greek literature, specifically Homer and Hesiod. Herington then argues against the position some have held that the *Prometheus Bound* is non-Aeschylean, considering that it reflects Aeschylus' late style of which no extant examples remain.

Ireland, S. "*Prometheus*." In his *Aeschylus. Greece and Rome*. New Surveys in the Classics 18. Oxford, England: Clarendon Press, 1986, pp. 34-38.
Cites the various arguments over authenticity, then considers how authorship may affect interpretation. Accepting Aeschylus as author might allow the play to stand as a commentary on the tyranny of Hiero of Syracuse. Ireland also notes the role of Zeus, apparently that of villain, and concludes that this unseen deity is more the focus of the play than its title character is.

Lucas, D. W. "The *Prometheus*." In his *The Greek Tragic Poets*, 2d ed. London: Cohen and West, 1950, rev. ed. 1959, pp. 102-108.
Deals with the extant play rather than attempting to reconstruct the trilogy. Considers that it has a theme as important and sweeping as that of the *Oresteia*. Lucas then makes comparisons with Prometheus in Hesiod's *Theogony*, noting that Hesiod provides the background Aeschylus assumes. After a summary and discussion, Lucas concludes that the essential conflict involves even Zeus' inability to escape what is ordained by fate. Lucas also notes the formidable objections to Aeschylean authorship, though he takes no position on the question.

Murray, Gilbert. "How Aeschylus Created Tragedy." In his *Aeschylus: The Creator of Tragedy*. Oxford, England: Clarendon Press, 1940, reprints 1951, 1958, pp. 1-36.
This first chapter of Murray's book argues that although others had written tragic dramas before him, Aeschylus created the form of literature the world thinks of as tragic drama. After a brief survey of the origins of tragedy, Murray illustrates his thesis through discussion of how Aeschylus shaped the raw material of the myth of Prometheus into a tragic drama. He resumes his discussion of the *Prometheus* in chapter 3 (cited below), as a play of ideas that one can compare with the *Suppliants* and the *Oresteia*.

Podlecki, Anthony J. "*Prometheus*." In his *The Political Background of Aeschylean Tragedy*. Ann Arbor: University of Michigan Press, 1966, pp. 101-129.
Having summarized the action of the play, Podlecki concludes that Aeschylus' real focus is on the tyranny of Zeus and argues that there is a resemblance in the plot of the *Prometheus* to Hiero's expulsion of the Naxians and Catanians in order to found Etna (on Sicily) for his son Deinomenes sometime after 476 B.C. Aeschylus could have witnessed the results of this forced exile or even have seen it at first hand since accounts of his life report his hav-

ing already visited Sicily by 474 B.C. as resident at Hiero's court. The second appendix of this volume, "The Date of the *Prometheus Bound*," argues against its being Aeschylus' final play.

Smyth, Herbert Weir. *"Prometheus."* In his *Aeschylean Tragedy.* Berkeley: University of California Press, 1924. Reprint. New York: Biblo and Tannen, 1969, pp. 92-122.
Following a brief survey of idealism as reflected in Western literature, Smyth discusses the figure of Prometheus in these terms and compares the more primitive Prometheus of Hesiod's *Theogony.* He notes that Io serves as an example of a mortal victim of Zeus' wrath and a character who complements that of Prometheus because of her plight, ironically caused by her having been Zeus' mistress. The Chorus, daughters of Ocean, serve to recall that Io is the mortal daughter of Inachus, a river god.

Spatz, Lois. *"Prometheus Bound:* Interpretation by Analogy." In her *Aeschylus.* Twayne's World Authors Series 675. Boston: Twayne, 1982, pp. 138-163.
Recounts the plot and its background, noting the provocative nature of the title character, then considers the objections to Aeschylean authorship, favoring Taplin's explanation that the play may have been completed by another author after Aeschylus' death. Spatz notes the use of spectacle against the physical stasis of Prometheus. Finally, she notes the allegorical nature of the play's symbolism, Prometheus as the rebel in conflict with the unjust tyranny of Zeus.

Taplin, Oliver. "Notes on the Title of *Prometheus Desmotes." Journal of Hellenic Studies* 95 (1975): 184-186.
Taplin argues against Aeschylean authorship based on the fact that the oldest manuscripts contain Alexandrian insertions and subtitles and that there is no external evidence for trilogies on the Prometheus myths. The article may be read against Conacher's book on the subject or against Spatz, who treats the question in terms more congenial for the general reader though she favors Aeschylean authorship. (Both works are cited above.)

Thomson, George. "Promethea." In his *Aeschylus and Athens: A Study in the Social Origins of Drama.* Cambridge, England: Cambridge University Press, 1940. Reprint. New York: Haskell House, 1967, pp. 317-346.
Thomson sees discovery of fire as marking the origins of civilization; hence, his analysis of the *Prometheus* focuses on this reason for Prometheus' punishment. He compares the popular Greek view of the tyrant with Aeschylus' portrait of Zeus, then conjectures on the lost plays of the trilogy, *Prometheus Unbound* and *Prometheus the Fire-bearer.*

_____ . "Prometheia." In *Aeschylus: A Collection of Critical Essays*, edited by Marsh McCall, Jr. Englewood Cliffs, N.J.: Prentice-Hall, 1972, pp. 124-147.

This essay, reprinted from Thomson's *Aeschylus and Athens: A Study in the Social Origins of Drama* (cited above), argues that the basis of the *Prometheus* is the emergence of civilization, symbolized in the fire Prometheus gives humanity. Thomson reads Aeschylus' portrait of Prometheus against the primitive myth and Hesiod's treatment of it in the *Theogony*. He makes further comparisons with the definitions of civilization offered by Hippocrates, the Pythagoreans, and the Orphics and shows that a harmony of opinion exists, despite radically different contexts.

Winnington-Ingram, R. P. "Towards an Interpretation of *Prometheus Bound*." In his *Studies in Aeschylus*. New York: Cambridge University Press, 1983, pp. 175-197.

Winnington-Ingram notes that he is not convinced of Aeschylean authorship, then observes that one of the play's major problems is that it admits so many interpretations, an un-Aeschylean feature. He has no difficulty understanding Zeus against the Zeus of the *Oresteia*. Based on the Io scene, which he considers to be in Aeschylean style, he conjectures that Aeschylus may have had some part in the play's composition, yet remains unconvinced that the play is wholly by Aeschylus.

Seven Against Thebes

Caldwell, Richard S. "The Misogyny of Eteocles." *Arethusa* 6 (1973): 197-231.

A literary and psychological interpretation of Eteocles' woman-hatred in Aeschylus' *Seven Against Thebes*. Caldwell examines the character, stressing Eteocles' relationship to Oedipus and considering the three generations of rejection by fathers in the House of Oedipus.

Gagarin, Michael. "*Septem, Supplices, Prometheus*." In his *Aeschylean Drama*. Berkeley: University of California Press, 1976, pp. 119-138.

Chapter 5 considers *Seven Against Thebes*, *Suppliants*, and *Prometheus* in turn. Gagarin notes that, like the *Oresteia*, the *Seven Against Thebes* presents sexual, ethical, and political conflicts. He cites examples of Eteocles' misogyny, notes his refusal to surrender the throne of Thebes despite the stipulation of the agreement with Polyneices, and considers Polyneices' attack on his own city and the death and suffering it causes.

Herington, John. "The Ancient Universe: *Seven Against Thebes*." In his *Aeschylus*. New Haven, Conn.: Yale University Press, 1986, pp. 78-93.

The concluding half of chapter 6 notes how different *Seven Against Thebes* is from *Persians*, primarily because the former play finds its inspiration in myth rather than in a historical event; moreover, the audience's familiarity with the myths of the House of Oedipus required that Aeschylus be faithful to the legends, yet to be innovative in his method of their presentation. The balance of Herington's discussion is his analysis of the play, illustrating how it conforms to the pattern he discerns in Aeschylus' works generally.

Ireland, S. *"Persae, Septem, Supplices."* In his *Aeschylus. Greece and Rome*: New Surveys in the Classics 18. Oxford, England: Clarendon Press, 1986, pp. 14-22.
Concentrates on the German scholarship that has appeared on the *Seven Against Thebes*. He notes that the self-sacrifice of Eteocles attracts particular critical notice, and he provides several ways of seeing the character, discussing as well Eteocles' relationship to Thebes and to the chorus.

Lucas, D. W. "The *Septem*." In his *The Greek Tragic Poets*. 2d ed.. London: Cohen and West, 1950, rev. ed. 1959, pp. 73-79.
Notes that the *Seven Against Thebes* was originally part of a trilogy that included the lost *Laius* and *Oedipus*, then recounts the background the play assumes. Lucas follows with a summary and straightforward discussion of plot. He leaves the reader with two questions: Why does Eteocles argue with the chorus for more than a hundred lines at the beginning of the play, and is Eteocles' death a heroic self-sacrifice that redeems his city or an insane crime that ensures only the destruction of himself and his brother Polyneices? Lucas notes that the chorus at no time shows admiration or gratitude to Eteocles, only horror at fratricide.

Murray, Gilbert. "The War Plays: *Persae* and *The Seven Against Thebes*." In his *Aeschylus: The Creator of Tragedy*. Oxford, England: Clarendon Press, 1940, reprints 1951, 1958, pp. 111-143.
Following his discussion of the *Persians*, Murray turns to Aeschylus' *Seven Against Thebes*, which he believes is written as a historical play. Murray considers that the ancient world saw it as Aeschylus' most distinguished work and bases his arguments partly on Aeschylus' remark in Aristophanes' *Frogs* that *Seven Against Thebes* most ennobled the characters of his countrymen. Following a brief discussion of the lost plays with which it was produced, Murray devotes the balance of this chapter to an examination of the play's character portraits.

Podlecki, Anthony J. *"Seven Against Thebes."* In his *The Political Background of Aeschylean Tragedy*. Ann Arbor: University of Michigan Press, pp. 27-41.
Chapter 3 considers the play at length, arguing that it has a general historical analogue in conditions at Athens during the Persian siege of 480 B.C. but that the personalities are largely Aeschylus' creations. Podlecki recounts the argument that the *Seven Against Thebes* had been intended as propaganda for Pericles but ultimately rejects the view.

Rosenmeyer, Thomas G. *"Seven Against Thebes*: The Tragedy of War." In *Aeschylus: A Collection of Critical Essays*, edited by Marsh McCall, Jr. Englewood Cliffs, N.J.: Prentice-Hall, 1972, pp. 40-62.

Rosenmeyer notes the several ways an author can choose to write about war: that fighting itself is a thing of beauty, but ultimately tragic (Homer); that war is an extension of diplomacy, the result of royal intrigue (Shakespeare); that it contains fear, suffering, misery, but also a desperate gentleness (Erich Maria Remarque); as lampoon (Aristophanes). Rosenmeyer then argues that *Seven Against Thebes* departs from all these ways since here war and the hero are not related as action and agent. His analysis proceeds to show that war in this play is an impersonal mechanism, an irresistible and brutal assault on human weakness.

Smyth, Herbert Weir. "The *Seven Against Thebes*." In his *Aeschylean Tragedy*. Berkeley: University of California Press, 1924. Reprint. New York: Biblo and Tannen, 1969, pp. 123-150.

Surveys the popular appeal of the Oedipus literature, citing ancient sources, then attempts to reconstruct the trilogy from what is known about the lost plays *Laius* and the *Epigoni*. Smyth then discusses characterization and, having noted the lack of spectacle, concludes that the play's primary focus resides with Eteocles.

Spatz, Lois. *"Seven Against Thebes*: Resolution." In her *Aeschylus*. Twayne's World Authors Series 675. Boston: Twayne, 1982, pp. 36-58.

Considers the play's relationship to its original trilogy and notes that the seven invaders of Thebes are not central to the play. Spatz then considers the myth itself and Aeschylus' treatment of it, noting the popularity of plays on the House of Oedipus in both the ancient and the modern world. There are discussions of the critics' objections that Aeschylus has joined two myths (the defense of Thebes and the curse of the descendants of Laius) without properly blending them, of possible inconsistencies in the character of Eteocles, of imagery that underlines the transition from war to curse, and of political interpretations.

Thalmann, William G. *Dramatic Art in Aeschylus' Seven Against Thebes*. New Haven, Conn.: Yale University Press, 1978.

Though Thalmann's book does not provide translations for the Greek quoted, its arguments on this little-discussed play make it worth inclusion here. He considers plot (role of the oracle, Laius' crime, Oedipus' sufferings, and the curse on Eteocles and Polyneices); then he examines important imagery, both of the city (nautical, walls, earth, blood) and of the family (lots and inheritance). Finally, he makes observations on manner of presentation and on the shield scene of the play's conclusion.

Thomson, George. "Earlier Plays." In his *Aeschylus and Athens: A Study in the Social Origins of Drama*. Cambridge, England: Cambridge University Press, 1940. Reprint. New York: Haskell House, 1967, pp. 298-316.

Sees the *Seven Against Thebes* as based on a myth that commemorates the evolution of clan to state. By bringing the story to an end with the deaths of both Polyneices and Eteocles, so Thomson argues, Aeschylus reduces its compass from four generations to three, adapting it to the form of a trilogy and producing the conclusion that the clan of Oedipus perishes but the state survives.

Vernant, Jean-Pierre, and Pierre Vidal-Naquet. "The Shields of the Heroes." In their *Tragedy and Myth in Ancient Greece*, translated by Janet Lloyd. Atlantic Highlands, N.J.: Humanities Press, 1981, pp. 120-149.

An essay on the central scene of *Seven Against Thebes* which examines the psychological reasons for the transformation in the character of Eteocles from collected military leader to desperate man haunted by the curse on the House of Oedipus. The essay then considers the relationship of Eteocles and the chorus; the female chorus' enthusiasm for war; and Eteocles' use of the first person plural pronoun, allying him to a group of women. Finally, there is discussion of the meaning of the sequence of the seven parallel speeches spoken by the Messenger and Eteocles, the former describing the enemy leaders, the latter turning these descriptions to the Theban leaders. This sequence contains descriptions of the seven Argive shields and the one Theban shield, the focus of this essay.

Winnington-Ingram, R. P. "*Septem contra Thebas*." In his *Studies in Aeschylus*. New York: Cambridge University Press, 1983, pp. 16-54.

Singles out Eteocles as the focus of the tragedy, noting that the *Seven Against Thebes* centers on the misfortunes of the man rather than his family or his city. Winnington-Ingram notes the play's completeness of action in contrast to the *Oresteia*, which requires the three plays of the trilogy to achieve full resolution. He conjectures that the polis (city) theme, which runs through this play, was likely a unifying element of the trilogy and present in the lost *Laius* and *Oedipus* as well. There is special attention to the rhetoric of the speeches of Eteocles and to the choral odes, specifically how they reveal Eteocles as an increasingly complex personality who fixes the blame for his plight on the madness of the gods.

The Suppliants

Buxton, R. G. A. "Aischylos: *Suppliants*." In his *Persuasion in Greek Tragedy: A Study of Peitho*. New York: Cambridge University Press, 1982, pp. 67-90.

Agrees with redating the play to between 467 and 456 B.C., allowing a political interpretation and veiled allusions to the ostracism of Cimon and the assassination of Ephialtes. Argues that the roles of *peitho* (persuasion) and *bia* (violence) appear in both the personal (particularly sexual) and political relationships of the play. The remainder of analysis is scene-by-scene summary and discussion, noting the antagonism of *peitho* and *bia* where it appears.

Finley, John H., Jr. "The *Suppliants*." In *Aeschylus: A Collection of Critical Essays*, edited by Marsh McCall, Jr. Englewood Cliffs, N.J.: Prentice-Hall, 1972, pp. 63-72.
Begins by noting the effect of knowing the last two plays of the trilogy (*Egyptians* and *Danaids*) only through conjecture and in outline. Finley then contrasts the relatively weak characterizations of the *Suppliants* with the detailed characterizations of the *Agamemnon*, remarking as well how different the *Suppliants* is from the abstract themes of the *Eumenides* and *Prometheus*. He then argues that the *Suppliants* is later in composition than many believe and analyzes its complexity scene by scene.

Gagarin, Michael. "*Septem, Supplices, Prometheus*." In his *Aeschylean Drama*. Berkeley: University of California Press, 1976, pp. 119-138.
The middle section of chapter 5 considers that the *Suppliants* portrays a triumph of female values in that the Danaids succeed in obtaining the support of Pelasgus and his city. He speculates on the opposing symbolism of Danaids (female dominance) and the Aegyptids (male dominance) and on the contents of the lost plays of the trilogy.

Herington, C. J. "Aeschylus: The Last Phase." In *Aeschylus: A Collection of Critical Essays*, edited by Marsh McCall, Jr. Englewood Cliffs, N.J.: Prentice-Hall, 1972, pp. 148-163.
Argues for a late dating of the *Suppliants*, a date that would place it close in date of composition to the *Oresteia* and the *Prometheus* as a group of works written toward the end of Aeschylus' career. He notes that all presuppose the same cosmology: a world in which the protagonists are haunted by outside malevolent forces. He also traces elements regularly found in Old Comedy; that comic elements could be tolerated in tragedy at all argues for late composition.

Herington, John. "No-Man's-Land of Dark and Light: *The Suppliants*." In his *Aeschylus*. New Haven, Conn.: Yale University Press, 1986, pp. 94-111.
Herington holds that the *Suppliants* is more difficult to interpret than Aeschylus' other extant plays, primarily because of its lyrical, dreamlike quality. He reviews the myth of the Danaids and the Aegyptids, notes that Aeschylus alludes to it in *Prometheus Bound* 856-869, and then analyzes the *Suppliants* section by section. He notes the recurring dream-deed imagery and argues that this antithesis ultimately resolves itself in the personality of Zeus.

Ireland, S. *"Persae, Septem, Supplices."* In his *Aeschylus. Greece and Rome*: New
   Surveys in the Classics 18. Oxford, England: Clarendon Press, 1986, pp. 14-22.
   Notes the embarrassment attending discovery in 1952 of the papyrus used to
   prove later composition of the *Suppliants* (c. 463 B.C.). He recounts the arguments offered by both sides in this controversy, then discusses the important
   and somewhat contradictory role of the chorus, made up of the Danaids. They
   appeal to Zeus to save them from marriage, yet they themselves are the descendants of Zeus and Io; while they collapse when faced by the Egyptian herald
   who demands they be given in marriage, the myth reveals that they will murder
   their husbands on their wedding night.

Lucas, D. W. "The *Supplices*." In his *The Greek Tragic Poets*, 2d ed. London:
   Cohen and West, 1950, rev. ed. 1959, pp. 79-85.
   Notes that the plot of the *Suppliants* is effectively summarized by Prometheus
   during that hero's prophecy of his own release from bondage; yet, Lucas notes
   the difficulties of reconstructing the theme of the trilogy to which the *Suppliants* belonged. It is difficult to account for the Danaids' objection to marriage with first cousins as such marriages were relatively common in the Greek
   world. The balance of the analysis discusses the *Suppliants* through plot summary and concludes with conjectures on the nature of the lost plays.

Murray, Gilbert. "Aeschylus as a Poet of Ideas: The Mystical Plays, *Supplices* and
   Prometheus: The *Oresteia*." In his *Aeschylus: The Creator of Tragedy*. Oxford,
   England: Clarendon Press, 1940, reprints 1951, 1958, pp. 72-110.
   Murray sees philosophical content in these plays, viewing Aeschylus as creator
   of tragedy because his plays deal with the problems of human life and recognize a mystical realm that controls human destiny. He concludes his discussion
   with illustrations from these plays and a more extended discussion of the *Suppliants*.

Murray, R. Duff. *The Motif of Io in Aeschylus' Suppliants*. Princeton, N.J.: Princeton University Press, 1958.
   Murray contends that the myth of Io, an unwilling victim forced to suffer
   because she submits to the will of Zeus, contains elements essential to
   Aeschylus' understanding of tragedy. Though the Io myth has little direct
   relevance to the *Suppliants*, aside from the fact that the Danaids are descendants of Zeus and Io, Murray argues that the fifty maidens are well aware of
   their genealogy and commit the murder of their husbands based on a misinterpretation of it. He shows how Aeschylus weaves elements of the Io myth
   into the plot of the *Suppliants*, and he considers the relationship between the
   Suppliants and *Prometheus Bound*, in which Io is explicitly compared to
   Prometheus.

Podlecki, Anthony J. *"Suppliants."* In his *The Political Background of Aeschylean Tragedy.* Ann Arbor: University of Michigan Press, 1966, pp. 42-62.
Dates the play's first presentation at 463 B.C., making it the earliest surviving drama of Aeschylus; this in contrast with H. D. F. Kitto, who rejects the early dating. Podlecki then summarizes and discusses stage action and reads the play against the Spartan accusation against Themistocles for treason, citing the historians Diodorus, Plutarch, and Thucydides.

Smyth, Herbert Weir. *"The Suppliant Maidens."* In his *Aeschylean Tragedy.* Berkeley: University of California Press, 1924. Reprint. New York: Biblo and Tannen, 1969, pp. 33-63.
Smyth accepts early dating of the play, a position not generally held since the discovery of the Aeschylus papyrus in 1952. He gives primary attention to the eloquence of the choral poetry and the central role the chorus of this play occupies. About half this chapter concerns the *Egyptians* and the *Danaids*, the two nonextant members of the original trilogy and what their contents (based on fragments and external testimonies) might have meant as a means of interpreting the *Suppliants.*

Spatz, Lois. *"Suppliants*: Beginnings." In her *Aeschylus.* Twayne's World Authors Series 675. Boston: Twayne, 1982, pp. 59-84.
Discusses plot and its problems: that it is difficult to interpret, that it is disconnected from the lost plays which once accompanied it, that the text is badly corrupt. Spatz mentions the 1952 discovery of the papyrus that allows dating as late as 456 B.C. She also discusses the play's production history and structure, seeing the *Suppliants* primarily as about rejection of a marriage; she then considers possible reasons offered for this rejection. Finally, Spatz notes the play's turn on patriotism and its symmetry, beginning and ending with Zeus.

Thomson, George. "Earlier Plays." In his *Aeschylus and Athens: A Study in the Social Origins of Drama.* Cambridge, England: Cambridge University Press, 1940. Reprint. New York: Haskell House, 1967, pp. 298-316.
Thomson interprets the *Suppliants* as based on a myth that celebrates endogamy in Egypt. He explains the Danaids' rejection of the Aegyptids as their reluctance to marry their first cousins, a hesitation he believes occurs at a major transitional period of every society. He further holds that the myth's change of setting from Egypt to Arcadia and the Argive tradition of associating the Danaids with irrigation can relate to the institution of the fertility festival which came to be the Thesmophoria.

Winnington-Ingram, R. P. "The Danaid Trilogy." In his *Studies in Aeschylus.* New York: Cambridge University Press, 1983, pp. 55-72.

Favors late dating of the *Suppliants* as the first play of a trilogy that included the lost *Aegyptids* and *Danaids* as its second and third constituents with *Amymone*, also lost, as the concluding satyr play. Winnington-Ingram conjectures, based on their portrait in the *Suppliants*, that the trilogy ended with the Danaids' reconciliation to marriage. He also reconstructs possible reasons for their original opposition, and he concludes by analyzing the character portrait of Hypermnestra.

General Criticism on Aeschylus

Gagarin, Michael. *Aeschylean Drama*. Berkeley: University of California Press, 1976.
Gagarin begins with an analysis of the Greek worldview as manifested in the Homeric poems and provides a related analysis of the *Persae*, Aeschylus' historical drama. He argues that this play has a dual perspective, both Persian and Athenian, and that this makes it a celebration as well as a tragedy. The focus of the book, however, is a discussion of the *Oresteia*, developed as the conflict of ethical forces eventually reconciled under law. Gagarin illustrates the connections between sexual and political conflict as linked in the *Oresteia* and demonstrates how they are reconciled in Aeschylus' own Athens. There is a brief concluding chapter that considers Aeschylus' three other surviving plays (*Seven Against Thebes*, *Suppliants*, and *Prometheus*) as parts of other trilogies whose companion plays are not extant. The first of two appendices considers the recurring motifs of wrath and vengeance in Aeschylean drama, while the second discusses the conflict between Eteocles and the chorus in *Seven Against Thebes*.

Garvie, A. F. "Aeschylus' Simple Plots." In *Dionysiaca: Nine Studies in Greek Poetry*, edited by R. D. Dawe, J. Diggle, and P. E. Easterling. Cambridge, England: Cambridge University Library, 1978, pp. 63-86.
Garvie considers each of the extant plays, notes their straightforward development, and concludes that Aeschylus creates dramatic intensity essentially by frustrating the audience's expectations concerning logical outcome. Clytemnestra, in the *Agamemnon*, thus emerges as both dutiful wife at play's beginning and revenge-intent mistress by play's end. Prometheus, literally stationary and figuratively static, is complemented by Io, another victim of Zeus, but one who is literally chased from continent to continent while enduring her suffering. This study nicely complements that of Caldwell, cited above.

Herington, John. *Aeschylus*. New Haven, Conn.: Yale University Press, 1986.
This text is an important and thoroughly modern study of the playwright and his works. It takes what little is known about the life of Aeschylus and reads

this against the considerably more specific information possessed on the period in which he wrote. An important conclusion is that Aeschylus is a more political playwright than generally believed, that questions of freedom challenged by both internal corruption (as in the *Oresteia*) and external aggression (*Persians, Seven Against Thebes*) figure importantly in his plays. Herington's work complements the Ireland study noted below.

Ireland, S. *Aeschylus. Greece and Rome*: New Surveys in the Classics 18. Oxford, England: Clarendon Press, 1986.
This survey, intended for student and general readers, begins by citing approaches various critics have taken in their analyses of Aeschylus' plays: literary, historical, and textual. It continues with a brief life of Aeschylus against his times and surveys the titles and possible order of his plays, then considers general themes which appear in his works. There are discrete discussions of the *Persians, Seven Against Thebes, Oresteia*, and *Prometheus*, cited above, and a selected bibliography. The overall intention of the survey is to direct readers to the approaches of various critics.

Jaeger, Werner. "The Drama of Aeschylus." In his *Paideia: The Ideals of Greek Culture*, translated by Gilbert Highet, 2d ed., vol. 1. New York: Oxford University Press, pp. 237-267.
Relates Aeschylus' developing a new form of dramatic poetry to the changed political circumstances of Athens, specifically, the fall of the Pisistratid dynasty and the rise of the new democracy. Jaeger discounts any conscious attempt on Aeschylus' part to portray the Eleusinian Mysteries of Demeter onstage, though the notes the words Aristophanes assigns Aeschylus in the *Frogs* 886-887, which imply Aeschylus was an Eleusinian initiate. Jaeger then reviews the plot of each of the extant plays, briefly, against their historical and social background.

McCall, Marsh, Jr., ed. *Aeschylus: A Collection of Critical Essays*. Englewood Cliffs, N.J.: Prentice-Hall, 1972.
This collection of essays on each of the surviving plays has the advantages of ready accessibility and sound scholarship by recognized critics. Each essay is written as a general introduction to some aspect of the playwright's work. C. M. Bowra writes on Aeschylus' conception of tragedy, Gilbert Murray on the *Persae*, Thomas G. Rosenmeyer on *Seven Against Thebes*, John H. Finley, Jr., on the *Suppliants*, and Richmond Lattimore on the *Oresteia*. Freedom and its limits is the subject of a particularly fine essay by N. G. L. Hammond, while George Thomson examines various treatments of the Prometheus myth, comparing them to that of Aeschylus. Those essays on the individual plays are cited above.

Murray, Gilbert. *Aeschylus: The Creator of Tragedy*. Oxford, England: Clarendon Press, 1940, reprints 1951, 1958.

This work remains an admirable study of how Aeschylus transformed myth to drama (specifically in the *Prometheus*) and of experimental staging techniques (such as the *mechané*). There is an important chapter on philosophical ideas and Aristophanes' misleading depiction of Aeschylus. Separate discussions of the war plays (*Persians* and *Seven Against Thebes*), satyr plays, the *Oresteia*, and a suggestive "scenario" on the *Agamemnon* conclude the volume.

Podlecki, Anthony J. *The Political Background of Aeschylean Tragedy*. Ann Arbor: University of Michigan Press, 1966.

Podlecki begins with the astute premise that political themes underlay the drama of every historical period. He focuses especially on the Persian wars and argues that Aeschylus was considerably more liberal than usually portrayed, that he was actually an ardent supporter of Themistocles in the attempt to restrict aristocratic privilege. There are separate chapters on biography, the *Persians*, *Seven Against Thebes*, *Suppliants*, *Oresteia*, and *Prometheus*, all cited above. The first of three appendices, "Aeschylus on Salamis," deduces historical information from *Persians* that Podlecki then reads against Herodotus.

Rosenmeyer, Thomas G. *The Art of Aeschylus*. Berkeley: University of California Press, 1982.

Most valuable to general readers are chapters 4 and 5, which analyze the style of Aeschylean verse and the set speech. Chapters 9 and 10 consider the role of the gods and the related themes of curse and guilt. There is discussion of timing, of the *Oresteia* as the only extant trilogy, a useful appendix on the life and times of Aeschylus, a comparative chronology, and a select bibliography. Discussion of text and manuscript transmission, with which the book begins, is considerably less technical than in many comparable works, making it suitable for the interested generalist. There are no discrete discussions of the plays. Each chapter considers passages, lines, and language to make overall conjectures on style, characterization of deities and mortals, and dramatic tension and timing.

Scott, William C. *Musical Design in Aeschylean Theatre*. Hanover, N.H.: University Press of New England, 1984.

An unusual study that considers the role of the chorus in the extant plays. Aeschylus, whose plays spring most directly from dithyramb, faced the problem of reconciling the musical tradition that he inherited with his own desire to create stage personalities rather than mere solo performances by a chorus member. He was neither inclined nor able to consign the chorus to an ancillary role, and the result is a blending and occasionally a contention of lyric and dramatic elements in his works.

Sheppard, John T. *Aeschylus and Sophocles: Their Work and Influence*. Our Debt to Greece and Rome Series. New York: Cooper Square, 1963.

This book, part of a series that examines antiquity against modern survivals, begins with three relatively short chapters. These discuss the work of Aeschylus and Sophocles and their combined influence in Greece and Rome. The focus of the book is its second part, on Italian, French, and German adaptations during the Renaissance, neoclassical, and Romantic periods. There is a short separate chapter on John Milton's use of Aeschylus' *Prometheus* for his own *Samson Agonistes* as an influence at least as profound as that of the Old Testament.

Smyth, Herbert Weir. *Aeschylean Tragedy*. Berkeley: University of California Press, 1924. Reprint. New York: Biblo and Tannen, 1969.

This work is a compendium of lectures prepared for the Sather series at the University of California at Berkeley by the author of what remains the standard in Attic Greek grammar texts. Though written in 1922, Smyth's introductions to the *Suppliants*, *Persians*, *Prometheus*, and *Seven Against Thebes* retain their clarity, strength, and logic. The final three chapters discuss separately the plays of the *Oresteia*. Despite its old-fashioned style and absence of documentation, Smyth's study is often cited in the critical literature and has become a standard volume.

Spatz, Lois. *Aeschylus*. Twayne's World Authors Series 675. Boston: Twayne, 1982.

Spatz here applies the regular Twayne series format to a study of Aeschylus. Her study includes a chronology, a sound and conservative first chapter on Aeschylus' times and the political atmosphere of fifth century Athens. She rightly focuses her discussion of the plays on the major historical events that shaped Aeschylus' retelling of the myths: the Persian wars. Separate chapters present excellent introductory discussions of *Persians*, *Seven Against Thebes*, *Suppliants*, and *Oresteia*. *Prometheus Bound*, whose style, language, and subject matter differ from other plays of Aeschylus, is often assigned a later date of composition or considered non-Aeschylean. Spatz discusses the basic evidence, accepts Aeschylus as author, though she notes the play might have been finished by another author, and provides a good discussion of Prometheus as archetype for human life. The volume concludes with a selected and briefly annotated bibliography.

Taplin, Oliver. "Aeschylean Silences and Silences in Aeschylus." *Harvard Studies in Classical Philology* 76 (1972): 57-97.

This article begins with the observation that most of the characters of any play are silent most of the time, but these silences in the hands of a playwright such as Aeschylus can hold considerable meaning in the context of a drama. Taplin cites Aristophanes' *Frogs*, specifically the debate between Aeschylus and Euripides, to prove that the ancient audience recognized the difference between the terse and quiet style of Aeschylus and the more loquacious characters of Euripides. The study employs all the extant plays, including fragments in the papyri, to argue that Aeschylus uses silence as a device that heightens dramatic intensity. Though somewhat technical, the arguments are straightforward and readily accessible to the general reader.

——————— . *The Stagecraft of Aeschylus: The Dramatic Use of Exits and Entrances in Greek Tragedy*. Oxford, England: Clarendon Press, 1977.
Considers the effect produced by sudden spectacular appearances, entrances, and exits. Paradoxically, despite Aeschylus' reliance on speeches and elegant dialogue, the variety of unusual entrances and exits is greatest in Aeschylus' plays. Taplin suggests that such spectacle serves to balance the relatively static Aeschylean dialogue.

Thomson, George. *Aeschylus and Athens: A Study in the Social Origins of Drama*. Cambridge, England: Cambridge University Press, 1940. Reprint. New York: Haskell House, 1967.
Parts 1 and 2 are an impressive exposition of the relation of ritual in tribal society and in the transitional period from tribe to state. Part 3 relates the evolution of these rituals to the beginnings of drama through the worship of Dionysus and Apollo. Part 4 traces the relationship of anthropological and social influences to Aeschylus' early style. All this appears in the style of J. G. Frazer's *The Golden Bough* (1890-1915). Essentially this approach is out of favor among contemporary critics. A group of such critics, known as the Cambridge Classical Anthropologists, influenced profoundly the study of classical literature and ancient history in the last twenty years of the nineteenth and the first quarter of the twentieth century. Another example of their approach to classical drama is that of Cornford, cited above under general works.

Turyn, Alexander. *The Manuscript Tradition of the Tragedies of Aeschylus*. Hildesheim, Germany: Georg Olms, 1943. Reprint. Cambridge, England: Cambridge University Press, 1968.
Though more technical than the average reader requires, Turyn's study remains the most complete analysis of variations in Aeschylus' texts, of how gaps and other lacunae have affected interpretation, and of how specific recensions have changed content. Each of Aeschylus' plays comes under scrutiny, and, though technical, Turyn's discussion is straightforward and engaging for the serious reader.

Winnington-Ingram, R. P. *Studies in Aeschylus*. New York: Cambridge University Press, 1983.
This assemblage of the author's previously published work on Aeschylus was

supplemented to include all the extant plays. Part 1 discusses all the earlier works with Zeus' role in *Persae*, the *Seven Against Thebes*, and the *Suppliants* each allotted one chapter. Part 2 considers aspects of the *Oresteia* in five chapters (general introduction to the trilogy; Agamemnon; Clytemnestra and Athena; Orestes and Apollo; Zeus and the Erinyes). A third part contains the author's arguments against Aeschylus' authorship of the *Prometheus Bound*, though Winnington-Ingram is willing to admit the influence or the authorship of Aeschylus in the Io scene.

ARISTOPHANES

Recommended Translations and Commentaries

Acharnians

Parker, Douglass, trans. *The Acharnians*. New American Library. New York: Mentor, 1961.

A sound translation, inexpensive, readily available, and designed for general readers and school use. The apparatus is not as complete as one might hope for in a play such as the *Acharnians*, though there is a short introduction that outlines crucial historical background.

Sommerstein, Alan H., ed., trans. *The Comedies of Aristophanes*. Vol. 1, *Aristophanes: Acharnians*. Wauconda, Ill.: Bolchazy-Carducci, 1980.

Designed for the broadest possible audience, this volume combines a Greek text with an English prose translation on facing pages and includes a commentary suitable for both students of Greek and general readers. The short apparatus contains only those variants and conjectures that present something worthy of discussion in the commentary. There is an introductory note as well as a selected bibliography. The translation, originally intended for the Loeb Classical Library, was published as the first volume of the complete plays of Aristophanes. See description of the complete set, below.

Starkie, W. J. M., ed., trans. *The Acharnians of Aristophanes*. London: Macmillan, 1909. Reprint. Salem, N.H.: Ayer, 1979.

Contains an introduction to the play and to Aristophanes, English prose translation, critical notes, and commentary. Though some of Starkie's commentaries seem dated and have gone out of print, this one remains an often-cited source. Its translation and the breadth of its commentary make it suitable for general readers as well as students of Greek.

Birds

Arnott, Peter D., ed., trans. *The Birds by Aristophanes and The Brothers Menaechmus by Plautus*. New York: Appleton-Century-Crofts, 1958.

Easily obtainable and a good translation of the two plays. The contrast of one of the best Old Comedy plays and one of the finest Roman New Comedy plays offers a good illustration of how ancient comedy evolves into the form that it assumes in the Roman world. Plautus' *The Brothers Menaechmus* inspired the plot of Shakespeare's *The Two Gentlemen of Verona*, and those familiar with the English play will enjoy making the contrasts. Arnott also provides a useful discussion of the two plays that can stand as a good introduction to Greek Old Comedy and New Comedy in its Roman form.

Merry, W. W., ed. *Birds: With Introduction and Notes*. Oxford, England: Clarendon Press, 1896.

This dated commentary with Greek text remains easily available, in effect its only virtue, for it has been effectively replaced by the Sommerstein commentary (1987), cited below. It follows the standard Oxford format, and readers unconcerned with recent scholarship will still find its introduction useful.

Sommerstein, Alan H., ed., trans. *The Comedies of Aristophanes*. Vol. 6, *Aristophanes: Birds*. Wauconda, Ill.: Bolchazy-Carducci, 1987.

This series of the complete extant plays contains separate volumes as published with Greek text and short apparatus on facing pages. It is suitable for general readers as well as students of Greek. See description of complete set, below.

Clouds

Arnott, Peter D., ed., trans. *The Clouds by Aristophanes and The Pot of Gold by Plautus*. New York: Appleton-Century-Crofts, 1967.

The companion volume to Arnott's translation of the *Birds*, cited above. It is inexpensive, readily available, and offers a good pairing with a Roman comedy that contains Aristophanic elements. Arnott's rationale is to contrast Old and New Comedy. The combination of an Aristophanes play and a comedy of Plautus makes this edition worthwhile for classroom use.

Dover, K. J. *Clouds: Edited with Introduction and Commentary*. Oxford, England: Clarendon Press, 1968.

Those without a knowledge of Greek may still profit from this commentary's extensive introduction, which begins by setting forth dates and events known about Aristophanes' career and discusses the different character and personalities of the *Clouds* (with good observations on Strepsiades, its protagonist). Another section provides background on Socrates with copious references both to the *Clouds* and the pre-Socratic philosophers. There is a good discussion of "Right" and "Wrong" and their debate, as well as of the chorus' role and production techniques. The revised version of the play is discussed, followed by a technical, but brief, consideration of text transmission. The Greek text and commentary constitute the heart of the volume, but readers without Greek may also use the commentary for its good observations on narrative and staging.

McLeish, Kenneth, trans. *Aristophanes: Clouds, Women in Power, Knights*. Translations from Greek and Roman Authors. New York: Cambridge University Press, 1980.

Strong, readable, and comparatively literal translations, though without detailed commentaries. The volume is available in paperback and hardcover format.

Sommerstein, Alan H., ed., trans. *The Comedies of Aristophanes*. Vol. 3, *Aristophanes: Clouds*. Wauconda, Ill.: Bolchazy-Carducci, 1982.

A reliable Greek text, short apparatus, translation, and commentary, intended both for students of Greek and for general readers. This volume's commentary particularly emphasizes idiom and dramatic structure. See description of complete set, below.

Starkie, W. J. M., ed., trans. *The Clouds of Aristophanes*. London: Macmillan, 1911. Reprint. Amsterdam: Hakkert, 1985.

Starkie's commentaries on the plays of Aristophanes remain often cited, despite their age and lack of modern scholarship. This volume contains a Greek text, an introductory essay on production history, prose translation, notes, and commentary. The commentary contains insights on interpretation as well as notes on the Greek text.

West, Thomas G., and Grace Starry West, trans. *Four Texts on Socrates: Plato's Euthyphro, Apology, and Crito, Aristophanes' Clouds*. Ithaca, N.Y.: Cornell University Press, 1984.

This volume is worthwhile for its convenient grouping of four texts on Socrates, literally translated and with notes intended for undergraduate and general readers. The lampooned Socrates of the *Clouds* stands as a stark contrast to the portrait in Plato's dialogues, and the translators provide a brief introduction that both compares and reconciles these different views. A selected bibliography, briefly annotated, accompanies the text.

Ecclesiazusae

Parker, Douglass, trans. *The Congresswomen*. Ann Arbor: University of Michigan Press, 1967.

One of the best translations of the *Ecclesiazusae*, prepared by one of the translators of the Mentor series. There is no apparatus, though there is a good introduction that covers background. Since relatively few translations in contemporary English are available, Parker's volume deserves special notice.

Usher, R. G. *Ecclesiazousae: Edited with Introduction and Commentary*. Oxford, England: Clarendon Press, 1973.

Follows the Oxford format of substantial introduction, which includes basic information on Aristophanes, production history and staging, and concluding with a more technical discussion of the manuscript tradition. The commentary emphasizes difficulties in the Greek text, but also traces stage action and elucidates plot complications.

Frogs

Stanford, W. B. *The Frogs: Edited with Introduction, Revised Text, Commentary, and Index*. 2d ed. London: Macmillan, 1963.

Stanford's edition, designed for readers of Greek, nevertheless has good comments useful for all readers on the debate of Aeschylus and Euripides, which is the focus of the play. There are worthwhile observations on the play's underworld setting, use of the chorus, and the more elusive sections of the debate.

Knights

Sommerstein, Alan H., ed., trans. *The Comedies of Aristophanes*. Vol. 2, *Aristophanes: Knights*. Wauconda, Ill.: Bolchazy-Carducci, 1981.
Greek text and short apparatus on facing pages with English translation. Intended for general readers as well as students of Greek, the commentary addresses problems of staging and production as well as of the text. See description of complete set, below.

Lysistrata

Beardsley, Aubrey, illus. *The Lysistrata of Aristophanes*. New York: St. Martin's Press, 1973.
Important more for the famous Aubrey Beardsley illustrations than for the awkward and nonliteral translation that accompanies them. *Lysistrata*, because of its premise that women using the primacy they have over love can bring peace to the world, has attained a new popularity and remains controversial as it was in fifth century Athens.

Henderson, Jeffrey, trans. *Aristophanes' Lysistrata*. Focus Classical Library. Cambridge, Mass.: Focus Information Group, 1988.
This translation includes a commentary simplified for general readers not concerned with the language and textual problems treated in Henderson's Greek edition and commentary cited below. The notes are particularly strong on the historical and cultural context of the play, and there are suggestions for further reading, notes on production, and a map.

_____ , ed. *Aristophanes' Lysistrata*. New York: Oxford University Press, 1987.
A sound Greek text with commentary and introductory. As with all Oxford commentaries, the focus is primarily textual; however, there is good information on stage problems, complications of plot, and background that can be useful for any reader. The introductory essay provides a history of the play and controversy attending its production.

Peace

Platnauer, Maurice, ed. *Aristophanes' Peace*. Oxford, England: Clarendon Press, 1964.
The commentary here is more keyed to problems in the Greek text than some of the other Oxford commentaries cited in this volume, but the introduction is

certainly accessible to all readers. It contains information on historical background, scenic arrangements, dating the play, and consideration of arguments for a second version. The brief structural analysis is also worthwhile for readers without Greek.

Sommerstein, Alan H., ed., trans. *The Comedies of Aristophanes*. Vol. 5, *Aristophanes: Peace*. Wauconda, Ill.: Bolchazy-Carducci, 1985.
Full Greek text, simplified apparatus, and English translation on facing pages. The commentary is suitable for both students of Greek and general readers. See description of the complete set, below.

Wasps

MacDowell, Douglas M. *Wasps: Edited with Introduction and Commentary*. Oxford, England: Clarendon Press, 1971.
A sound edition of the Greek text. The introduction treats background and production history. Both the introduction and line commentary are subdivided in a way that allows general readers to use them with a good translation, though the Oxford commentaries are intended for students of the language. Sommerstein's commentary, volume 4 of the series listed below, has an updated and more thorough bibliography as well as an accompanying translation, but MacDowell's remains stronger on language and textual matters.

Parker, Douglass. *The Wasps*. New American Library. New York: Mentor, 1962.
Designed for school and general use and offering the advantages of ready availability and contemporary English. There is a short introduction, basic notes, and a glossary of names.

Sommerstein, Alan H., ed., trans. *The Comedies of Aristophanes*. Vol. 4, *Aristophanes: Wasps*. Wauconda, Ill.: Bolchazy-Carducci, 1983.
Greek text and short apparatus facing English prose translation. The commentary is suitable for general readers as well as students of Greek. See description of complete set, below.

Complete Collections

Arrowsmith, William, Richmond Lattimore, and Douglass Parker, trans. *Aristophanes: Four Plays*. New York: Meridian, 1986.
This collection, which includes the *Birds*, *Clouds*, *Frogs*, and *Lysistrata*, deserves special mention because it overcomes many of the difficulties associated with rendering a witty yet faithful translation of Aristophanes' topical humor for students not thoroughly acquainted with the political background against which the plays were written. Though not burdened with apparatus (which can sometimes be more intrusive than helpful), there are notes when translation alone cannot convey full meaning. Arrowsmith's idiom in his translation of

Birds and *Clouds* suits Aristophanes' style best of all. Lattimore's rendering of *Frogs* is somewhat more formal but also more literal. Parker's *Lysistrata* falls somewhere in between these two styles of translation. All these translations have appeared separately in earlier Mentor editions.

Arrowsmith, William, and Douglass Parker, trans. *Three Comedies by Aristophanes*. Ann Arbor: University of Michigan Press, 1969.
Contains Arrowsmith's distinguished translations of the *Birds* and the *Clouds* and Parker's translation of the *Wasps*, brief notes, and short introduction. Trade paperback format. See the Arrowsmith, Lattimore, Parker volume, cited above.

Barrett, David, trans. *Aristophanes: Lysistrata and Other Plays*. New York: Penguin Books, 1974.
Includes translations of the *Acharnians* and the *Clouds*, as well as the *Lysistrata*, and contains an introduction and short notes. One of the three Penguin volumes that, taken together, provide translations of all the extant plays.

_____ . *Aristophanes: The Frogs and Other Plays*. New York: Penguin Books, 1964.
Contains a brief introduction, short notes, and good translations of the *Frogs*, the *Wasps*, and the *Thesmophoriazusae*. One of three Penguin volumes that, taken together, provide translations of all the extant plays.

Barrett, David, and Alan H. Sommerstein, trans. *Aristophanes: The Knights, Peace, The Birds, The Assemblywomen, Wealth*. New York: Penguin Books, 1978.
One of the three volumes that, as a collection, contain translations of all the extant plays. See also Sommerstein's commentaries with Greek texts and translations, cited below.

Hadas, Moses, ed., trans. *The Complete Plays of Aristophanes*. New York: Bantam, 1962.
The strengths of this collection are Hadas' own translations of the *Clouds* and the *Wasps* and his introduction (brief yet excellent). The volume itself is inexpensive, an asset for classroom use; yet, its weaknesses are considerable. Foremost among these is the unevenness of the translations, all by various hands. Benjamin Bickley Rogers' translations of the *Acharnians* and the *Plutus* depart considerably from the Greek and are in an Edwardian verse idiom. Robert H. Webb's translations of the *Knights* and the *Frogs* read more smoothly, but they, too, retain rhymed verse form. The volume is entirely without commentary or notes, and this lack discourages readers unfamiliar with the historical, social, and political references upon which Aristophanes bases much of his humor.

Parker, Douglass, and Richmond Lattimore, trans. *Four Comedies by Aristophanes*. Ann Arbor: University of Michigan Press, 1969.

Contains Parker's excellent translations of *Lysistrata*, *Acharnians*, and *Congresswomen* (*Ecclesiazusae*) and Lattimore's translation of the *Frogs*, brief notes, and introduction. Trade paperback format. See the Arrowsmith, Lattimore, Parker volume and the Arrowsmith, Parker volume, both cited above.

Rogers, Benjamin Bickley, trans. *Aristophanes*. 3 vols. Loeb Classical Library. Cambridge, Mass.: Harvard University Press, 1924.

Contains all the plays in verse translation with Greek text on facing pages. Though it remains in print as part of the Loeb Classical Library, the Sommerstein editions, noted herein, contain infinitely better translations and have the advantages of commentaries and later scholarship.

Sommerstein, Alan H., ed., trans. *The Comedies of Aristophanes*. 11 vols. Warminster, Wiltshire, England: Aris and Phillips, 1980-   ; Wauconda, Ill.: Bolchazy-Carducci, 1980-

This set is the much-praised major edition of all the comedies of Aristophanes, the first since that of Benjamin Bickley Rogers in 1915. It contains a full Greek text and apparatus for each of the eleven extant plays, a readable translation, and a commentary that concentrates on the theatrical, literary, social, and historical background of each work. It presents the plays in chronological order, starting with *Acharnians*. The general introduction in the first volume considers Aristophanes' life, work, and thought; the structure and production of the comedies; transmission of text; a selected bibliography. The final volume presents a complete index. The middle volumes present discrete texts and commentaries of the other ten surviving plays. Available as separate volumes in both hardcover and paperbound format. See citations above for the individual volumes.

Recommended Criticism on Aristophanes

Acharnians

Dover, K. J. "*Acharnians*." In his *Aristophanic Comedy*. Berkeley: University of California Press, 1972, pp. 78-88.

Begins with a synopsis that recounts the play against the background of the Peloponnesian War and then analyzes its production, noting the relatively large cast it requires and commenting on staging problems. Dover disdains arguments for the pacifism that some have seen as its theme and argues instead that the issue is the willingness to continue war for an uncertain and marginal gain when it is possible to make peace at a trivial cost.

Edmunds, Lowell. "Aristophanes' *Acharnians*." In *Yale Classical Studies, Volume XXVI: Aristophanes, Essays in Interpretation*, edited by Jeffrey Henderson. New York: Cambridge University Press, 1981, pp. 1-41.

Edmunds contends that Aristophanes has a clear political program in this play, beginning with the title, for the Acharnians were the most hawkish demesmen of the period. Dicaeopolis (whose name translates to "just-city") makes peace with Sparta as an act of whimsy and self-assertion, and his name justifies his action. Edmunds argues that one cannot separate the poetry of the *Acharnians* from its political message and analyzes the connections of plot and language to theme.

Gomme, Arnold Wycombe. "Aristophanes and Politics." In *More Essays in Greek History and Literature*, edited by David A. Campbell. Oxford, England: Basil Blackwell, 1962, pp. 70-91.

This collection of essays on various classical subjects contains Gomme's "Aristophanes and Politics," which appeared originally in 1938. Gomme analyzes the extent to which Aristophanes considered himself a political playwright and argues that a didactic moral sense and basic conservatism pervade the extant plays. He considers that Aristophanes admired the old ways, that Miltiades, Cimon, and Myronides were his military heroes, Marathon and Salamis his great battles. The article presents a good analysis of several plays (*Acharnians*, *Knights*, and *Peace* especially) along these lines.

Murray, Gilbert. "Ancient Greek Comedy: Aristophanes' Background." In his *Aristophanes: A Study*. Oxford, England: Clarendon Press, 1933. Reprint. New York: Russell and Russell, 1964, pp. 1-38.

Discusses the *Acharnians* as an early play, noting its daring political nature and indicating the great freedom of expression possible in the Athenian theater. Dicaiopolis, in effect, argues in defence of an enemy and against state policy. The Spartans, so Dicaiopolis says, are not the cause of all the troubles and in some respects have been unfairly treated. Murray uses the *Acharnians* and what is known about the lost plays *Daitales* and *Babylonians* to describe the degree of toleration in Athenian Old Comedy.

Reckford, Kenneth J. "*Acharnians*: The Creative Word; The See-through Rags; Comic Integrity." In his *Aristophanes' Old-and-New Comedy: Six Essays in Perspective*, vol. 1. Chapel Hill: University of North Carolina Press, 1987, pp. 162-196.

Compares the *Acharnians* to Tom Stoppard's *Travesties* in that both have two interwoven comic ideas superimposing art on politics. The more obvious is the separate peace Dicaeopolis negotiates. Reckford then analyzes wordplay and innuendo and argues that *Acharnians* is about art as well as politics; he goes on to show how Aristophanes repeatedly mixes the two in suggestive ways.

Spatz, Lois. "War and Peace: *Acharnians* (*Akharnes*) and *Peace* (*Eirene*)." In her *Aristophanes*. Twayne's World Authors Series 482. Boston: Twayne, 1978, pp. 30-45.

Chapter 2 of this study examines both plays. There is a summary of *Acharnians*, followed by discussion of the play as a satire that attacks corrupt politicians, inefficient government, the degeneration of poetry, and materialism in urban life. Spatz then examines the *Peace* as a variation on these themes, summarizing the plot and noting similarities.

Strauss, Leo. "The Other Plays: The *Acharnians*." In his *Socrates and Aristophanes*. New York: Basic Books, 1966, pp. 57-79.

Notes that the plot concerns matters that are public and that they are discussed in public, in contrast to the plot of the *Clouds*. Dikaeopolis (whose name means "just-city") is not conscious of any guilt or betrayal of his city in making a separate treaty; he has simply forgotten his city. Dikaeopolis is the contemporary of, and even more unerotic than, Strepsiades; yet, he sings a phallic song to Dionysus. Essentially, everything he does in some way implies unjust speech, a parody of demagogic oratory.

Whitman, Cedric H. "City and Individual: *Acharnians*." In his *Aristophanes and the Comic Hero*. Martin Classical Lectures 19. Cambridge, Mass.: Harvard University Press, 1964, pp. 59-80.

Notes that the *Acharnians* is usually analyzed either as a peace play or as propaganda rather than as poetry, that this obscures a larger range of meanings, among them the portrait of Dicaeopolis as a comic hero. Whitman reads the play as a heroic fantasy that focuses on Dicaeopolis as "Just City."

Birds

Dover, K. J. "*Birds*." In his *Aristophanic Comedy*. Berkeley: University of California Press, 1972, pp. 140-149.

The synopsis recounts the establishment of *Nephelokokkygía* (cloudcuckooland), noting the huge cast of major and minor actors and considering production problems. Dover notes the implied criticism of life at Athens but also observes that Aristophanes does not direct the attention of the community to any specific policy changes or political reforms.

Murray, Gilbert. "The Plays of Escape." In his *Aristophanes: A Study*. Oxford, England: Clarendon Press, 1933. Reprint. New York: Russell and Russell, 1964, pp. 135-163.

Murray rejects the argument that the *Birds* refers to the debacle of the Sicilian Expedition, remarking that its failure would not have been known until the winter of 413 B.C., one year after the play's production. He also rejects the view that the play represents the sanguine hopes of the period immediately before the expedition, arguing that critics expect strongly political themes in every Aristophanes play and have read strong political implications into the *Birds*. He prefers to see good-natured humor, comparing its tone to Shakespeare's *A Midsummer Night's Dream*.

Reckford, Kenneth J. "Utopia Unlimited: *Birds*." In his *Aristophanes' Old-and-New Comedy: Six Essays in Perspective*, vol. 1. Chapel Hill: University of North Carolina Press, 1987, pp. 330-343.
Having noted the play's striking reversal (two refugees from Athens seeking a quiet town fortify a bird metropolis, blockade the gods, and win control of the universe), Reckford emphasizes the escape theme, often overlooked. Cloud-cuckooland is a lovely, recreative, green world, and Reckford shows how the sights and sounds of nature are represented in poetry and dramatic movement. He notes that imagination is prey to deception and delusion, for the pastoral world the Athenians discover becomes, through their own doing, precisely like the city from which they had fled.

Spatz, Lois. "Dirty Politics: *Knights* (*Hippēs*) and *Birds* (*Ornithēs*)." In her *Aristophanes*. Twayne's World Authors Series 482. Boston: Twayne, 1978, pp. 71-90.
Spatz relates *Birds* to *Knights* through the plays' political themes. *Birds* is a satire of political life in general with the hero as persuasive and egotistical demagogue. The birds represent the fickle mob who rush from craze to craze and allow themselves to be victimized. The gods, too, can be manipulated because they incorporate all the worst features of human nature.

Strauss, Leo. "The Other Plays: The *Birds*." In his *Socrates and Aristophanes*. New York: Basic Books, 1966, pp. 160-194.
Strauss notes the location, the only play whose entire action takes place far from Athens. His analysis focuses on wily speech that implies half-truths. For example, when Peisthetaerus explains his plan to find the ideal state to the birds, he proceeds very differently from the way he did when he explained it to Tereus. He makes no attempt to convince Tereus that the idea of birds ruling men and destroying gods is just. For Tereus, a tyrant himself, the proposal is eminently right.

Whitman, Cedric H. "The Anatomy of Nothingness: *Birds*." In his *Aristophanes and the Comic Hero*. Martin Classical Lectures 19. Cambridge, Mass.: Harvard University Press, 1964, pp. 167-199.
Rejects the play as an allegory on the Sicilian Expedition, as what some have called irrelevant fantasy and others a condemnation of Athenian gullibility, fickleness, waywardness, and superstition. Whitman considers that the play's allusions are topical rather than political. The hero is Peithetaerus (whose name means "companion-persuader"), who exercises resourceful wickedness in the company of his naïve companion, Euelpides.

Clouds
Dover, K. J. *"Clouds."* In his *Aristophanic Comedy*. Berkeley: University of California Press, 1972, pp. 101-120.
Offers a short production history and a synopsis and discusses the nature of the revision, referred to by the chorus. Dover notes that four actors are required, remarking that the large part given to the fourth actor constitutes an abnormality. He then considers the stage setting against problem scenes and notes that the Socratic logic this play spoofs was unsettling to conservative Greek beliefs and practices and that this, plus the increasing emphasis on persuasion in law courts and political assemblies, provided inspiration for the play.

Glen, R. S. *The Two Muses: An Introduction to Fifth-Century Athens by Way of the Drama*. New York: St. Martin's Press, 1968.
The two Muses of the title are Melpomene (Tragedy) and Thalia (Comedy). Emphasizing the *Medea* of Euripides and the *Clouds* of Aristophanes (both of which it presents in translations and with introductions by the author), the book is intended as an undergraduate's or general reader's introduction to the life of fifth century Athens. The two plays are preceded by chapters on the social and historical background of the Greek world, on the fifth century Athenian theater, and on the intellectual climate of the period. There is a very satisfactory map of Greece as well as photographs of drama-related pottery, statuary, and modern productions of ancient dramas.

Harriott, Rosemary M. *"Clouds."* In her *Aristophanes: Poet and Dramatist*. Baltimore: Johns Hopkins University Press, 1986, pp. 165-186.
Discusses the contrast of Strepsiades and Pheidippides, noting that Pheidippides acquires intellectual and physical superiority over his father at the same moment and that rhetoric and family relationships come together when the boy strikes his father. Harriott provides a discrete chapter analysis of this play considering the impact of rhetoric, and specifically Socratic dialectic, on the theme of the play.

Marrou, H. I. "The 'Old' Athenian Education." In his *A History of Education in Antiquity*, translated by George Lamb. New York: Sheed and Ward, 1956. Reprint. New American Library. New York: Mentor, 1964, pp. 63-75.
Marrou borrows the term "old Athenian education" from Aristophanes' *Clouds* 961 and understands it to denote the type of education that prevailed before the changes initiated by the Sophists and Socrates. He discusses its aristocratic associations with the military and notes references to it in Thucydides, Xenophon, and especially in the plot of the *Clouds*.

Murray, Gilbert. "The New Learning: Socrates." In his *Aristophanes: A Study*. Oxford, England: Clarendon Press, 1933. Reprint. New York: Russell and

Russell, 1964, pp. 85-110.

Considers the *Clouds* as a development of the *Daitales*, that the play adds to questions about how Socrates was viewed by his contemporaries. Notes the contrast Aristophanes makes between the methods of intellectual training then practiced in Athens and Socrates as symbol of new and, some said, radical methods. Murray considers this an elaboration of the good young man and the corrupt young man in the fragmentary *Daitales*.

Nussbaum, Martha C. "Aristophanes and Socrates on Learning Practical Wisdom." In *Yale Classical Studies, Volume XXVI: Aristophanes: Essays in Interpretation*, edited by Jeffrey Henderson. New York: Cambridge University Press, 1981, pp. 43-97.

Notes that the uncompromising praise of Socrates in the twentieth century has caused many critics to scorn Aristophanes' portrait of him in the *Clouds*. Nussbaum focuses on traditional and expert-centered conception of moral education and holds that Socrates' assimilation with the Sophists in Aristophanes' play constitutes an interesting criticism of his thought, that the criticism can legitimately be found in the play, and that the *Clouds* anticipates the main lines along which Plato, in the *Republic*, modifies the Socratic program of moral education.

Reckford, Kenneth J. "Aristophanes' Old-and-New Comedy: *Clouds*." In his *Aristophanes' Old-and-New Comedy: Six Essays in Perspective*, vol. 1. Chapel Hill: University of North Carolina Press, 1987, pp. 388-402.

Sees all Aristophanes' works as representing late Old Comedy, and this play, produced in 423 B.C., as incorporating much of what would be called New Comedy, the result being that *Clouds* falls, by Reckford's parameters, somewhere between Old and New Comedy, despite its composition in the early period of the playwright's career. *Clouds* is high comedy, more than criticism of Socrates, the Sophists, or new education.

Spatz, Lois. "School for Life: *Clouds* (*Nephelai*)." In her *Aristophanes*. Twayne's World Authors Series 482. Boston: Twayne, 1978, pp. 46-59.

Provides a plot summary, then interprets the play as representing the conflict of old and new and an indictment of the Sophists. Spatz considers that Socrates was merely a convenient caricature of the new philosopher, that Aristophanes is not specifically attacking Socrates or Socratic thought. She concludes by noting the play's comic coherence and some inconsistencies of plot.

Strauss, Leo. "The *Clouds*." In his *Socrates and Aristophanes*. New York: Basic Books, 1966, pp. 11-53.

Strauss argues that despite his lampooning of Socrates, Aristophanes does not champion unreason over reason. Socrates' downfall is brought about by Strepsiades, who does not even know Socrates' name when the play begins. The Clouds occupy a pivotal role as the chorus, being predisposed intellectually to Socrates but morally supporting the old man Strepsiades when his son Pheidippides strikes him. Strauss concludes that Pheidippides is not a follower of Socrates; he remains unconverted to Socratic continence and endurance. That Strepsiades is represented as not understanding Socrates' assertion that Zeus does not exist and, hence, cannot face the question is proof that Aristophanes himself had faced it.

Whitman, Cedric H. "The War Between the Generations: *Clouds.*" In his *Aristophanes and the Comic Hero*. Martin Classical Lectures 19. Cambridge, Mass.: Harvard University Press, 1964, pp. 119-143.
  Strepsiades never attains any stature greater than he starts with; he never reaches the wily unscrupulousness of an Aristophanic hero; essentially, he is a failed student of Socrates. His son Pheidippides, however, has fully mastered Socratic wickedness. Whitman illustrates by comparing the confrontations of Strepsiades and Socrates, and Strepsiades and Pheidippides.

Ecclesiazusae
Dover, K. J. "*Women in Assembly.*" In his *Aristophanic Comedy*. Berkeley: University of California Press, 1972, pp. 190-201.
  The synopsis notes problems of dating and discusses the chorus as the play's most unusual feature, since it enters in silence at line 30 but says nothing until line 285 when it goes out of the theater to the Assembly. Dover follows with a list and discussion of characters, staging problems, and the play's theme of women and property.

Murray, Gilbert. "The Beginning of the Fourth Century." In his *Aristophanes: A Study*. Oxford, England: Clarendon Press, 1933. Reprint. New York: Russell and Russell, 1964, pp. 181-198.
  Murray notes that both the *Ecclesiazusae* and the *Plutus* show a new fourth century style, lacking bold speech and outspoken criticism and showing a greatly reduced chorus. He analyzes the dialogue of the *Ecclesiazusae* to show Aristophanes' attempt to write somewhere between the strong humor of Old Comedy and the subtle tone that had caused some of his earlier plays to fail.

Reckford, Kenneth J. "Utopia Limited: *Ecclesiazusae.*" In his *Aristophanes' Old-and-New Comedy: Six Essays in Perspective*, vol. 1. Chapel Hill: University of North Carolina Press, 1987, pp. 344-353.
  Noting that most critics cite the serious and changed style of the *Ecclesiazusae* and *Plutus* and label them as Middle Comedy, Reckford illustrates the recurrence of familiar Aristophanes themes. In the *Ecclesiazusae*, Praxagora's demonstration speech begins, like Lysistrata's, by recounting the wretched state of

public affairs. The theme of community remains, seen through the borrowed men's clothes and preparation for the Assembly, and constitutes strong political satire.

Spatz, Lois. "New Comedy for Old: *Ekklesiazousai* and *Wealth (Ploutos)*." In her *Aristophanes*. Twayne's World Authors Series 482. Boston: Twayne, 1978, pp. 131-145.
Remarks on the state of Athens after the Peloponnesian War precede Spatz's summary of the *Ecclesiazusae*. She notes similarities with the women's theme of the *Lysistrata* and that the battle of the sexes in the *Ecclesiazusae* lacks the bitterness of that in the *Thesmophoriazusae*. The *Ecclesiazusae* is social satire, and Aristophanes has chosen women as his main characters because they are the most appropriate dominated group to institute what is, in effect, a communist reform. Spatz groups this play with her discussion of the *Plutus*.

Strauss, Leo. "The Other Plays: The *Assembly of Women*." In his *Socrates and Aristophanes*. New York: Basic Books, 1966, pp. 263-282.
Sees the youth of Praxagora against the age of her erotically repulsive husband. Since her new laws are meant for the sexual gratification of free women, they apply to her as well. Adultery can no longer be prohibited. This new order brings happiness to all, repulsive hags as well as pretty young wives. The humor thus essentially derives from sophistry. Strauss notes Socrates' correction of Praxagora's scheme in Plato's *Republic*, where sex is presented as entirely of male origin.

Frogs

Dover, K. J. "*Frogs*." In his *Aristophanic Comedy*. Berkeley: University of California Press, 1972, pp. 173-189.
A synopsis of the play, followed by an analysis of the role of the frog chorus, whether they appear onstage and the nature of their songs. Dover also considers properties (Charon's boat, the donkey on which Xanthias appears) and problems of composition (possible conflation of versions). He concludes by noting the Aeschylus-Euripides debate as indicative of the clear demarcation between types of tragic drama.

Littlefield, David J., ed. *Twentieth Century Interpretations of The Frogs: A Collection of Critical Essays*. Englewood Cliffs, N.J.: Prentice-Hall, 1968.
As other volumes in this series, this collection contains a series of essays, all of which have previously appeared, each by a recognized scholar with a distinctive view. Noteworthy are Leo Strauss's essay (from his *Socrates and Aristophanes*, cited below), George E. Mylonas on the Eleusinian Mysteries references, Charles Paul Segal on the character of Dionysus, G. M. A. Grube on Greek literary criticism, and a series of briefly stated "View Points," one a quotation from Henry David Thoreau on the frogs of Walden Pond.

McLeish, Kenneth. "Characterization in Aristophanes." In his *The Theatre of Aristophanes*. New York: Taplinger, 1980, pp. 127-143.

A comparison of the *Women at the Festival* (*Thesmophoriazusae*) and *Frogs* that notes their similarities of characterization and construction, resembling contemporary character comedy rather than the stereotypes of Old Comedy. The characters resemble those of Euripides' late plays; they develop with the plot, and both plays feature more than one central character.

Reckford, Kenneth J. "Festive Play Revisited: *Frogs*." In his *Aristophanes' Old-and-New Comedy: Six Essays in Perspective*, vol. 1. Chapel Hill: University of North Carolina Press, 1987, pp. 403-432.

Sees the conflict between Aeschylus and Euripides, upon which the play focuses, as symbolic of a renewal in spirit and perspective, that Aristophanes was at first inclined to favor Euripides in his writing of the debate, but he recognized the value of conservatism as he continued.

Spatz, Lois. "Poets and Purgatory: *Frogs* (*Batrakhoi*)." In her *Aristophanes*. Twayne's World Authors Series 482. Boston: Twayne, 1978, pp. 116-130.

Summarizes the play against the period in which it appeared (overthrow of the old democracy by the oligarchic Council of Four Hundred, their replacement by the Five Thousand as a futile attempt to combine oligarchy and democracy, and, ultimately, the appearance of the demagogue Cleophon). The death of Euripides likely provided the immediate inspiration for the play. Spatz argues that the mythic descent to the realm of the dead, where Aeschylus and Euripides debate, implies hope, that in choosing Aeschylus over Euripides, Dionysus celebrates the eternal verities of Athens.

Strauss, Leo. "The Other Plays: The *Frogs*." In his *Socrates and Aristophanes*. New York: Basic Books, 1966, pp. 236-262.

Concludes that the play presents the education of Aristophanes' educator. Dionysus moves from unqualified admiration for Euripides to a preference for Aeschylus. Significantly, his education takes place in Hades and in the guise of Heracles, in other words through a blunder that leads to the whipping contest that compares and contrasts with the intellectual test of Aeschylus and Euripides.

Whitman, Cedric H. "Death and Life: *Frogs*." In his *Aristophanes and the Comic Hero*. Martin Classical Lectures 19. Cambridge, Mass.: Harvard University Press, 1964, pp. 228-258.

In one sense, the journey to Hades is Dionysus' initiation, though the play acquires its power in the confrontation of Aeschylus and Euripides, both dead. Charon, the boatman of the Styx, collects two obels for his passage, the price of entrance to the theater. Whitman notes that the play is artistic self-scrutiny, that Xanthias shows tricky wickedness that allows him to turn the tables on his master, Dionysus.

Knights

Dover, K. J. "*Knights.*" In his *Aristophanic Comedy*. Berkeley: University of California Press, 1972, pp. 89-100.

Provides a synopsis and production history, then notes the allegory as a portrait of Cleon, its economy as a play that can be performed with only three actors. Dover believes that the play distinguishes among criticism of political structure, of political style, and of individual decisions on policy. Athenian democracy in the 420's B.C. could be changed only by restricting power to something less than the total citizen body and by a diminution in the accountability of magistrates. *Knights*, so Dover holds, contains no suggestion that such changes be made.

Edmunds, Lowell. *Cleon, Knights, and Aristophanes' Politics*. Lanham, Md.: University Press of America, 1988.

This study of Aristophanes' *Knights* relies extensively on external historical evidence to explain the themes and action of the play. Edmunds presents sound arguments on Aristophanes' political ideology, includes a chapter on Cleon in *Wasps*, discusses *stasis* (static elements) in Aristophanes' comedies, and contrasts what he calls the recurring element of "disturbance" in contemporary ideology. Class conflict is the subject of another chapter, entitled "Rapproachement Between the Knights and the *Demos*," as is Pindaric *hesychía* (stillness) and its relation to Athenian *aprágmones* (freedom from business).

Murray, Gilbert. "Cleon." In his *Aristophanes: A Study*. Oxford, England: Clarendon Press, 1933. Reprint. New York: Russell and Russell, 1964, pp. 39-68.

A discussion of Aristophanes' portrayal of Cleon in the *Knights* and the *Peace*. In the *Knights*, Aristophanes is able to portray Cleon with rollicking humor, even as he shows the tragedy to the state of Cleon's overbearing behavior. Murray cites the double implications of Aristophanes' descriptions of Cleon: He walks like a colossus, one leg in Pylos, the other in the Athenian Assembly; he is an eagle hovering in the air; the rich and poor alike dread him; he counts the people as his property.

Reckford, Kenneth J. "Wine-drinking and Recovery: Euripides' *Cyclops* and Aristophanes' *Knights*." In his *Aristophanes' Old-and-New Comedy: Six Essays in Perspective*, vol. 1. Chapel Hill: University of North Carolina Press, 1987, pp. 105-112.

Considers that the drinking scene in *Knights* raises questions of meaning and value of the human imagination. It is a warning against the tricks of deceptive imagining and a suggestion that relaxation, such as wine confers, brings a hopefulness, a power of conception, that is a prerequisite for successful action in civic life. Reckford refuses to read the play purely as satire on Cleon.

Spatz, Lois. "Dirty Politics: *Knights* (*Hippēs*) and *Birds* (*Ornithēs*)." In her *Aristophanes*. Twayne's World Authors Series 482. Boston: Twayne, 1978, pp. 71-90.
Begins by noting the historical incident that inspired the *Knights*: Cleon's having persuaded the Athenians to hold out for total surrender of the Spartans, Nicias' calling Cleon's bluff by resigning his command in Cleon's favor, and Demosthenes' victory for which Cleon took credit. Spatz thus sees the *Knights* as a bitter satire on politics and politicians. She provides a related discussion of the *Birds* as criticism of the disastrous Sicilian Expedition.

Strauss, Leo. "The Other Plays: The *Knights*." In his *Socrates and Aristophanes*. New York: Basic Books, 1966, pp. 80-111.
Strauss continues his survey of the place of just and unjust speech by noting the contrast between Nicias and Demosthenes, both slaves of Demos plagued by the new slave Cleon. He notes that Nicias so arranges things that Demosthenes is the one who actually pronounces Nicias' own proposal to desert to the enemy. When their discussion considers suicide as a means of escape, Demosthenes remarks he is willing to drink unmixed wine rather than poisonous bull's blood; thus Demosthenes transforms the means for dying into a means for living, though he is unable to convince the sober Nicias that drunkenness is conducive to sound deliberation. Strauss considers such turns of argument a manifestation of Socratic dialectic and examines the entire play in these terms.

Whitman, Cedric H. "City and Individual: *Knights*." In his *Aristophanes and the Comic Hero*. Martin Classical Lectures 19. Cambridge, Mass.: Harvard University Press, 1964, pp. 80-103.
Although a highly political play, *Knights* offers neither a program of reform nor responsible criticism. Though it relies less on fantasy than other plays of Aristophanes, this element surrounds the portrait of Cleon. Whitman's discussion focuses on this portrait, citing the degree to which fantastic elements dominate political aspects.

Lysistrata
Dover, K. J. "*Lysistrata*." In his *Aristophanic Comedy*. Berkeley: University of California Press, 1972, pp. 150-161.
Summarizes the play, then focuses on its bawdy scenes, which have earned the *Lysistrata* a certain notoriety. Dover then turns to the choral poetry and the characters, concluding with observations on the women and the war theme. He holds that, as in the cases of *Acharnians* and *Peace*, there are difficulties with

asserting that the *Lysistrata* positively advocates peace by setting a portrait of war through women's eyes.

Henderson, Jeffrey. "*Lysistrate*: The Play and Its Themes." In *Yale Classical Studies, Volume XXVI: Aristophanes, Essays in Interpretation*. New York: Cambridge University Press, 1981, pp. 153-218.
A critical essay that discusses production history, Aristophanes' use of theater resources, and staging. Henderson considers recent scholarship, discusses the use of two or three stage doors as well as the number of actors and costumes. He argues that this play requires more than three actors, outlines it, and analyzes it by scene. He then discusses plot and characterization and emphasizes that Aristophanes does not argue for the superiority or even the equality of women.

Murray, Gilbert. "The Last Effort for Peace." In his *Aristophanes: A Study*. Oxford, England: Clarendon Press, 1933. Reprint. New York: Russell and Russell, 1964, pp. 164-180.
Dating the *Lysistrata* at February, 411 B.C., Murray reads the play against the Sicilian Expedition of 413 B.C., in which Athens lost its army, its ships, and many of its young men. The oligarchy of the Four Hundred was largely ineffective in securing peace, and so the *Lysistrata* becomes a farce in which the women withhold their favors until their men decide to end the war.

Reckford, Kenneth J. "Loyalty to *Communitas*: *Lysistrata*, *Thesmophoriazusae*." In his *Aristophanes' Old-and-New Comedy: Six Essays in Perspective*, vol. 1. Chapel Hill: University of North Carolina Press, 1987, pp. 301-311.
A comparison of the role of *communitas* (fellowship) in these two plays. Reckford cites the anthropological study of *communitas* made by R. S. Rattray in 1923 and applies it to specific elements of the Aristophanes plays that imply tribalism (such as sexual separation, the exchange of clothing). Reckford notes that the women secede from family and household duties, compares elements of the actual Thesmophoria, and sees fruitful conflict of the sexes as a common theme.

Spatz, Lois. "The Battle of the Sexes: *Lysistrata* (*Lysistrate*)." In her *Aristophanes*. Twayne's World Authors Series 482. Boston: Twayne, 1978, pp. 91-102.
Provides a plot summary that emphasizes the play's irony. Spatz follows it by discussing the place women occupied in male-dominated classical Greece. Aristophanes, she notes, ignores the fact that both prostitution and homosexuality were tolerated in Athens. To admit that men could have recourse to one or the other would have undermined the power of the wives of the play. The *Lysistrata* also implies, Spatz contends, that sexual drive is more potent even than the desire for political power.

Strauss, Leo. "The Other Plays: The *Lysistrate*." In his *Socrates and Aristophanes*. New York: Basic Books, 1966, pp. 195-213.

Notes the immediate distinction made between Lysistrata and the women she calls together; she is impatient that their home duties delay them, and Strauss wonders whether Lysistrata has such obligations herself. Strauss examines the degrees of warmth or coldness with which Lysistrata receives the women; her warmest words are reserved for the Spartan Lampito, for the enemies of Athens. He concludes, having closely examined all the major speeches, that Aristophanes intentionally implies the only way to obtain peace would be through a major change in Athenian policy, the coming to power of men who would need the support of Sparta to control the Athenian populace and would, for this reason, have already made contacts with Sparta, just as Lysistrata.

Whitman, Cedric H. "The War Between the Sexes: *Lysistrata*." In his *Aristophanes and the Comic Hero*. Martin Classical Lectures 19. Cambridge, Mass.: Harvard University Press, 1964, pp. 200-216.

Notes the collective nature of Lysistrata; she represents not only women in general but also a historical and political view of Athens, perhaps something of the Panhellenic ideal. Lysistrata is not a grotesque figure; she does not possess the animal and divine dimensions one often sees in the Aristophanic hero. Whitman studies her character portrait, noting that Lysistrata radically reforms her society, while she herself remains within it.

Peace

Dover, K. J. "*Peace*." In his *Aristophanic Comedy*. Berkeley: University of California Press, 1972, pp. 132-139.

Starts with a straightforward synopsis and discusses stage settings and production problems, then considers the question of whether peace and Panhellenism are reconcilable, noting that ending the war is the common theme of *Acharnians* and *Peace*.

Murray, Gilbert. "Cleon." In his *Aristophanes: A Study*. Oxford, England: Clarendon Press, 1933. Reprint. New York: Russell and Russell, 1964, pp. 39-68.

Compares Cleon in the *Knights* and the *Peace*. Murray notes the greater subtlety of the references to Cleon in the *Peace*: the tanner, now dead; the infernal Cerberus who may rise from his grave. He also considers the social background against which the *Peace* first appeared. Though Aristophanes did not forget his feud with Cleon, this play shows Aristophanes' willingness to place old grievances to one side in favor of domestic reconciliation.

Reckford, Kenneth J. "Relaxation, Recovery, and Recognition: *Peace*." In his *Aristophanes' Old-and-New Comedy: Six Essays in Perspective*, vol. 1. Chapel Hill: University of North Carolina Press, 1987, pp. 3-13.

Recounts the two historically based interpretations of the *Peace*: as reflecting the real hopes for peace between Athens and Sparta in 421 B.C., the result of protracted negotiations, and as indicating Aristophanes' strong doubts whether that peace can be lasting, then notes that both these views are misleading insofar as they treat comedy as merely a reflection of historical events. This said, Reckford analyzes the play's humor, as a recovering of good feelings and the harbinger of the pleasant elements of life.

Strauss, Leo. "The Other Plays: The *Peace*." In his *Socrates and Aristophanes*. New York: Basic Books, 1966, pp. 136-159.
Strauss considers the beginning of the play in which the two servants are busy feeding a dung beetle. The second servant, who actually prepares the food from ass dung, does not answer the question posed by the first about what the beetle means. He explains the *logos* of the play (its narrative level alone) and leaves interpretation to the audience. (Though one fairly clear interpretation is that the beetle is Cleon the demagogue.) Their master suffers from his own form of madness, railing at the harm the gods do to the Greeks and threatening to fly to Zeus to ask what his further intentions may be. Strauss notes that the master, Trygaeus, remains unnamed as do the servants, and this anonymity obscures his relationship to the unnamed servants; the master is "Trygedy," that is, comic parody.

Whitman, Cedric H. "City and Individual: *Peace*." In his *Aristophanes and the Comic Hero*. Martin Classical Lectures 19. Cambridge, Mass.: Harvard University Press, 1964, pp. 103-118.
Analyzes the character portrait of Trygaeus as a creature of *poneria* (wickedness that implies the ability to get the advantage of somebody or something in an unscrupulous but enjoyable way). Whitman notes that Aristophanes succeeds in making Trygaeus unscrupulously wicked without sacrificing the character's plausible humanity.

Plutus

Dover, K. J. "*Wealth*." In his *Aristophanic Comedy*. Berkeley: University of California Press, 1972, pp. 202-209.
Begins with brief production history and synopsis, then considers the role of slave characters, specifically that Carion and Chremylus act more like friends than slave and master. Dover concludes by noting that in this play the relation between virtue and prosperity is inverse; to create a direct relation is to fly in the face of reality.

Murray, Gilbert. "The *Plutus* and After: Aristophanes and the Ancient Critics." In his *Aristophanes: A Study*. Oxford, England: Clarendon Press, 1933. Reprint. New York: Russell and Russell, 1964, pp. 199-220.

Analyzes the play as Aristophanes' final extant contribution to the Greek theater. Murray summarizes the play, noting how it had to conform to the reduced resources available for production of comedy. He discerns a change in tone between the first and second scenes; Chremylus' visit to Apollo's oracle to inquire how to become rich as the thieves, burglars, and politicians who surround him recalls the thrust of Old Comedy, while the chorus of farmers receives only a small lyric to sing, and this in a relatively simple meter. The chorus becomes only a shadow of what it was in Old Comedy, signaling the arrival of new comic forms realized in Menander's works.

Reckford, Kenneth J. "Utopia Still Wanted: *Plutus*." In his *Aristophanes' Old-and-New Comedy: Six Essays in Perspective*, vol. 1. Chapel Hill: University of North Carolina Press, 1987, pp. 354-363.
Reckford objects that critics have assigned the play to Middle Comedy, preferring to see familiar Old Comedy themes. Reckford argues that the differences between the *Plutus* and Menander's *Dyscolus* are so striking that it is misleading to seem to make the play less than classically Aristophanic. The *Plutus*, he contends, rejects moral allegory, moral purpose, and philosophical compromise. It escalates revolutionary change until Zeus himself is dethroned, yet it affirms the Olympians through the healing Asclepius and the present savior Zeus.

Spatz, Lois. "New Comedy for Old: *Ekklesiazousai* and *Wealth (Ploutos)*." In her *Aristophanes*. Twayne's World Authors Series 482. Boston: Twayne, 1978, pp. 131-145.
Considers the play a utopian folk tale that develops from the proverb that wealth must be blind since it attaches itself to the undeserving. Spatz summarizes the action, noting that the diminished role of the chorus makes it different from Old Comedy, though she notes Aristophanes' retention of Old Comedy's traditional structure: prologue, *parodus*, *agon*, episodes, and *exodus*.

Strauss, Leo. "The Other Plays: The *Plutos*." In his *Socrates and Aristophanes*. New York: Basic Books, 1966, pp. 283-307.
Notes the sophistic logic implied by replacing Zeus with the god Wealth as a means of eliminating injustice among human beings. At the beginning of the play, Wealth was half convinced that Zeus was wise in blinding him; yet, while believing that wealth corrupts absolutely, Wealth also believes Zeus is unjust and ascribes the blinding to envy. Poverty vindicates Zeus by arguing that the chief god of the Olympians cannot be unjust; hence, Zeus must be poor.

Thesmophoriazusae
Dover, K. J. "*Women at the Thesmophoria*." In his *Aristophanic Comedy*. Berkeley: University of California Press, 1972, pp. 162-172.

Contains a synopsis and brief production history, discussion of characters, and an analysis of the play as parody of Euripides' *Helen* and *Andromeda*, of at least one play by Agathon, and of proceedings of the Athenian Assembly. Dover describes the precarious political atmosphere of Athens and concludes with remarks on the final choral ode.

McLeish, Kenneth. "Characterization in Aristophanes." In his *The Theatre of Aristophanes*. New York: Taplinger, 1980, pp. 127-143.
Sees *Women at the Festival (Thesmophoriazusae)* and *Frogs* as plays in which Aristophanes laid aside the stereotyped character-drawing of his other plays to produce characters partly in a mode like that of the late Euripides, fore-shadowing the character comedy most familiar to modern audiences. McLeish compares the two plays, noting that the characters develop organically with the plot and that there is more than one central character.

Reckford, Kenneth J. "Loyalty to *Communitas*: *Lysistrata, Thesmophoriazusae*." In his *Aristophanes' Old-and-New Comedy: Six Essays in Perspective*, vol. 1. Chapel Hill: University of North Carolina Press, 1987, pp. 301-311.
Relates the two plays through the theme of fellowship in a discussion based on anthropological studies of the first quarter of the twentieth century. Cited above under studies on the *Lysistrata*.

Spatz, Lois. "Playgirls and Poets: *Thesmophoriazusai*." In her *Aristophanes*. Twayne's World Authors Series 482. Boston: Twayne, 1978, pp. 103-115.
Spatz follows a plot summary with discussion of the women of the play. She notes the implication of the prologue that inspired tragic poets can penetrate and conquer the mystery of the cosmos; this idea develops through the visit of Euripides and Mnesilochus to the house of the tragic playwright Agathon. The transvestitism of Mnesilochus in his joining the women of the Thesmophoria parodies the opening of the all-male Athenian Assembly. Spatz concludes that this emasculation is a metaphor. Pure tragedy and pure comedy lay at opposite poles, tragedy as masculine, but without compromise tragedy sets human action against the mysterious and incomprehensible.

Strauss, Leo. "The Other Plays: The *Thesmophoriazusai*." In his *Socrates and Aristophanes*. New York: Basic Books, 1966, pp. 214-235.
Strauss notes the impossibility of the premise: Euripides could not have possibly persuaded the average Athenian that there are no gods (any more than Socrates could have done so). The most that Euripides could have achieved would have been to convince some of the truth of atheism. Strauss concludes that it is a superior play to the *Clouds*. The dramatic poet is able to appear in various disguises because the concerns of drama are practical; this ability is denied the philosopher, whose lofty concerns remove him from the world of average people.

Whitman, Cedric H. "The War Between the Sexes: *Thesmophoriazusae.*" In his *Aristophanes and the Comic Hero*. Martin Classical Lectures 19. Cambridge, Mass.: Harvard University Press, 1964, pp. 216-227.

Agathon becomes the symbol of the emasculated art of new tragedy, that of Euripides. This symbolism becomes clear, so Whitman argues, in the transvestitism imagery of the play. The character Euripides, however, is the embodiment of trick-filled wickedness, primarily apparent in his ability to use rhetoric to deceive.

Wasps

Dover, K. J. "*Wasps.*" In his *Aristophanic Comedy*. Berkeley: University of California Press, 1972, pp. 121-131.

The synopsis notes that this play, like the *Clouds*, portrays a father and son but in a decidedly more political way: Philokleon (love-Cleon) and Bdelykleon (despise-Cleon). Dover considers production and staging, observing that four actors are probably necessary, though with quick changes three might suffice. He then analyzes the portrait of Philokleon and concludes by considering the play against procedures of the Athenian law courts.

McLeish, Kenneth. "Leading Actors and Leading Roles." In his *The Theatre of Aristophanes*. New York: Taplinger, 1980, pp. 113-121.

Calculates that the total performance time for an ancient staging of the *Wasps* at about one hundred minutes with Philocleon on stage for about seventy of the hundred. A time chart divides scenes by line numbers and calculates their duration. McLeish shows that the actor playing Philocleon had to be gifted in slapstick clowning, dancing, singing, and acting. He continues by analyzing several of these key scenes.

Murray, Gilbert. "The Jury Courts." In his *Aristophanes: A Study*. Oxford, England: Clarendon Press, 1933. Reprint. New York: Russell and Russell, 1964, pp. 69-84.

Analyzes the *Wasps* as Aristophanes' protest against the Dicasteria, the Athenian law courts. The play emphasizes the age and poverty of the jurors, who are past military age, unable to find ordinary employment, and dependent upon the three obels per day that jury service brings. The play thus focuses on social disparities not envisioned when the courts themselves were created.

Reckford, Kenneth J. "Dream Transformations and Comic Recognitions: *Wasps.*" In his *Aristophanes' Old-and-New Comedy: Six Essays in Perspective*, vol. 1. Chapel Hill: University of North Carolina Press, 1987, pp. 217-282.

Begins with an analysis of the dream section (lines 1-53), noting the relaxed but attentive effect it produces on the audience. Reckford argues for a strong connection between dream and comedy and considers that Aristophanes repeatedly, in this and other plays, uses a process that entails relaxation, transformation, and recognition. He then discusses the play's running metaphor (the "stings" of the jurymen-wasps) and concludes with observations on the connections of physical violence, farce, and verbal violence.

Spatz, Lois. "Jurymen on Trial: *Wasps* (*Sphēkes*)." In her *Aristophanes*. Twayne's World Authors Series 482. Boston: Twayne, 1978, pp. 60-70.
Offers a plot summary followed by the interpretation that Aristophanes places the Athenian court system on trial in this play, aiming particularly at Cleon's introduction of a raised fee for jury service. Spatz describes the Athenian court system in brief, then discusses applications of the wasp metaphor. She concludes by discussing the final scenes where the satire is dropped, noting the implication that reform is futile, even on an individual basis, but that ridicule of the important business of poets, parents, and citizens provides a sacred release.

Strauss, Leo. "The Other Plays: The *Wasps*." In his *Socrates and Aristophanes*. New York: Basic Books, 1966, pp. 112-135.
While in *Knights* the slaves are in truth political men, in *Wasps* the slaves are political men in their dreams. Strauss contrasts the dreams of Xanthias and Sosias. The latter slave's dream is more overtly political; its subjects are a pernicious measure intended by the demagogue Cleon, one of Cleon's lackeys, and Alcibiades' lisp. Xanthias convinces a doubtful Sosias that the dream is a good omen, and this dubiousness foreshadows the end of the play, which, while politically satisfactory, will be neither ethically nor morally satisfactory. Strauss continues in like vein, examining the speeches of Philocleon and Bdelycleon as just and unjust rhetoric.

Whitman, Cedric H. "The War Between the Generations: *Wasps*." In his *Aristophanes and the Comic Hero*. Martin Classical Lectures 19. Cambridge, Mass.: Harvard University Press, 1964, pp. 143-166.
Analyzes the play through Aristophanes' contrasting portraits of Philocleon and Bdelycleon. Whitman notes that Philocleon is considerably more than a stock curmudgeon, that he repeatedly appears as something contrary to nature. Bdelycleon tries to mend his father's ways, but the effort is a failure, precisely because nature is intractable.

General Criticism on Aristophanes

Anderson, Warren D. "From Pindar to Aristophanes." In his *Ethos and Education in Greek Music: The Evidence of Poetry and Philosophy*. Cambridge, Mass.:

Harvard University Press, 1966. 2d ed., 1968, pp. 34-63.

Traces the appearance of the *nomos* (law), or *nome* (a term referring to any traditionally established melodic pattern), in the extant plays. Anderson argues that the extant comedies of Aristophanes also indicate marked shifts of musical taste, the lyre ranking low in popular esteem by the end of the fifth century. Traditional musical education appears in the plays as an indication of character. Worthless individuals are raised in an atmosphere devoid of choral song and music. Anderson then surveys and discusses references to music in the extant plays.

Croiset, Maurice. *Aristophanes and the Political Parties at Athens.* Translated by J. Loeb. London: Macmillan, 1909. Reprint. Salem, N.H.: Ayer, 1987.

An old but frequently cited work. Croiset was the first modern critic to consider the degree to which Aristophanes' use of political satire reflects his own involvement in the political life of Athens. He sees Aristophanes as a defender of conservative, traditional values, that this feature emerges in his parodies of both Cleon and Socrates, and that the potent criticism in his plays so antagonized political factions within the city that it provoked the antisatire laws that hastened the development of New Comedy. An alternative view, that economic circumstances, as much if not more, caused this evolution, appears in Whitman's volume, cited below.

Dearden, C. W. *The Stage of Aristophanes.* London: Athlone Press, 1976.

Analyzes the components of Aristophanes' productions: actors, unusual entrances and exits, use of the chorus, parodic elements within the plays, the roles of didacticism and pure humor. Dearden traces this development through the plays, then contrasts the much leaner and less politically volatile New Comedy. There are photographs, illustrations, and a good, selected bibliography.

Dover, K. J. *Aristophanic Comedy.* Berkeley: University of California Press, 1972.

An excellent introduction to Greek comedy intended for those interested in Greek culture or the history of comedy but unable to read the ancient language. The book contains a simplified account of text transmission, including indications of staging and a chronology. There are larger, more substantive chapters on theater conditions (organization, theater buildings, and actors), Aristophanes' use of fantasy (with a good discussion of the *Birds*), techniques of illusion, instruction, and entertainment (concentrating on the chorus), parody, then separate chapters on each of the extant plays. Two final chapters discuss Aristophanes' predecessors and contemporaries and Middle and New Comedy. There is a selected bibliography, index of passages, and a general index.

Ehrenberg, Victor. *The People of Aristophanes: A Sociology of Old Comedy*. New York: Schocken, 1962.

Examines the characters of the plays, concentrating on types and farcical elements, to show how they represent broadly the social atmosphere in which Aristophanes wrote. Ehrenberg argues convincingly that the fast-talking swindlers, impudent slaves, and dim heroes of New Comedy actually make their appearance much earlier, that there is a stronger connection between Old and New Comedy than is usually thought.

Forman, Robert J. "Aristophanes." In *Research Guide to Biography and Criticism: Dramatists Supplement*, edited by Walton Beacham. Washington, D.C.: Research Publishing, 1986, pp. 16-20.

Contains an author's chronology, list of major editions, an overview of biographical sources, brief evaluations of selected biographical sources, important criticism, and miscellaneous articles on other topics relevant to Aristophanes. The emphasis is on translations and article-length works largely omitted from this volume as well as noteworthy articles in French, German, and Italian, also not treated in this bibliography.

Harriott, Rosemary M. *Aristophanes: Poet and Dramatist*. Baltimore: Johns Hopkins University Press, 1986.

Discusses Aristophanes' ability as a story-teller, focusing on narrative elements in *Acharnians*, *Knights*, *Clouds*, *Wasps*, and *Frogs*, all considered together in the first chapter. Harriott then analyzes Aristophanes' rhetoric and dialogue, his use of myth, and the recurring theme of peace. She concludes by noting Aristophanes' parody of institutions and with a discrete analysis of *Clouds*.

Henderson, Jeffrey, ed. *Yale Classical Studies, Volume XXVI: Aristophanes, Essays in Interpretation*. New York: Cambridge University Press, 1981.

This volume, devoted entirely to Aristophanes studies, contains five good essays suitable for general readers as well as specialists. Michael Silk's "Aristophanes as a Lyric Poet" notes that although most critics cite the beauty of the lyrics, they almost never support this thesis. Silk thus analyzes passages from the *Birds*, the *Clouds*, the *Frogs*, the *Knights*, the *Lysistrata*, and the *Acharnians* against passages from Euripides and Pindar to show the distinctiveness of Aristophanes' verse. Hans-Joachim Newiger's "War and Peace in the Comedy of Aristophanes" examines the *Peace*, the *Acharnians*, and the *Lysistrata* to show how Aristophanes represents war and peace and how he brings these concepts to dramatic life on the stage. The essays by Lowell Edmunds (on *Acharnians*), Martha Nussbaum (on the *Clouds*), and Jeffrey Henderson (on the *Lysistrata*) are discussed above.

Jaeger, Werner. "The Comic Poetry of Aristophanes." In his *Paideia: The Ideals of Greek Culture*, translated by Gilbert Highet, 2d ed., vol. 1. New York: Oxford

University Press, 1949, pp. 358-381.

Jaeger cautions readers of Aristophanes that Old Comedy sprang from tragedy and was not merely a crude but actually a brilliant precursor of the New Comedy of manners. He reviews the origins of comedy, notes the predecessors of Aristophanes, Cratinus and Eupolis (whose works are no longer extant), and discusses the figures of Crates, Cratinus, and Aristophanes as portrayed in Plato's *Symposium*. Brief summary discussions of Aristophanes' plays follow, against their political and social background.

Lever, Katherine. "Aristophanes: The Servant of Dionysos; Comic Dramatist; Comic Poet." In her *The Art of Greek Comedy*. London: Methuen, 1956, pp. 88-159.

This substantial introductory survey considers how Aristophanes saw his own plays against those of his predecessors. Lever observes Aristophanes' recurring concern for Athens, the extent to which he represented Dionysian ritual, and the varieties of comic madness in his works. She examines the interplay of drama and humor in his works and considers Aristophanes' theater and audience. Finally, she notes the recurring motif of reconciliation, considering all these topics with integrated illustrations from all the extant plays.

Lord, Louis E. *Aristophanes: His Plays and Influence*. Our Debt to Greece and Rome. New York: Cooper Square, 1963.

A good, general introduction, written in the standard format of the Our Debt to Greece and Rome series. There is an introductory chapter on origins of Greek comedy; others follow on the Athens of Aristophanes, his influence on Greece and Rome, on the Renaissance, on German, French, and English writers. The treatment is necessarily superficial, but the volume is helpful as a guide to those beginning comparative study in any of these areas.

McLeish, Kenneth. *The Theatre of Aristophanes*. New York: Taplinger, 1980.

Outlines categories of Aristophanic comedy (farce, literary and nonliterary), then considers practical problems of production Aristophanes faced (festivals, financing, performers, judges, and audience). One section considers staging and theater use as well as Aristophanes' utilization of stage machinery. There follows a chapter on dramatic form, the comic hero, and the traditional role of the comic dramatist. There is a full three-chapter section on aesthetics: the real world and the fantasy world, stage illusion, and bawdy plot lines. The final section (of four chapters) considers leading actors and their roles, characterization, stage conventions, and Aristophanes' use of metaphor and language.

Murphy, C. T. "A Survey of Recent Works on Aristophanes and Old Comedy." *Classical World* 49 (1956): 201-211; 65 (1972): 261-273.

Murphy's work is a two-part updating of the bibliography by K. J. Dover,

"Aristophanes: 1938-1955." *Lustrum* 2 (1957): 52-112. Much has appeared since these two bibliographies were published, and Murphy's listing covers material only as recent as 1967. Brief annotations accompany each item in the general list, followed by annotations of articles on the individual plays. These surveys are intended for teachers of undergraduate students, primarily to assemble class reading lists.

Murray, Gilbert. *Aristophanes: A Study*. Oxford, England: Clarendon Press, 1933. Reprint. New York: Russell and Russell, 1964.
Remains an often-cited popular introduction to the comedies. There is a chapter on background, including references to the fragmentary *Daitales* and *Babylonians*, followed by discrete analyses of the surviving plays, each allotted separate chapters. The study concludes with the *Plutus* and the ancient critics as well as a chapter on Menander's innovations. There is a chronological table of Aristophanes' plays paired with historical events concurrent with them, and a brief index. The book is not intended as original scholarship and so lacks extensive notes and apparatus.

Reckford, Kenneth J. *Aristophanes' Old-and-New Comedy: Six Essays in Perspective*. Vol. 1. Chapel Hill: University of North Carolina Press, 1987.
Written from the viewpoint of a theater director, this book, intended as the first volume of a two-volume set, presents six extended essays analyzing six important elements of the comedies. These are religious aspects (Old Comedy as derived from festive plays); psychological (suggesting that Aristophanes humor repeatedly builds upon elements of wishing and hoping, similar to fairy tales); theatrical (tracing the idea of the playwright to its comic realization); poetic and fantastic (concentrating on symbolic transformations and comic recognitions in the *Wasps* and comparing these with dream experience and interpretation); political (arguing for recurring basic loyalties and ideals in all the plays); and literary-historical (on defining the achievement and place of the playwright and his works).

Sifakis, G. M. *Parabasis and Animal Choruses: A Contribution to the History of Attic Comedy*. London: Athlone Press, 1971.
Examines Aristophanes' use of theriomorphic choruses within the context of the *parabasis* (in which the chorus came forward to address directly the audience). Sifakis considers possible evolution in the form of the *parabasis*, then discusses participation of animal choruses in dramatic action and their functions outside plot. A second part of the study examines archaeological evidence for use of animal choruses before Aristophanes.

Spatz, Lois. *Aristophanes*. Twayne's World Authors Series 482. Boston: Twayne, 1978.

This volume, another in Twayne's World Authors series, was written by the same author as the companion Twayne volume on Aeschylus. It follows a similar format and is useful as an introduction to Aristophanes and his comedies. There is a chronology of events contemporary to Aristophanes' life and ten subsequent chapters. The first of these discusses what is known of Aristophanes' life but concentrates on parallel historical events that affected the plots of his plays. Subsequent chapters offer solid basic discussions of the individual comedies, and there is a concluding summary and a selected bibliography that briefly annotates the critical works used in the study.

Strauss, Leo. *Socrates and Aristophanes*. New York: Basic Books, 1966.
A brilliantly eccentric study of Socratic dialectic as deduced from direct and oblique references in the plays of Aristophanes. Strauss begins with the well-taken assumption that the principal sources of information on Socratic thought, (Plato's dialogues, remarks in Aristotle, and Xenophon's *Symposium* and *Memorabilia*) are by friends and admirers of Socrates. Aristophanes' parodic view of Socrates, portraying him essentially as a sophist, and using Socrates' own definition of the word to do so, leads Strauss to argue for an essentially hostile and hence contrasting view. Strauss thoroughly discusses the *Clouds* in these terms in one large chapter and the remaining ten plays in a second substantial chapter, each of these ten in chronological order.

Sutton, Dana Ferrin. *Self and Society in Aristophanes*. Washington, D.C.: University Press of America, 1980.
Discusses the characters, plots, and techniques of Aristophanes against the society that produced them and traces comedy's development and appearance of Aristophanes' persona through passages from the comedies. There are frequent comparisons to Plautus, Terence, and Shakespeare as well as comparative discussions of Aristophanes' heroes, antagonists, and the comic catharsis. There is a good final chapter on tragicomic elements in Euripides' *Bacchae*, the characters of this play being read against comic types. The book is intended for undergraduates with some knowledge of Greek. Though quoted passages are untranslated, line numbers are clearly indicated, and the discussion is straightforward.

Whitman, Cedric H. *Aristophanes and the Comic Hero*. Martin Classical Lectures 19. Cambridge, Mass.: Harvard University Press, 1964.
A straightforward volume that emphasizes the role of the comic hero and accompanies the author's previous books on the tragic hero in Sophocles and the epic hero in Homer. Whitman rejects the argument that Aristophanes was a social or political reformer and argues that Aristophanes' heroes are either resourceful and unscrupulous or that they transcend a threatening society by

imposing some boundless, satisfying fantasy upon it. Whitman sees the *Clouds* as an unsatisfying portrayal of war between the generations, reflecting the appearance of sophistical educational methods at Athens. For a contrasting view, compare Reckford's volume, cited above.

ENNIUS

Recommended Translations and Commentaries

Jocelyn, H. D. *The Tragedies of Ennius*. Cambridge Classical Texts and Commentaries. Cambridge, England: Cambridge University Press, 1969.
Contains a Latin text of the fragments. The general reader, however, will find Jocelyn's introduction useful, for it provides a good discussion of Ennius and the historical background against which he wrote. The English commentary elucidates the contexts of the fragments as well as language difficulties, and so it can be read against the fragments in E. H. Warmington's translation, cited below. The introduction has seven subdivisions, all of considerable interest to readers interested in the development of Roman drama: "Athenian Drama and the Roman Festivals"; "The Hellenising of the Roman Stage"; "Athenian Drama and the Roman Poets"; "The Form of Roman Tragedy"; "Ennius"; "The History of the Text of Ennius' Tragedies"; and "The Titles of Ennius' Tragedies."

Vahlen, I. *Ennianae poesis reliquiae*. Leipzig, Germany: Teubner, 1928, reprint 1968.
This volume remains the standard major edition of Ennius' poetry, both epic and dramatic.

Warmington, E. H. *Remains of Old Latin*. Vol. 1. Loeb Classical Library. Cambridge, Mass.: Harvard University Press, 1956.
This volume, the first of four on the earliest Latin authors, contains all the extant Ennian fragments in its first half with English and Latin texts on facing pages. It is kept in print as part of the Loeb Classical Library, separate volumes with original texts and English translations of the major Greek and Latin authors. The volumes of the set provide otherwise unavailable translations of the fragments of Ennius (the *Annales* as well as the dramas) and Caecilius in volume 1; of Livius Andronicus, Naevius, Pacuvius, and Accius in volume 2; of Lucilius and the Twelve Tables of Roman Law in volume 3; and of archaic inscriptions in volume 4. Warmington's text for his Ennius translations is that of I. Vahlen, cited above.

General Criticism on Ennius

Beare, W. *The Roman Stage: A Short History of Latin Drama in the Time of the Republic*. London: Methuen, 1950, 3d ed. 1964.
Cited above under "General Studies." Beare's study, though well documented

and scholarly, is nontechnical and worthwhile for general readers as well as specialists. It contains a good discussion of Ennius as successor of Livius Andronicus and Gnaeus Naevius and places these playwrights in context as pioneers in the development of Roman drama. Information on these authors and their works appears in chapter 2, "The Italian Origins of Latin Drama"; chapter 3, "Livius Andronicus and the Coming of Literary Drama to Rome"; chapter 4, "Naevius"; and chapter 9, "The General Character of Roman Tragedy."

Duckett, Eleanor Shirley. *Studies in Ennius*. Bryn Mawr: Bryn Mawr College, 1915.
Though written as a dissertation, Duckett's approach is not intimidating, and she provides more detail than most other sources. She first discusses Ennius as a writer of history, then considers how he uses history in his *praetextae* (historical dramas). A second half analyzes Ennius' influence on the chorus of Roman tragedy, comparing that of Naevius, Pacuvius, and Accius. Despite its date, this volume often appears in the critical literature, and Duckett's reputation has kept it available.

Duff, J. Wight, and A. M. Duff. *A Literary History of Rome from the Origins to the Close of the Golden Age*. 3d ed. New York: Barnes and Noble Books, 1963.
This first volume of a two-volume study (cited above under "General Studies") contains as much information on the early Roman dramatists Livius Andronicus, Naevius, and Ennius as most general readers will likely require in chapter 3: "The Pioneers of Roman Poetry." Brief sketches containing what is known of their lives precede analyses of the major fragments. Chapter 5, "Roman Tragedy After Ennius," traces Ennius' influence on Pacuvius, Accius, the chorus in Roman tragedy, and the *praetextae* (historical dramas in which the *toga praetexta*, or senatorial toga with purple hem, was the costume).

Forman, Robert J. "Quintus Ennius." In *Critical Survey of Drama: Foreign Language Series*, edited by Frank N. Magill. Pasadena, Calif.: Salem Press, 1986, pp. 546-551.
Lists the principal dramas, discusses Ennius' contribution to epic poetry, his personal achievements as soldier and writer, provides a biography, and surveys the fragments to assess Ennius' importance in Latin literature.

_____ . "Quintus Ennius." In *Great Lives from History: Ancient and Medieval Series*, edited by Frank N. Magill. Pasadena, Calif.: Salem Press, 1988, pp. 665-669.
A brief essay written for general readers. It sets forth basic information on Ennius' life, his contribution to Latin literature (in epic poetry as well as drama), and describes his efforts to make Latin a literary language comparable to Greek. The largest section of the essay discusses what is known of Ennius'

works through the extant fragments, enumerates the certain titles of plays for which little or no text survives, and assesses his influence on subsequent writers.

Frank, Tenney. "Early Tragedy and Epic." In his *Life and Literature in the Roman Republic*. Sather Classical Lectures 7. Berkeley: University of California Press, 1930, reprint 1971.

Frank's study analyzes the social forces that create the various types of literature that emerge during the Roman Republic. Students of Roman drama will find chapter 2 especially worthwhile, for it features a discussion of Ennius and Naevius, contrasting the two and surveying the extant fragments. General readers will enjoy Frank's straightforward style and freedom from the apparatus and overly technical arguments that can discourage further inquiry.

Skutsch, Otto. *Studia Enniana*. London: Athlone Press, 1968.

The first half of the book presents a coherent study of the *Annales* fragments. "The Soldiers' Chorus in the *Iphigenia*" analyzes possible emendations and restorations for one of the better known fragments. "On the *Medea* of Ennius" compares the Ennius fragment with the Euripides original in a series of conjectures on possible restorations in Ennius' text. "Notes on Ennian Tragedy" considers possible sources for Ennius and makes conjectures on the degree to which Plautus and Terence show Ennian vocabulary in their adaptations of Greek comedy.

EURIPIDES

Recommended Translations and Commentaries

Alcestis

Arrowsmith, William, trans. *Euripides: Alcestis.* Greek Tragedy in New Translations Series. New York: Oxford University Press, 1974.

Perhaps the best translation of this play for American readers. Arrowsmith's
version reads well, remains reasonably faithful to the Greek, and provides a
good introduction to the play.

Dale, A. M., ed. *Euripides: Alcestis.* Oxford, England: Oxford University Press,
1954.

A Greek text with English commentary and introduction. This volume remains
in print and is one of the few commentaries on the play ever published. The
commentary and introduction follow the regular Oxford format and contain
much information, such as production history and background on Euripides
and his times, that is of interest to general readers. Available in relatively
inexpensive paperbound form.

Andromache

Stevens, P. T., ed. *Andromache: Edited with Introduction and Commentary.* Oxford, England: Clarendon Press, 1971.

One of the few extended studies of the *Andromache*, which itself is an under-
rated and much criticized play. General readers will find useful those portions
of the commentary that elucidate stage action as well as a large part of the
introductory essay, which discusses production history, Euripides' adaptation
of the myth, and the characterizations he provides. A Greek text accompanies
the English commentary.

Bacchae

Dodds, E. R. *Bacchae: Edited with Introduction and Commentary.* 2d ed. Oxford,
England: Clarendon Press, 1960.

The most acclaimed of all the Oxford commentaries on Euripides, primarily
for its excellent introduction, which focuses on the character of Pentheus and
Dionysian ritual as viewed against modern psychology. The more technical
elements regularly a part of this series also appear here; these include discussion of manuscript tradition, meter, and the Greek text with short apparatus.

Kirk, G. S. *The Bacchae of Euripides: Translated with an Introduction and Commentary.* New York: Cambridge University Press, 1979.

A very good translation and commentary on Euripides' last play. Modern psychology has roused new interest in Euripides' portrait of Pentheus as a repressed personality who persecutes the Maenads primarily because he is so intrigued by their *orgia* (rituals). Kirk's commentary concentrates on developing this contemporary view of the *Bacchae*. The translation is literal and reads well, and there is a good selected bibliography.

Sutherland, Donald, trans. *The Bacchae of Euripides: A New Translation with a Critical Essay.* Lincoln: University of Nebraska Press, 1968.
    Sutherland's good translation is followed by notes for general readers on the meters of the *Bacchae* as adapted for the translation, on staging problems, and on the fifty-line gap that occurs at the climax of the play. There is also an extended essay on the composition of the *Bacchae*, Euripides' final play, which makes contrasts with the style of Aeschylean drama; it also discusses the characters of the *Bacchae*, comparing them with other characters of Euripides' plays.

Children of Heracles (Heracleidae)
Taylor, Henry, and Robert Brooks, trans. *The Children of Heracles.* Greek Tragedy in New Translations Series. Edited by William Arrowsmith. New York: Oxford University Press, 1981.
    One of the few separate translations of this play, it is a very readable translation with brief introduction by the translators, essential notes, and a general introduction to the series by Arrowsmith.

Cyclops
Seaford, Richard, ed. *Euripides: Cyclops.* Oxford, England: Oxford University Press, 1988.
    A Greek text with English commentary and introduction. The commentary is excellent, and the volume contains illustrations that trace the cyclops figure in art.

Electra
Denniston, J. D., ed. *Euripides: Electra.* Oxford, England: Oxford University Press, 1973.
    A Greek text with English commentary, available in paperbound form.

Ferguson, John. *Euripides, Medea and Electra: A Companion to the Penguin Translation.* Cambridge, Mass.: Bristol Classical Press, 1988.
    A commentary on the two plays, it is keyed to the Vellacott translation. See full description of this volume, listed with *Medea* entries, below.

Hecuba

Tierney, M., ed. *Euripides: Hecuba*. London: Browne and Nolan, 1946. Reprint. Cambridge, Mass.: Bristol Classical Press, 1979.

A Greek text that includes one of the few English commentaries available on this play. There is a good introduction to the play itself, information on the life of Euripides, his style, and his understanding of tragic drama.

Helen

Dale, A. M., ed. *Helen: Edited with Introduction and Commentary*. Oxford, England: Clarendon Press, 1967. Reprint. Cambridge, Mass.: Bristol Classical Press, 1981.

This volume is primarily for students of Greek but does much to discuss difficulties of interpretation in this problem-filled play. There is a good introductory section on the figure of Helen, the legend of the phantom Helen, and the place of the *Helen* in the sequence of Euripides' plays. The accompanying Greek text is that of Gilbert Murray, reprinted unaltered but with some suggested dialogue revisions offered in a second appendix.

Michie, James, and Colin Leach, trans. *Euripides: Helen*. Greek Tragedy in New Translations Series. Edited by William Arrowsmith. New York: Oxford University Press, 1981.

A particularly good translation of this play that captures the farce of its surface yet is restrained and shows the wasted existence of Euripides' rescued Helen. There is a short introduction, brief notes, and Arrowsmith's general introduction to the series.

Heracles

Bond, Godfrey, ed. *Euripides' Heracles: With Introduction and Commentary*. Oxford England: Oxford University Press, 1981.

A major edition of the play with Greek text and full apparatus, commentary, and major introductory essay. The volume is comparable to Barrett's edition of the *Hippolytus*, noted below. Designed as a scholar's edition, the volume may be helpful for general readers seeking answers to questions not resolved in the Halleran text, cited below.

Halleran, Michael R., ed., trans. *The Heracles of Euripides*. Cambridge, Mass.: Focus Classical Library, 1988.

A translation, introduction, notes, and interpretive essay designed for courses in Greek civilization, mythology, and ancient drama. This volume is ideal for general readers; it is inexpensive, paperbound, and the best available introduction to the play.

Hippolytus

Bagg, Robert, trans. *Euripides: Hippolytus*. Greek Tragedy in New Translations

Series. Edited by William Arrowsmith. New York: Oxford University Press, 1973.
A good translation, in the regular format of this series: short introduction to the play, brief notes at the end of the volume, and a general introduction to the series by Arrowsmith.

Barrett, W. S., ed. *Euripides: Hippolytus*. Oxford, England: Clarendon Press, 1964.
Barrett's major commentary remains the most complete available on the *Hippolytus*. It is intended for undergraduates and scholars, though any reader with questions regarding interpretation, staging, variant readings, and the like will find a thorough discussion in its line-by-line citations. Students of Greek will find its detailed analysis of the lyric meters worthwhile. All readers will discover its full discussion of both the history of the Hippolytus myth and of the two lost tragedies on the Hippolytus theme profitable.

Ferguson, J., ed. *Euripides: Hippolytus*. Cambridge, Mass.: Bristol Classical Press, 1984.
A Greek text with English commentary. The introductory section is excellent and contains essays on Euripides, the Greek theater, early tragedy, Aeschylus and Sophocles as predecessors of Euripides, the Hippolytus myth, Euripidean drama and the structure, textual tradition, and mythic focus of his plays.

Lawall, Gilbert, and S. Lawall, eds., trans. *Euripides' Hippolytus: A Companion with Translation*. Cambridge, Mass.: Bristol Classical Press, 1986.
The best-available introduction to the play expressly designed for general readers. The translation is good, the commentary strong, and the introduction as thorough as most general readers would likely desire.

Sutherland, Donald, trans. *Hippolytus in Drama and Myth*. Lincoln: University of Nebraska Press, 1960.
This attractive volume translates the play and traces the myth, how Euripides modified it, and how subsequent playwrights (including Jean Racine) altered it again.

Ion
Owen, A. S. *Ion: Edited with Introduction and Commentary*. Oxford, England: Clarendon Press, 1939, reprints 1957, 1963. Reprint. Cambridge, Mass.: Bristol Classical Press, 1987.
One of the few commentaries available on the *Ion*. It was carried forward from work begun by E. E. Genner. Owen reviews the myth of Ion, eponym of the Ionian race, discussing its late introduction into the canon of classical mythology. He then considers the play as romance rather than tragedy. The Greek text followed by scholarly commentary, metrical analysis (valuable for readers of

Greek), and an appendix (useful for all) on tribal (or caste) names used within the play complete the volume.

Iphigenia in Aulis

England, E. B., ed. *The Iphigeneia at Aulis of Euripides*. London: Macmillan, 1891. Reprint. Salem, N.H.: Ayer, 1979.

A Greek text with an excellent English commentary, returned to print after relative unavailability. Notes are explanatory as well as critical, and general readers will find them useful. The commentary shows an excellent understanding of Euripidean language and contains many citations of parallel passages.

Kennedy, E. C., ed. *Euripides: Scenes from Iphigenia in Aulis and Iphigenia in Tauris*. London: Macmillan, 1954. Reprint. Cambridge, Mass.: Bristol Classical Press, 1981.

A student edition that contains selections, in Greek, from the two Iphigenia plays. Useful for all readers are the English commentary, essays on Euripides, the origin and development of tragedy, Greek theater the legend of Iphigenia, staging problems, and the plot summaries.

Merwin, W. S. and George Dimock, trans. *Euripides: Iphigeneia at Aulis*. Greek Tragedy in New Translations Series. Edited by William Arrowsmith. New York: Oxford University Press, 1978.

A straightforward, modern translation, short introduction to the play, essential notes, and a glossary of names; also contains Arrowsmith's introduction, standard in each of the series volumes.

Iphigenia in Tauris

Kennedy, E. C., ed. *Euripides: Scenes from Iphigenia in Aulis and Iphigenia in Tauris*. London: Macmillan, 1954. Reprint. Cambridge, Mass.: Bristol Classical Press, 1981.

This volume contains selections, in Greek, from the two Iphigenia plays. Its purpose is to illustrate the range of Euripidean tragedy by contrasting the playwright's treatment of the mythic variants. See full description of this volume, listed with *Iphigenia in Aulis* entries, above.

Lattimore, Richmond. *Euripides: Iphigenia in Tauris*. Greek Tragedy in New Translations Series. Edited by William Arrowsmith. New York: Oxford University Press, 1973.

Lattimore's own excellent translation (the translation in the collection edited by him and David Grene, cited below, being that of Witter Bynner). The Lattimore translation includes a short but good introduction to the play, essential notes, and a general introduction to the series by Arrowsmith.

Platnauer, M. *Iphigenia in Tauris: Edited with Introduction and Commentary*. Oxford, England: Clarendon Press, 1938. Reprint. Wauconda, Ill.: Bolchazy-Carducci, 1984.

Another in the Oxford series, reproducing the Greek text with an English line-by-line commentary. General readers will find useful those portions of the commentary that elucidate stage action as well as the first half of Platnauer's introduction, which discusses Euripides' life briefly, then turns to the production history of the *Iphigenia in Tauris*, considers Euripides' adaptation of the myth, and provides discussion of the characters, assessing the merits of the play.

Medea

Ferguson, John. *Euripides, Medea and Electra: A Companion to the Penguin Translation*. Cambridge, Mass.: Bristol Classical Press, 1988.

Keyed to the Vellacott translation, this volume provides the good commentary the Penguin edition lacks. It includes an introduction to Euripides, historical background, special discussions of key passages, and references to modern scholarship.

McDermott, Emily A. *Euripides' Medea: The Incarnation of Disorder*. University Park: Pennsylvania State University Press, 1989.

Considers the contradictory qualities of Medea as tragic heroine who is simultaneously majestic, sympathetic, and morally repugnant. Medea paradoxically elicits audience sympathy even as her actions during the course of the play range from deceitful to morally repellent. Jason, on the other hand, descends through Euripides' conception to a nonhero. McDermott's study explicates elements of the play in terms of its overarching sense of disorder, a characteristic the author believes is an abiding element in Euripidean drama.

Page, Denys L. *Medea: Edited with Introduction and Commentary*. Oxford, England: Clarendon Press, 1938.

An important commentary with Greek text, intended for students of the language but useful for all for its introduction, which covers production history and provides basic information on Euripides. The commentary itself, in addition to problems of text and language, also considers staging and interpretation. Available in paperbound form.

Orestes

West, M. L., ed., trans. *Orestes of Euripides*. Warminster, Wiltshire, England: Aris and Phillips, 1987.

A suitable student's edition of the Greek text, along with a less technical commentary prepared in part from the more scholarly volume of C. W. Willink, cited below. There is a fairly literal, rather British, English translation on facing pages. This volume is one of a series of commentaries with Greek texts and translations of the plays of Euripides. There is a good general introduction to the play and a selected bibliography of articles on *Orestes*. General readers will find the commentary easier to use than that of Willink.

Willink, C. W., ed. *Orestes*. Oxford, England: Clarendon Press, 1986.

A Greek text and English commentary on the most popular of Euripides' plays during the playwright's lifetime. Since no major English commentary has appeared since 1895, Willink's is important to note. General readers will profit from most of the long introductory essay, which covers historical events that impelled the writing of the play and includes a general discussion of plot and staging. Those sections of the commentary that elucidate stage action will help general readers who desire to closely read the text in English translation. Willink's commentary is more technical than that of West, cited above, and lacks the translation that West's volume provides on facing pages. The West commentary was prepared with the help of drafts from Willink's original manuscript.

Phoenician Women

Burian, Peter, and Brian Swann, trans. *Euripides: The Phoenician Women*. Greek Tragedy in New Translations. Edited by William Arrowsmith. New York: Oxford University Press, 1981.

A sound translation that contains a short introduction to the play, discussing structure and dramatic action. Also includes brief notes at the end of the text.

Trojan Women

Barlow, Shirley A., trans. *Trojan Women*. Wauconda, Ill.: Bolchazy-Carducci, 1986.

Those unable to read Greek, as well as students of the language, can easily use this edition. Contains a Greek text (a photographic reproduction of J. Diggle's 1981 Oxford Classical Text), an English translation on facing pages, and a general bibliography of works on the play under discussion. Barlow's translation is sound and lively, relying less than other volumes of this series on British idiom.

Fragmentary and Pseudo-Euripidean Plays

Bond, G. W., ed. *Euripides' Hypsipyle*. London: Oxford University Press, 1963.

A reconstruction of Euripides' lost play, based on the fragmentary papyrus role first discovered in 1908 and now in the Bodleian Library, Oxford University. The volume contains a Greek text with emendations as well as a commentary that is rather more technical than general readers would prefer; nevertheless, this remains the only significant study of an important fragment. Euripides appears to have combined the story of Jason's concubine with the legend of the Seven against Thebes.

Braun, Richard E., trans. *Euripides: Rhesos*. Greek Tragedy in New Translations Series. Edited by William Arrowsmith. New York: Oxford University Press, 1978.

An unusual discrete translation of this play, generally considered pseudo-

Euripidean. The volume contains a brief introduction and essential notes with Arrowsmith's introduction to the series.

Diggle, James, ed. *Euripides: Phaethon*. Cambridge, England: Cambridge University Press, 1970.

The fragmentary text of the *Phaethon* depends upon two pages from a Euripides manuscript that dates to about A.D. 500 and a third century B.C. papyrus that contains a substantial portion of the play's *parodos* (entrance song of the chorus). External evidence in the form of citations by classical authors and a prefatory *hypothesis* (plot outline), not by Euripides and itself in fragmentary form. Diggle presents all this evidence, providing a Greek text of the fragment and fragmentary hypothesis. Of interest to those unable to read Greek are the exegetical commentary, the prolegomena, and the appendices that discuss the Phaethon myth in classical literature and art and that reconstruct the play based on available materials. There are plates of both the manuscript and papyrus, and general readers will enjoy following the techniques by which Diggle reconstructs the play.

Complete Collections

Grene, David, and Richmond Lattimore, eds., trans. *Euripides*. 5 vols. The Complete Greek Tragedies. Chicago: University of Chicago Press, 1955.

These excellent translations of the extant plays remain standards and are kept in print. The disadvantages are that they are without substantial introductions and have no commentaries or notes; still, they are inexpensive, readily available, and can be purchased separately. Volume 1 includes *Alcestis, Medea, Heracleidae, Hippolytus*; volume 2, *Cyclops, Heracles, Iphigenia in Tauris, Helen*; volume 3, *Hecuba, Andromache, Trojan Women, Ion*; volume 4, *Rhesus, Suppliant Women, Orestes, Iphigenia in Aulis*; and volume 5, *Electra, Phoenician Women, Bacchae*.

Hadas, Moses, and John McLean, trans. *Ten Plays by Euripides*. New York: Bantam Books, 1960.

An inexpensive volume with good translations of the *Alcestis, Medea, Hippolytus, Andromache, Ion, Trojan Women, Electra, Iphigenia at Tauris, Bacchae*, and *Iphigenia at Aulis*. There is a general introduction by Hadas that considers the various types of Euripidean drama, a short introduction to each play, and a glossary of proper names.

Vellacott, Philip, trans. *Euripides: Alcestis and Other Plays*. New York: Penguin Books, 1953.

This serviceable translation is kept in print and includes the *Iphigenia in Tauris* and the *Hippolytus*. There is a good introduction and some essential notes. This volume is the companion of three others, listed below, which collectively offer Vellacott's translations of the extant plays of Euripides.

_____ . *Euripides: The Bacchae and Other Plays.* New York: Penguin Books, 1954.

Contains, as well, translations of the *Ion, Trojan Women,* and *Helen.* There is an introduction that considers each play, the section on the *Bacchae* being particularly good. Essential notes appear at the end of the volume.

_____ . *Euripides: Medea and Other Plays.* New York: Penguin Books, 1963.

Includes translations of the *Hecuba, Electra,* and *Heracles.* There are very short introductions to each play, much less than they demand, and brief notes at the end of the volume. The Ferguson companion, keyed to this volume, provides commentaries for the *Medea* and *Electra.* Cited above with individual plays.

_____ . *Euripides: Orestes and Other Plays.* New York: Penguin Books, 1972.

The other plays translated are the *Children of Heracles, Andromache, Suppliants, Phoenician Women,* and *Iphigenia in Aulis.* The introduction is fuller than in the companion volumes, and the notes more generous.

Way, A. S., trans. *Euripides.* 4 vols. Loeb Classical Library. Cambridge, Mass.: Harvard University Press, 1912.

Convenience of Greek and English texts on facing pages and ready availability are, unfortunately, the only reasons to recommend this complete collection of the plays. The translations are stiff, antiquated, in verse, and take great liberties with the Greek of Euripides. There are only brief introductions, no apparatus, and no notes. Volume 1 includes *Iphigeneia at Aulis, Rhesus, Hecuba, Trojan Women, Helen*; volume 2, *Electra, Orestes, Iphigeneia in Tauris, Andromache, Cyclops*; volume 3, *Bacchae, Heracles, Phoenician Women, Heracleidae*; and volume 4, *Ion, Hippolytus, Medea, Alcestis.*

Recommended Criticism on Euripides

Alcestis

Bates, William Nickerson. "The Extant Plays: The *Alcestis.*" In his *Euripides: A Student of Human Nature,* 58-65. New York: Atheneum, 1930. Reprint. New York: Russell and Russell, 1969.

A straightforward plot summary followed by basic commentary that notes the prevailing supernatural element of the return to life. Admetus' lines comprise nearly one-third of the play, but he is in no sense a tragic hero. He shows his weakness in accepting Alcestis' offer to die for him, though, Bates argues, Admetus could not have changed the situation once the fated day for him to die finally arrives. Bates also notes the clarity of Alcestis' character portrait, conveyed without an extensive speaking part, the combination of buffoon and superhuman strong man in Euripides' *Heracles*, and the common sense of Admetus' father Pheres.

Burnett, Anne Pippin. "*Alcestis*." In her *Catastrophe Survived: Euripides' Plays of Mixed Reversal*. Oxford, England: Clarendon Press, 1971, pp. 22-46.
The oldest surviving play of Euripides and a completely successful experiment with a compound plot. The first half of the play is a tragedy of Alcestis' willing sacrifice; yet, Heracles' determination to reclaim Alcestis from the dead reverses the traditional tragic theme of sacrifice and makes it a rescue play. The effect is also changed; the true friendship of Heracles contrasts with the false friendship of Pheres, and Admetus and Alcestis have a better life than they had known before.

_____ . "The Virtues of Admetus." In *Euripides: A Collection of Critical Essays*, edited by Erich Segal. Englewood Cliffs, N.J.: Prentice-Hall, 1968, pp. 51-69.
A sympathetic view of Admetus' role in the *Alcestis*. Alcestis, Burnett notes, agrees to die only after Admetus promises not to give their children a step-mother. Admetus not only agrees but also adds that he will grieve for Alcestis forever and sacrifice all joys: music, masculine company, and feminine companionship. He will have a statue of Alcestis made, place it upon his bed, and call it by her name. Burnett calls the *Alcestis* a mystery play for the uninitiate, revelation of a world in which friendship may resurrect itself and virtue is the key to blessedness.

Conacher, D. J. "Satyric (and Pro-satyric?) Drama: The *Alcestis*." In his *Euripidean Drama: Myth, Theme, and Structure*. Toronto: University of Toronto Press, 1967, pp. 327-339.
Contrasts Euripides' version of the myth with a passing reference in Homer's *Iliad* and a fuller account in the Hesiodic *Ehoiai* (*Catalogue of Famous Women*). In Euripides' play, there is the addition of the role of Artemis and the alternative explanations for the restoration of Alcestis. Conacher concludes that the myth leading to the enslavement of Apollo to Admetus and the myth involving Alcestis' substitute death for Admetus were originally of fundamentally different origins.

Grube, G. M. A. "*Alcestis*." In his *The Drama of Euripides*. London: Bradford and Dickens, 1941. Reprint. New York: Barnes and Noble Books, 1961, pp. 129-146.
Grube notes the tragicomic elements of the play, observing that these make the

play disconcerting for readers who expect a traditional tragic plot. He provides sketches of Alcestis, Admetus, Heracles, and Apollo that note their Euripidean absurdities, though he rejects the notion that the play was written as farce.

Wilson, John Richard, ed. *Twentieth Century Interpretations of Euripides' Alcestis: A Collection of Critical Essays*. Englewood Cliffs, N.J.: Prentice-Hall, 1968.

Because the *Alcestis* contains tragicomic and parodic elements, its nature is often discussed. This survey, by various critics, takes a variety of positions and is divided into two parts. The first contains a series of interpretations and covers such fundamental questions as whether the protagonist is Alcestis or Admetus, whether Alcestis is as noble as she appears, whether Admetus is worthy of her, and whether Admetus deserves his father Pheres' blame. The second section presents more general points of view on Euripidean drama; these are quite brief and drawn from larger works. William Arrowsmith discusses "turbulence," the absence of rational thinking; A. M. Dale considers tragic conventions and "a rhetoric of death" in the *Alcestis*.

Andromache

Bates, William Nickerson. "The Extant Plays: The *Andromache*." In his *Euripides: A Student of Human Nature*. New York: Atheneum, 1930. Reprint. New York: Russell and Russell, 1969, pp. 65-70.

Notes that Euripides attacks the Spartans rather than praising Athens and conjectures that the *Andromache* can plausibly have reflected Athenian feelings at the start of the Peloponnesian War. Bates then provides a simple plot summary, acknowledges the weaknesses of its two parts (the struggle between Hermione and Andromache and the events connected with the death of Neoptolemus). He concludes with analyses of the portraits of Andromache, Hermione, and Neoptolemus.

Burnett, Anne Pippin. "*Andromache*." In her *Catastrophe Survived: Euripides' Plays of Mixed Reversal*. Oxford, England: Clarendon Press, 1971, pp. 130-156.

Argues that Euripides here eschews regularity and proportion in favor of the effects produced by intentional distortion of character and situation. The *Andromache* employs blatant mutations of character. The play begins with a suppliant tragedy played by Andromache as helpless heroine, but continues, after the first action comes to successful conclusion, as a rescue play in which one of her tormentors, Hermione, herself becomes the helpless heroine.

Conacher, D. J. "War and Its Aftermath: The *Andromache*." In his *Euripidean Drama: Myth, Theme, and Structure*. Toronto: University of Toronto Press, 1967, pp. 166-180.

Observes that this play, with the *Hecuba* and the *Trojan Women*, continues the theme of personal and dynastic relationships between victors and vanquished. Conacher notes that all the conflicts in the *Andromache* lead to one conclusion: defeat is changed to victory by the addition, first to one side then to the other, of some powerful new ally. One sees examples of this in the appearances of Orestes and later of Thetis.

Grube, G. M. A. "*Andromache.*" In his *The Drama of Euripides*. London: Bradford and Dickens. Reprint. New York: Barnes and Noble Books, 1961, pp. 198-213.

A negative criticism of the play, primarily because of what Grube perceives as its lack of unity. He believes that the narrative sections, such as the introductory monologue and the choral odes, succeed better than the characterizations, though he criticizes even these for lack of relevance.

Bacchae

Arthur, Marylin. "The Choral Odes of the *Bacchae* of Euripides." In *Yale Classical Studies, Volume XXII: Studies in Fifth-Century Thought and Literature*, edited by Adam Parry. Cambridge, England: Cambridge University Press, 1972, pp. 145-175.

Considers that Euripides' last play reflects a more conventional, Aeschylean type of drama than his earlier works and notes that the subject matter of the choral odes, unlike those in his other plays, relates directly to the concerns of the drama. Arthur examines each choral ode, showing how it indicates the forward movement of plot.

Bates, William Nickerson. "The Extant Plays: The *Bacchae.*" In his *Euripides: A Student of Human Nature*. New York: Atheneum, 1930. Reprint. New York: Russell and Russell, 1969, pp. 71-79.

Notes the lacuna in the text, affecting the final scene, but acknowledges the play as a masterpiece despite its incomplete text. Bates provides a plot summary, notes the paraphrase of the myth of Pentheus in the *Dionysiaca* of Nonnus and similar themes in the medieval play *Christus Patiens* (*The Suffering Christ*). There is no attempt to analyze the play's psychological theme. Bates sees Pentheus merely as a typical symbol of feeble humanity before the overwhelming might of a higher power.

Conacher, D. J. "Mythological Tragedy: The *Bacchae.*" In his *Euripidean Drama: Myth, Theme, and Structure*. Toronto: University of Toronto Press, 1967, pp. 56-77.

Considers how Euripides adapted the traditional mythic material on Dionysus' punishment of mortals and that the playwright went beyond this material to portray his own interpretations of Dionysian ritual. Conacher provides a full dramatic analysis of the play followed by discussion, in an appendix, of the place of law, knowledge, awareness, and wisdom.

Decharme, Paul. "The Drama of the *Bacchanals*." In his *Euripides and the Spirit of His Dramas*, translated by J. Loeb. London: Macmillan, 1906. Reprint. Port Washington, N.Y.: Kennikat Press, 1968, pp. 46-66.
Decharme sees the *Bacchae* as Euripides' criticism of mythological legends condemned by common sense and opposed to morality. He rejects arguments that Euripides had ever felt attraction to the Orphic sect and sees the *Bacchae* as an indication of the playwright's uneasy feelings about ecstatic, cultic religious practices.

Foley, Helene P. "The *Bacchae*." In her *Ritual Irony: Poetry and Sacrifice in Euripides*. Ithaca, N.Y.: Cornell University Press, 1985, pp. 205-258.
The obvious ambiguity resides in the interpretation of the play as a justification of the retributive Dionysus or as an attack on Dionysian and other mystery cults. Foley notes Dionysus' associations with ritualized release of self-control and with madness, with women and the natural world outside of the city-state, with Apollo, with the ambivalent yet civilizing gifts of wine and festival, and with the theater itself. She argues, through examination of the text, that the play concerns the ritual aspects of tragedy, specifically the rituals of the god of tragic festival.

Grube, G. M. A. "The *Bacchants*." In *The Drama of Euripides*. London: Bradford and Dickens, 1941. Reprint. New York: Barnes and Noble Books, 1961, pp. 398-420.
Surveys the wide variety of interpretations given the play while acknowledging that it is a masterpiece. Grube believes that Euripides here provides a portrait of the extremes that the personality of Dionysus implies. He offers a complete analysis by scene.

Lucas, D. W. "The *Bacchae*." In his *The Greek Tragic Poets*. 2d ed.. London: Cohen and West, 1950, rev. ed. 1959, pp. 209-214.
A summary-analysis that reads the play as punishment of Pentheus for denying what he should have acknowledged: the place of ecstatic sensuality in life as well as in religious ritual. Lucas provides no more definite suggestions regarding Euripides' own feelings about religion, the fact that this play was written in Euripides' old age and during his Macedonian exile, or that Dionysus emerges as a vindictive god who punishes his worshippers as well as his opponents.

Norwood, Gilbert. "The *Bacchae* and Its Riddle." In his *Essays on Euripidean Drama*. Berkeley: University of California Press, 1954, pp. 52-73.
A restatement, updated and revised, of the author's early study, *The Riddle of the Bacchae* (1908). Norwood examines ambiguous language, apparent contra-

dictions, and problems of staging and characterization and offers his solutions; he considers indications of stage spectacle implied by the text of the play and notes where his opinions have changed.

Rosenmeyer, Thomas G. "Tragedy and Religion: The *Bacchae*." In *Euripides: A Collection of Critical Essays*, edited by Erich Segal. Englewood Cliffs, N.J.: Prentice-Hall, 1968, pp. 150-170.
Demonstrates Euripides' exploitation and distortion of the Dionysian ritual, designed as a means to help spectators consider the mystery and precariousness of their own existence. The play reverses the pattern of Aesopic fable; its mortals are identified with animals and irrationality supercedes rational behavior.

Sale, William. "The Psychoanalysis of Pentheus in the *Bacchae* of Euripides." In *Yale Classical Studies, Volume XXII: Studies in Fifth-Century Thought and Literature*, edited by Adam Parry. Cambridge, England: Cambridge University Press, 1972, pp. 63-82.
Analyzes the character of Pentheus in the tone of Sigmund Freud's casebooks, using the pseudonym "Mr. P." The first emotion one feels upon meeting "Mr. P." is dislike; then, as his defenses break down, sympathy. Just as one likes him, he is destroyed, and one wishes to be angry with someone. Dionysus has simply acted in line with his function and so cannot be blamed for Pentheus' death. One cannot blame Agave, especially after she sees what she has done to her son. Sale concludes that the culprit is humanity's desire to transcend the bestial.

Segal, Charles. "The *Bacchae* as Metatragedy." In *Directions in Euripidean Criticism: A Collection of Essays*, edited by Peter Burian. Durham, N.C.: Duke University Press, 1985, pp. 156-174.
The figure of Dionysus in this play reflects the paradoxical nature of tragedy itself: by creating illusion it seeks to convey truth; by causing the audience to lose itself, it gives the audience a deeper perception of self; by representing intense pain, it gives pleasure. Segal examines antitheses and contradictions in characterization and plot and relates these to the god's seen and unseen presence as patron deity of drama.

——————————— . *Dionysiac Poetics and Euripides' Bacchae*. Princeton, N.J.: Princeton University Press, 1982.
An important structuralist study of one of Euripides. Segal calls the *Bacchae* "metatragedy," noting that Euripides intends Dionysus' dual associations with fertility of the wine vine and with theater itself to represent the paradoxical nature of tragedy. The mythic persona of the stage Dionysus is different from the god to whom the Maenads surrender themselves in the *orgia*. Segal sug-

gests that by creating illusion, tragedy seeks to convey truth; by causing the audience to lose itself, it gives the members of the audience a deeper perception of themselves as individuals; by representing events filled with intense pain, it gives pleasure. Dionysus is, therefore, "liminal," between truth and delusion, sanity and madness, civilization and wildness, order and chaos; these are, also, the paradoxes of tragedy.

Verrall, A. W. *The Bacchants of Euripides and Other Essays*. Cambridge, England: Cambridge University Press, 1910.
This study remains readily available. It is regularly cited (though often negatively) in the critical literature and contains Verrall's Victorian interpretation of the *Bacchae*, his notes on the play, and miscellaneous essays on subjects unrelated to Euripides' last play. There is very little documentation, and the reader should be prepared for highly the ideocentric views of the author.

Children of Heracles (Heracleidae)

Bates, William Nickerson. "The Extant Plays: The *Heraclidae*." In his *Euripides: A Student of Human Nature*. New York: Atheneum, 1930. Reprint. New York: Russell and Russell, 1969, pp. 107-111.
The play resembles the *Suppliants* and contains patriotic elements. Bates follows this observation with a simple plot summary and concludes by noting the brevity of the *Heraclidae*. He suggests that there may be a lacuna after line 629 and that part of the play may, therefore, be lost.

Conacher, D. J. "Political Tragedy: The *Heracleidae*." In his *Euripidean Drama: Myth, Theme, and Structure*. Toronto: University of Toronto Press, 1967, pp. 109-124.
In both the *Heracleidae* and the *Suppliants*, Euripides emphasizes, through myth, the piety of Athens, especially its willingness to defend a weaker state against a stronger one. Conacher supports this view through an analysis that notes that the children of the dead Heracles seek protection at Marathon (allied with Athens) and from the Argive King Eurystheus; yet, Eurystheus would, for self-protection, exterminate the children of the hero he had persecuted. Iolaus, on the other hand, is a man who is just by nature and who is equally determined to defend the children of his dead lord; the play builds on this opposition.

Decharme, Paul. "Foreign Policy: The *Children of Heracles* and the *Suppliants*." In his *Euripides and the Spirit of His Dramas*, translated by J. Loeb. London: Macmillan, 1906. Reprint. Port Washington, N.Y.: Kennikat Press, 1968, pp. 128-142.
Summarizes the *Heracleidae* and discusses it as a play which reflects political questions then current at Athens. Decharme notes the various explanations of

critics: that the play is a thrust at either the Argives, or the Spartans, or both. Decisive for him, however, is the final speech of Eurystheus, in which he shows his gratitude to Athens for refusing to put him to death. Eurystheus' revelation of Apollo's prophecy regarding burial on Attic soil helps date the play at 427 B.C., three years after Athenian resistance to Spartan and Argive provocations. The play thus becomes a glorification of Athens as a city willing to defend its principles.

Grube, G. M. A. "The *Children of Heracles.*" In his *The Drama of Euripides.* London: Bradford and Dickens, 1941. Reprint. New York: Barnes and Noble Books, 1961, pp. 166-176.
Criticizes the play for disunity while acknowledging the worth of certain speeches such as that of the Argive herald. Grube is puzzled by what he considers inconsistencies (Eurystheus) and failures (Alcmene) of characterization. He believes that Demophon and Macaria are among the most consistently drawn characters.

Lesky, Albin. "On the *Heraclidae* of Euripides." In *Yale Classical Studies, Volume XXV: Greek Tragedy*, edited by T. F. Gould and C. J. Herington. New York: Cambridge University Press, 1977, pp. 227-238.
Considers how five fragments generally understood to be from this play might affect its action depending upon their inclusion or their placement in the text.

Zuntz, Gunther. *The Political Plays of Euripides.* Manchester, England: Manchester University Press, 1963.
Thorough discussion of two almost unconsidered plays, the *Suppliant Women* and the *Heraclidae (Children of Heracles)* comprise this excellent book. Zuntz begins with his political interpretation of each play, then situates to place in history, citing allusions to fifth century events, considering the larger relationship between tragedy and history, and the dating of both works. Part 2 focuses on the setting of the *Heraclidae*, provides a scholarly but not intimidating commentary on selected lines from its text, and concludes by discussing the *hypothesis* (argument-summary) affixed by scribal addition in Codex L.

Cyclops
Bates, William Nickerson. "The Extant Plays: The *Cyclops.*" In his *Euripides: A Student of Human Nature.* New York: Atheneum, 1930. Reprint. New York: Russell and Russell, 1969, pp. 80-85.
Discusses the *Cyclops* as the only complete example of a satyr play, then summarizes plot, notes the brevity of the play, and concludes that shortness likely characterized all the plays written in this genre since fantasy is hard to sustain. Bates makes comparisons with Homer's narrative of Odysseus and Polyphemus in the *Odyssey* and concludes with conjectures on the costuming of the Cyclops and on the staging of the blinded Polyphemus scene.

Conacher, D. J. "Satyric (and Pro-satyric?) Drama: The *Cyclops*." In his *Euripidean Drama: Myth, Theme, and Structure*. Toronto: University of Toronto Press, 1967, pp. 317-326.

Conacher's analysis sees the play as a blending of slapstick and verbal wit, comic incongruities in the placing of serious subjects in absurd contexts, and various ingenious adaptations of Homeric material to satyric situations. Based on particulars from his analysis, Conacher deduces aspects of the satyr play as a genre and considers that Euripides wrote at least seven plays which might be classed as satyric or pro-satyric.

Reckford, Kenneth J. "Wine-drinking and Recovery: Euripides' *Cyclops* and Aristophanes' *Knights*." In his *Aristophanes' Old-and-New Comedy: Six Essays in Perspective*. Vol. 1. Chapel Hill: University of North Carolina Press, 1987, pp. 105-112.

Reads the *Cyclops* as a satyr play, a Dionysian fairy tale, and compares elements of its playfulness with Homer's account of Odysseus and Polyphemus in the *Odyssey*. Reckford notes the play's sexual innuendo and vulgarity and compares its simplicity to the "Jack and the Beanstalk" tale: The hero outwits the foolish giant and escapes. He considers that Euripides makes more positive use of the wine-motif than Homer, connecting it with the Dionysian elements of recovery, encouragement, and celebration.

Electra
Bates, William Nickerson. "The Extant Plays: The *Electra*." In his *Euripides: A Student of Human Nature*, 85-91. New York: Atheneum, 1930. Reprint. New York: Russell and Russell, 1969.

Notes the popularity of the Electra theme, that it appears in the *Libation Bearers* of Aeschylus and the *Electra* of Sophocles. Bates follows with a simple plot summary. He describes the major characters, though without any psychological insight, seeing Electra as "a high spirited and highly excitable young woman who is quite carried away by her emotions" and Orestes as "a manly young prince."

Conacher, D. J. "Realistic Tragedy: The *Electra*." In his *Euripidean Drama: Myth, Theme, and Structure*. Toronto: University of Toronto Press, 1967, pp. 199-212.

Euripides' heroine is the negation of both Aeschylean and Sophoclean conceptions of Electra as avenger. In Euripides' play, Electra acts independently from the command of Apollo. Conacher argues that the play has its unity through a deft and damning portrait of a matricidal woman. Every detail contributes to this characterization.

Grube, G. M. A. "*Electra*." In his *The Drama of Euripides*. London: Bradford and Dickens, 1941. Reprint. New York: Barnes and Noble Books, 1961, pp. 297-314.

Considers the shock value of the peasant farmer's monologue, in which he announces that he is the husband of Electra, noting that the farmer's words imply a good deal as well about the relationship of Aegisthus and Clytemnestra. Aegisthus clearly dominates his partner, very different from the portrait of Aegisthus in Aeschylus' *Oresteia*.

Walsh, George B. "The First *Stasimon* of Euripides' *Electra*." In *Yale Classical Studies, Volume XXV: Greek Tragedy*, edited by T. F. Gould and C. J. Herington. New York: Cambridge University Press, 1977, pp. 227-289.
Examines the play's first choral ode, emphasizing its contrast with the immediate dramatic context. The ode provides a contrast by turning from the present to the remote past. It also suggests verbal echoes that give dimension to the action of the play. Walsh identifies this as an example of a variety of choral lyrics he calls "escape odes." He makes comparisons with others in Euripides' plays that he considers belong to this category.

Hecuba

Bates, William Nickerson. "The Extant Plays: The *Hecuba*." In his *Euripides: A Student of Human Nature*. New York: Atheneum, 1930. Reprint. New York: Russell and Russell, 1969, pp. 91-95.
Contrasts the play's popularity during the Middle Ages with the relatively little attention it has received in the modern world. Bates notes its distinctly tragic nature and its two-part plot: the sacrifice of Polyxena and the news of the death of Polydorus. A simple plot summary follows and concludes with observations on Hecuba as central character and Polymestor as villain.

Buxton, R. G. A. "Euripides: *Hekabe*." In his *Persuasion in Greek Tragedy: A Study of Peitho*. New York: Cambridge University Press, 1982, pp. 170-186.
Peitho (persuasion) is coarsened in the *Hecuba* to match the qualities of the play's characters. It becomes the quality that determines survival. Buxton supports this thesis by discussing the speeches of Hecuba and the language of the Chorus. He notes that neither Polyxena nor Odysseus play the game of supplication; she disdains to supplicate, and Odysseus moves both hand and chin to make impossible the physical contact that ritual supplication requires.

Conacher, D. J. "War and Its Aftermath: The *Hecuba*." In his *Euripidean Drama: Myth, Theme, and Structure*. Toronto: University of Toronto Press, 1967, pp. 146-165.
Conacher notes the objections many have made to the play's double plot: the sacrifice of Polyxena to the shade of Achilles and the vengeance of Hecuba on the Thracian king, Polymestor, for the murder of her son, Polydorus. He observes that there are two ways of responding: first, that Hecuba provides the real unity because she experiences both actions; or second, that the sacrifice of

Polyxena is an example of community justice, while the revenge of Hecuba is an example of individual, primitive justice. The strongest link, however, is the thematic use of rhetoric, seen as early as Odysseus' cynical instruction of Hecuba on the political aspect of how to recompense one's friends.

Decharme, Paul. "Double Plots: *Hecuba*." In his *Euripides and the Spirit of His Dramas*, translated by J. Loeb. London: Macmillan, 1906. Reprint. Port Washington, N.Y.: Kennikat Press, 1968, pp. 224-229.
Argues that all the double plots of Euripides' plays grow from a single action. Hecuba is both the crushed and despairing mother after the death of Polyxena; yet, as a result of this loss, she becomes a woman excited by a desire for revenge, which causes her to blind Polymestor and slay his children. Decharme then briefly compares the double plots of the *Heracles*, *Trojan Women*, and *Phoenician Women* to that of the *Hecuba*.

Grube, G. M. A. "*Hecuba*." In his *The Drama of Euripides*. London: Bradford and Dickens. Reprint. New York: Barnes and Noble Books, 1961, pp. 214-228.
Finds structural unity in the portrait of Hecuba, the Chorus providing an effective extension of Hecuba's personality. Grube then summarizes the plot and examines the scenes in the order in which the play presents them.

Kovacs, David. "Dynasts and Democrats in the *Hecuba*." In his *The Heroic Muse: Studies in the Hippolytus and the Hecuba of Euripides*. Baltimore: Johns Hopkins University Press, 1987, pp. 78-114.
Kovacs suggests answers for several questions implicit in the play: why the ghost of Polydorus says that Polyxena's death is fated for that very day (lines 43-44); that the ghost's finding its corpse is the result of his entreaties to the gods of the Underworld (lines 49-50); that Hecuba's fall from power is compensation for her former prosperity (lines 55-58); whether Achilles demanded Polyxena by name, as Polydorus maintains (line 40); or simply one of the Trojan women, as Hecuba believes (line 95); and, finally, whether Achilles prevents the Greeks from sailing by windlessness or by the force of words.

Reckford, Kenneth J. "Concepts of Demoralization in the *Hecuba*." In *Directions in Euripidean Criticism: A Collection of Essays*, edited by Peter Burian. Durham, N.C.: Duke University Press, 1985, pp. 112-128.
A careful analysis of the play's speeches. Hecuba remarks repeatedly on human nobility, then supplicates Agamemnon. The meditation on Polyxena's nobility catches Hecuba in a moment of poise before the drastic change. The later speeches show Hecuba's deterioration, associated with the destruction of the moral universe. Her remarks on law, morality, persuasion, and freedom are designed not to persuade a weak Agamemnon but to indicate that Hecuba is

pursuing her private and primitive vengeance, that she is living in a world without grace, pity, or meaning.

Helen

Bates, William Nickerson. "The Extant Plays: The *Helen*." In his *Euripides: A Student of Human Nature*. New York: Atheneum, 1930. Reprint. New York: Russell and Russell, 1969, pp. 95-103.
Notes that it is not a tragedy, though the simple plot summary and character descriptions which follow it do little to convey its elements of romantic comedy. Bates compares it in general terms to the *Iphigeneia*. He concludes by objecting to Verrall's argument (largely discredited among contemporary critics) that the *Helen* is a jest and mockery of serious drama.

Burnett, Anne Pippin. *"Helen."* In her *Catastrophe Survived: Euripides' Plays of Mixed Reversal*. Oxford, England: Clarendon Press, 1971, pp. 76-100.
Beneath the smiling surface of the suppliant-rescue theme surrounding Helen's reunion with Menelaus are the more serious parallel scenes involving Teucer and Theonoe. Burnett's analysis shows how a negative reversal, revealed only for a moment, is about to take place, only to be interrupted and a happy conclusion allowed.

Conacher, D. J. *"Tragédie Manquée*: The *Helena*." In his *Euripidean Drama: Myth, Theme, and Structure*. Toronto: University of Toronto Press, 1967, pp. 286-302.
Considers that the structure of the play depends upon the numerous variations of the appearance and reality dichotomy. The shade of Helen was at Troy, the real woman in Egypt and longing for her husband Menelaus' return; yet, when Menelaus finally sees the real Helen, he refuses to accept that it is she. Helen anticipates Menelaus' arrival by recounting Zeus' deception of her mother, Leda, the very seduction that resulted in her birth, but adds an aside that leaves Helen's own divine origins open to question.

Grube, G. M. A. *"Helen."* In his *The Drama of Euripides*. London: Bradford and Dickens, 1941. Reprint. New York: Barnes and Noble Books, 1961, pp. 332-352.
Grube questions how to treat the play, for it is clearly not tragedy and has important comic elements. He firmly rejects the notion that it is farce. His analysis focuses on the humorous reunion of Menelaus and the real Helen, and he compares the use of irony and irreverent comic thrusts at the gods to similar elements in other Euripides plays.

Vellacott, Philip. "Helen." In his *Ironic Drama: A Study of Euripides' Method and Meaning*. London: Cambridge University Press, 1975, pp. 127-152.
Attempts to discover a consistent portrait of Helen as described in the Trojan

plays. Vellacott examines the Helen references in *Andromache*, *Orestes*, *Hecuba*, *Iphigeneia in Tauris*, *Iphigeneia in Aulis*, *Electra*, the *Trojan Women*, and the *Helen* itself. He concludes that Euripides does not consider Helen's leaving Menelaus the act of a whore, that she simply refuses to accept the laws men set for marriage. Though Euripides' treatment of Helen varies with the tone of the individual plays and the degree to which Helen participates in the dramatic action, the playwright maintains remarkable impartiality.

Heracles

Bates, William Nickerson. "The Extant Plays: The *Heracles Furens*." In his *Euripides: A Student of Human Nature*. New York: Atheneum, 1930. Reprint. New York: Russell and Russell, 1969, pp. 103-107.
Considers the *Heracles* an unappreciated and neglected play and provides a simple plot summary. Bates notes the tragic element of the hero overpowered by outside forces and remarks on the play's reversal of fortune, observing that Heracles himself provides the element of unity.

Burnett, Anne Pippin. "The *Madness of Heracles*." In her *Catastrophe Survived: Euripides' Plays of Mixed Reversal*. Oxford, England: Clarendon Press, 1971, pp. 157-182.
Notes that *Heracles* is a play of triple action, with the final overturn from bad fortune to good; nevertheless, there is real tragedy here, for Heracles has had the role of destroyer of his wife and children forced upon him, so his own final survival is mixed with bitterness.

Conacher, D. J. "Mythological Tragedy: The *Heracles*." In his *Euripidean Drama: Myth, Theme, and Structure*. Toronto: University of Toronto Press, 1967, pp. 78-90.
Examines the ironic and parodic relationship between theme and plot. Conacher argues that Euripides here implies the inferiority of the gods of myth to human heroes, especially with regard to the related qualities of *philia* (friendship and family affection) and of *charis* (gratitude). He provides an analysis of the play to show that even the triumph over the unfriendly gods of the essentially human qualities in Heracles' heroism contributes to this larger theme.

Foley, Helene P. "The *Heracles*." In her *Ritual Irony: Poetry and Sacrifice in Euripides*. Ithaca, N.Y.: Cornell University Press, 1985, pp. 147-204.
Foley notes that the reversal in this play begins with a purificatory ritual that becomes a perverted sacrifice in which the divinely maddened Heracles destroys his own wife and children. Examination of the play's language ties Heracles' action perversely and ironically to religious sacrifice and Dionysian ritual.

Gregory, Justina. "Euripides' *Heracles*." In *Yale Classical Studies, Volume XXV: Greek Tragedy*, edited by T. F. Gould and C. J. Herington. New York: Cambridge University Press, 1977, pp. 259-275.

Argues that the play shows a structural and thematic unity, even though it is usually considered to fall into two or three parts. Gregory uses the motif of genealogy as an element that informs the play to provide cohesiveness. She focuses particularly on Heracles' two fathers: Zeus and the mortal Amphitryon.

Grube, G. M. A. "*Heracles*." In his *The Drama of Euripides*. London: Bradford and Dickens, 1941. Reprint. New York: Barnes and Noble Books, 1961, pp. 244-260.

Considers that Amphitryon's monologue, his boast that his wife has just given birth to the son of a god, constitutes the central problem of the play. Can one understand his words as natural, or is it Euripides' intention to make Amphitryon appear ridiculous? Grube prefers to believe that they set a heroic framework against which to understand the play.

Lucas, D. W. "The *Heracles*." In his *The Greek Tragic Poets*. 2d ed.. London: Cohen and West, 1950, rev. ed. 1959, pp. 214-223.

Notes Euripides' transference of Heracles' madness and murder of his family to the end of the hero's career. This switch increases the irony, for at the time of the murders Heracles is at the peak of his heroic career. Lucas then provides a plot summary that outlines the play by scenes.

Hippolytus

Bates, William Nickerson. "The Extant Plays: The *Hippolytus*." In his *Euripides: A Student of Human Nature*. New York: Atheneum, 1930. Reprint. New York: Russell and Russell, 1969, pp. 111-117.

Notes the strength and pacing of the play, the use of a secondary chorus, and provides a simple plot summary. Bates mentions the failure of an earlier Euripides play on the Hippolytus myth but suggests neither anything of the lost play's content nor reasons for its failure. The conclusion identifies Phaedra as the true tragic character and makes some general comparisons with Seneca's *Hippolytus*, Sophocles' lost *Phaedra*, and Jean Racine's *Phèdre*.

Conacher, D. J. "Mythological Tragedy: The *Hippolytus*." In his *Euripidean Drama: Myth, Theme, and Structure*. Toronto: University of Toronto Press, 1967, pp. 27-55.

Considers the degree to which human beings possess any freedom of action given the apparent power of all the deities in this play. There is a good summary discussion followed by consideration of how the antagonism of Aphrodite and Artemis appears in Phaedra's forbidden love for Hippolytus. The first of two appendices examines a variety of modern interpretations. The second considers what Euripides may imply on a philosophical level about the source of human wrongdoing.

Dimock, George E., Jr. "Euripides' *Hippolytus*, or Virtue Rewarded." In *Yale Classical Studies, Volume XXV: Greek Tragedy*. Edited by T. F. Gould and C. J. Herington. New York: Cambridge University Press, pp. 239-258.
Relates the action of the play to the two great civic calamities that parallel the time of its writing: the Peloponnesian War and the plague of Athens. Both Euripides' *Hippolytus* and Sophocles' *Oedipus the King* date from this period, and in both the relevance, or even existence, of divine law is called into question. Dimock contends that both playwrights were concerned with what it might mean for an essentially innocent man, or city, to be apparently doomed by the gods.

Grube, G. M. A. "*Hippolytus*." In his *The Drama of Euripides*. London: Bradford and Dickens, 1941. Reprint. New York: Barnes and Noble Books, 1961, pp. 177-197.
Holds that this play is the greatest of Euripides' extant plays and that it forms a perfect unity. Grube considers Hippolytus, not Phaedra, the character of primary interest, discusses the Aphrodite-Artemis conflict that the play mirrors, and provides a straightforward plot summary.

Knox, Bernard M. W. "The *Hippolytus* of Euripides." In *Euripides: A Collection of Critical Essays*, edited by Erich Segal. Englewood Cliffs, N.J.: Prentice-Hall, 1968, pp. 90-114.
Contends that there is no single tragic character in the play, that freedom of the human will and the importance of human choice are both expressly denied in the prologue. The action is divided among Hippolytus, Phaedra, Theseus, and the Nurse, and the tragedy exists in the relationship of all four.

Kovacs, David. "Hippolytus, Phaedra, and Heroism." In his *The Heroic Muse: Studies in the Hippolytus and Hecuba of Euripides*. Baltimore: Johns Hopkins University Press, 1987, pp. 22-77.
Considers several crucial questions: the reason Aphrodite (lines 7-8) maintains gods and mortals are similar; the reason Hippolytus becomes an Eleusinian initiate (line 25); why Aphrodite lays such stress on Phaedra's good name (line 47); why Hippolytus insists on the untaught nature of his chastity (lines 79-81); why the servant emphasizes the similarity between gods and mortals (lines 91-97); the reason the servant uses the word *semnós* ("revered" or "august" but also "proud" or "haughty") in all of its different senses within six lines; and why the Nurse discourses, without any apparent relevance, on the uncertainty of any life beyond death (lines 191-197).

Lucas, D. W. "The Significant Plays: The *Hippolytus.*" In his *The Greek Tragic Poets*. 2d ed. London: Cohen and West, 1950, rev. ed. 1959, pp. 201-209.

A summary-discussion that notes unity of structure, the two divine epiphanies that frame the play becoming an impulse for human action. Hippolytus' asceticism is an ideal championed by few if any in Euripidean Greece; if anything, it was a requirement associated with certain religious rituals, though Lucas rejects firmly the argument that Hippolytus as portrayed by Euripides is an Orphic or Pythagorean.

Norwood, Gilbert. "God and Man in *Hippolytus.*" In his *Essays on Euripidean Drama*. Berkeley: University of California Press, 1954, pp. 74-111.

Analyzes the portraits of Phaedra, Hippolytus, and Theseus while noting that though each engages audience sympathy in varying degrees, all are blameworthy; their own characters collectively account for all the misunderstanding and pain in the play. He concludes by relating the human level to the three deities of the play (Aphrodite, Artemis, and Poseidon) and determines that the tragedy is an entirely human one, that human beings ruin their lives through their virtues as well as their faults.

Zeitlin, Fromma I. "The Power of Aphrodite: Eros and the Boundaries of the Self in the *Hippolytus.*" In *Directions in Euripidean Criticism: A Collection of Essays*, edited by Peter Burian. Durham, N.C.: Duke University Press, 1985, pp. 52-111.

Notes the play as a unique second treatment of the myth Euripides had already represented onstage. Zeitlin judges the failure of the first version probably resulted from portrayal of Phaedra as brazenly lustful. Zeitlin then analyzes the Phaedra of the second play and demonstrates that Phaedra carefully observes social conventions. The author shows how Phaedra is trapped by the knot of her own words and illustrates with an analysis of the large number of words, all associated with Phaedra, which imply tying or binding as well as loosening, and notes the conflict between desire and language.

Ion

Bates, William Nickerson. "The Extant Plays: The *Ion.*" In his *Euripides: A Student of Human Nature*. New York: Atheneum, 1930. Reprint. New York: Russell and Russell, 1969, pp. 117-138.

Observes the lack of critical attention given the play, notes its happy conclusion and its unusual plot, and provides extended quotations from the play with a simple plot summary. Bates notes but does not comment on Ion's decision to remain at Delphi rather than journey to Athens, where Ion is sure envy and hatred await him; Bates sees the play as a simple retelling of the myth that accounts for the founding of the Ionian race.

Burnett, Anne Pippin. *"Ion."* In her *Catastrophe Survived: Euripides' Plays of Mixed Reversal*. Oxford, England: Clarendon Press, 1971, pp. 101-129.
Burnett notes that the multiple actions of the play run simultaneously rather than in sequence. Creusa moves as principal through a vengeance plot with catastrophe interrupted, but she is also victim-heroine of a release. Ion, meanwhile, plays the primary role in a "drama of return"—to wealth and power.

Conacher, D. J. *"Tragédie Manquée*: The *Ion."* In his *Euripidean Drama: Myth, Theme, and Structure*. Toronto: University of Toronto Press, 1967, pp. 267-285.
Notes the brilliant paradoxes upon which the play rests. Ion is the son of Apollo and Creusa. Since he is destined to become the eponymous ancestor of the Ionian race, the tale reflects glory on the Athenians. On the other hand, the source of all this glory is the inadequate, shifty Apollo of the play. Conacher concludes that Euripides used the inherent possibilities of political propaganda and theological satire because they contributed best to the tragicomic tone the playwright sought. The political element is a superstructure that readers need not reject.

Grube, G. M. A. *"Ion."* In his *The Drama of Euripides*. London: Bradford and Dickens, 1941. Reprint. New York: Barnes and Noble Books, 1961, pp. 261-279.
Grube focuses on the light-hearted tone of Hermes' introductory monologue; this lack of intensity creates a mood in spectators that allows less deeply moving feelings than in strictly tragic drama. He also notes the care with which Euripides describes the meeting of Ion and Creusa.

Lucas, D. W. "The *Ion* and Related Plays." In his *The Greek Tragic Poets*. 2d ed. London: Cohen and West, 1950, rev. ed. 1959, pp. 223-229.
A plot summary and discussion that discounts the argument that the play represents a rejection of religion. Lucas sees it as comic farce, relating the play to the tone of the *Helen* and the *Electra*.

Saxenhouse, Arlene W. "Myths and the Origins of Cities: Reflections on the Autochthony Theme in Euripides' *Ion*." In *Greek Tragedy and Political Theory*, edited by J. Peter Euben. Berkeley: University of California Press, 1986, pp. 252-273.
Cites the common birth from earth rather than from human mothers and fathers, which Socrates describes in *Republic* 3. The myth gives the city unity, order, cohesion, and hierarchy. Saxenhouse argues that the *Ion* confronts the issue of lies-become-myth that controls the Athenians' image of themselves. Autochthony enables Euripides to present Athenians with the foundations of their prejudices regarding the privileged position of the Ionian race.

Iphigenia in Aulis

Bates, William Nickerson. "The Extant Plays: *The Iphigenia at Aulis.*" In his
    Euripides: A Student of Human Nature. New York: Atheneum, 1930. Reprint.
    New York: Russell and Russell, 1969, pp. 146-154.

The plot summary notes the play's conservative structure, more like traditional
tragic form than other Euripides plays. Bates indicates that the play shows
reworking by another hand, cites the excellence of Iphigenia's character portrait, and discusses her tragic nobility, contrasting it with Clytemnestra's
haughty pride.

Conacher, D. J. "*Tragédie Manquée*: The *Iphigeneia at Aulis.*" In his *Euripidean
    Drama: Myth, Theme, and Structure*. Toronto: University of Toronto Press,
    1967, pp. 249-264.

Conacher identifies three movements in the play that lead to Iphigenia's sudden
and surprising decision to sacrifice herself willingly for the success of the
expedition. The entire action of the play, he argues, takes place for the sake of
this romantic transformation scene. The characterizations of the variously corrupt or counterfeit heroes contribute by contrast to the greater glorification of
the heroine.

Foley, Helene P. "The *Iphigenia in Aulis.*" In her *Ritual Irony: Poetry and Sacrifice
    in Euripides*. Ithaca, N.Y.: Cornell University Press, 1985, pp. 65-105.

Foley notes the common theme in Euripides of voluntary sacrifice of young
people to save family, city, or nation in a situation of social crisis. She observes
the victim is always a virgin and usually young. In this play, the irony is that
Iphigenia's sacrifice and the rhetoric of Panhellenism do not finally change the
realities of the world.

Grube, G. M. A. "*Iphigenia at Aulis.*" In his *The Drama of Euripides*. London:
    Bradford and Dickens, 1941. Reprint. New York: Barnes and Noble Books,
    1961, pp. 421-438.

Holds that it is an attractive but not a great play, with the characterization at a
considerably lower level than in Euripides' strongest plays. Grube notes what
he considers spurious additions to the text and conjectures that others may
have finished the play. He provides an analysis by scene, noting especially
unsatisfactory poetry at the play's conclusion.

Iphigenia in Tauris

Bates, William Nickerson. "The Extant Plays: The *Iphigenia Among the Taurians.*"
    In his *Euripides: A Student of Human Nature*. New York: Atheneum, 1930.
    Reprint. New York: Russell and Russell, 1962, pp. 138-146.

Bates observes the nontragic, romantic nature of the play in a simple plot
summary and notes the unexpected portrayals of Iphigenia, Orestes, and the

Furies. Aristotle, Bates reports, favors the play because of its well-drawn characters, though, Bates contends, there is no attempt at subtle psychological analysis.

Burnett, Anne Pippin. "*Iphigeneia amongst the Taurians.*" In her *Catastrophe Survived: Euripides' Plays of Mixed Reversal*. Oxford, England: Clarendon Press, 1971, pp. 47-75.

Compares the fates of Iphigenia and Orestes in that both were snatched from misfortune by divine intervention. Burnett notes the contingency of Orestes' rescue: that he himself must rescue the cult statue of Artemis from the Taurians and that his attempt leads to his capture by the power he had hoped to liberate. She further shows how the linked fraternal rescues, each the reverse image of the other, are crossed by the kin-murder of Iphigenia, itself interrupted in its catastrophe.

Conacher, D. J. "*Tragédie Manquée*: The *Iphigenia among the Taurians.*" In his *Euripidean Drama: Myth, Theme, and Structure*. Toronto: University of Toronto Press, 1967, pp. 303-313.

Considers that the play is romantic tragicomedy, based on the ironic interplay of illusion and reality. It depends on two successive delusions: Iphigenia, deluded by a dream, believes that Orestes is dead; Orestes, deluded by the sacrifice at Aulis, believes that Iphigenia dead and considers the woman he sees as a mortal enemy. Conacher refuses to look for hidden meanings in the play; he considers that it rests upon the tragicomic elements of the double recognition scenes.

Grube, G. M. A. "*Iphigenia Among the Taurians.*" In his *The Drama of Euripides*. London: Bradford and Dickens, 1941. Reprint. New York: Barnes and Noble Books, 1961, pp. 315-331.

Criticizes the play for lack of subtlety in characterization, noting the romantic tone and general lack of terror. Grube finds Iphigenia's description of her dream worthwhile for its fantastic elements and symbolism, and he considers Iphigenia's misinterpretation of it particularly compelling.

Medea

Bates, William Nickerson. "The Extant Plays: The *Medea.*" In his *Euripides: A Student of Human Nature*. New York: Atheneum, 1930. Reprint. New York: Russell and Russell, 1969, pp. 154-166.

Extended quotations from Medea's speeches fill the simple plot summary. Bates notes the complexity of Medea's character portrait and other treatments of the myth, by Ennius and Seneca especially. He cites Euripides' use of *deus ex machina* (divine intervention) and concludes that the playwright was evidently willing to sacrifice logic for spectacle in the play's final scene.

Buxton, R. G. A. "Euripides: *Medea.*" In his *Persuasion in Greek Tragedy: A Study of Peitho*. New York: Cambridge University Press, 1982, pp. 153-170.
Notes Medea's use of *peitho* (persuasion) resembles the demonic wiliness of Aeschylus' Clytemnestra but also that it underscores her position as a barbarian and the rejected wife of Jason. Buxton then notes the formalized ritual patters, such as supplication, through which one person persuades another to acquiesce. Finally, Buxton considers a quintessentially Euripidean use of *peitho*: characters who exist as noteworthy according to the effectiveness with which they are able to present their cases to the audience. This paradox occurs especially in the confrontations between Jason and Medea. Though Medea uses *peitho* for murderous purposes, she never entirely forfeits audience sympathy because of what she has suffered at the hands of Jason.

Conacher, D. J. "Realistic Tragedy: The *Medea.*" In his *Euripidean Drama: Myth, Theme, and Structure*. Toronto: University of Toronto Press, 1967, pp. 183-198.
Medea is a victim of circumstances but not in the same way as Andromache or Hecuba. Medea initiates the events that frame her life and shape her fate, and Conacher illustrates that this pattern continues even after Jason announces his intention to wed Glauce. The tragedy remains with Medea's moral destruction, evident both in her infanticide and in the murder of Glauce. Conacher notes that the spectacular nature of Medea's departure merely reinforces Medea's mythic identification with magic and in no way detracts from the moral tragedy.

Easterling, P. E. "The Infanticide in Euripides' *Medea.*" In *Yale Classical Studies, Volume XXV: Greek Tragedy*, edited by T. F. Gould and C. J. Herington. New York: Cambridge University Press, 1977, pp. 177-191.
Though Euripides recognized that his audience would recoil from Medea's horrific act, he manipulates the portrait he presents of her so that the audience may at least understand why she kills her children. Easterling focuses on her foreign origin, that she equates violence and love when she kills her brother Apsyrtus, that the marriage of Jason and Medea had dubious legality among the Greeks. There is a good analysis of the exchange with Creon that emphasizes his harshness and of that with Jason that notes his insensitivity.

Grube, G. M. A. "*Medea.*" In his *The Drama of Euripides*. London: Bradford and Dickens, 1941. Reprint. New York: Barnes and Noble Books, 1961, pp. 147-165.
Grube's analysis focuses on the extremes of Medea's temperament, how her lust for vengeance overpowers even maternal love. He emphasizes Medea's foreign origins and considers how the Greek attitude toward barbarians in general and Eastern women in particular provide important background against which to understand the play.

Knox, B. M. W. "The *Medea* of Euripides." In *Yale Classical Studies, Volume XXV: Greek Tragedy*, edited by T. F. Gould and C. J. Herington. New York: Cambridge University Press, 1977, pp. 193-225.

Out of all the mythic variants available to him, Euripides created a new one, more shocking and physically violent than anything in the tradition. Knox considers that Euripides' greatest challenge was how to present this version successfully to conservative Athenian audiences. This study discusses the alternative methods Euripides could have used to portray Medea and contrasts Euripides' approach with the techniques and language of Sophoclean tragedy.

Lucas, D. W. "The Significant Plays: The *Medea*." In his *The Greek Tragic Poets*. 2d ed. London: Cohen and West, 1950, rev. ed. 1959, pp. 193-201.

Following a straightforward plot summary, Lucas asks several provocative questions about the play's ending (though he answers none of these). Medea's sun chariot carries her away. Helios, god of the sun, is Medea's grandfather. While Lucas notes this point, he still does not account for the reason Medea's departure is apposite. The general function and varieties of endings by divine intervention is, however, neatly discussed in simple terms.

Pucci, Pietro. *The Violence of Pity in Euripides' Medea*. Ithaca, N.Y.: Cornell University Press, 1980.

Medea's abandonment by Jason inspires sympathy, yet this emotion is mitigated by her vindictive murder of their children. Pucci's structural analysis focuses on this tension, which he examines through crucial scenes in Euripides' play: the Nurse's speech, Medea's discovery of Jason's intentions, her plans for survival and revenge, and the murder/sacrifice of the children. Pucci argues, drawing upon the ideas of Jacques Derrida and other poststructuralists, that the ambiguity and ambivalence of the play's language achieve the pity and fear that Aristotle contends in the *Poetics* are elements crucial to drama. All Greek citations are translated, and the author presents these subtle arguments in straightforward and nontechnical ways suitable for general readers.

Schlesinger, Eilhard. "On Euripides' *Medea*." In *Euripides: A Collection of Critical Essays*, edited by Erich Segal. Englewood Cliffs, N.J.: Prentice-Hall, 1968, pp. 70-89.

Argues that critics have focused too exclusively on Medea's monologue (lines 1020-1080) to discover the essence of the tragedy, that Medea, once she sees the monstrosity of her plan, recognizes her children's death as something that fate, rather than she, has decided.

Orestes

Bates, William Nickerson. "The Extant Plays: The *Orestes*." In his *Euripides: A Student of Human Nature*. New York: Atheneum, 1930. Reprint. New York:

Russell and Russell, 1969, pp. 167-176.
The summary notes Euripides' untraditional retelling of the myth and the unsympathetic elements of all the characters except Pylades. Bates notes unusual features of staging deduced from the text, such as the Phrygian slave's climbing out of the house over the triglyphs, indicating more substantial scenery than usually associated with productions of Greek drama. Neither Orestes nor Electra arouses audience sympathy; Orestes is quite willing to add the murders of Helen and her daughter Hermione to that of Clytemnestra and Aegisthus, and Electra is willing to be an accomplice in her brother's plan.

Burnett, Anne Pippin. *"Orestes."* In her *Catastrophe Survived: Euripides' Plays of Mixed Reversal.* Oxford, England: Clarendon Press, 1971, pp. 183-222.
No situation is allowed to resolve itself in the ordinary tragic way, and no character behaves in the way the audience expects. Orestes and Electra inspire less sympathy, not more, as the play progresses, and both are ready to murder again if need be. Menelaus, a totally repulsive figure, is willing to allow the death of Hermione, his only daughter, in order to safeguard his own power. Orestes will eventually marry Hermione, a woman he was willing to allow Electra to kill only moments before.

Conacher, D. J. "Realistic Tragedy: The *Orestes*." In his *Euripidean Drama: Myth, Theme, and Structure.* Toronto: University of Toronto Press, 1967, pp. 213-224.
Conacher establishes that a unified sequence of actions results in a withdrawal of sympathy for Orestes as the play proceeds: suffering of Orestes; the social justification of Orestes' deed; the savage plans for escape at whatever cost in murder and destruction. He concludes that the play describes Orestes' evolution from patient, to self-defender, to aggressor, his experience traveling the full cycle from remorse to the vengeful violence that first caused his suffering.

Euben, J. Peter. "Political Corruption in Euripides' *Orestes*." In *Greek Tragedy and Political Theory*, edited by Euben. Berkeley: University of California Press, 1986, pp. 222-251.
Considers that the play is about political corruption, the corrupt city, Argos, a substitute for Euripides' Athens. Corruption also exists in the play's departure from traditional myth and the Aeschylean-Sophoclean view of Orestes, and Euben illustrates this by comparing the Aeschylean Orestes with Euripides' conception.

Grube, G. M. A. *"Orestes."* In his *The Drama of Euripides.* London: Bradford and Dickens, 1941. Reprint. New York: Barnes and Noble Books, 1961, pp. 374-397.
Notes Euripidean changes in the traditional myth: Menelaus and Helen arrive in Argos about a week after the murder of Clytemnestra. Grube observes the

ironic detachment of Electra's speech in which she acknowledges her part in the murder of Clytemnestra and in which she even doubts Agamemnon's glory. Grube considers the divinely engineered marriage of Orestes and Hermione a particularly unsatisfying ending.

Parry, Hugh. "Euripides' *Orestes.*" *Transactions of the American Philological Association* 100 (1960): 333-353.
Parry examines the clash between the play's surface and subsurface form, its Apollonian and Dionysian elements. His thesis is that the play has even more to do with irrationality than the *Bacchae*, and he considers the jarring effect of Apollo's entrance at the conclusion of the *Orestes*, noting its irony and black humor.

Vellacott, Philip. "The Ironic Method 2—*Orestes.*" In his *Ironic Drama: A Study of Euripides' Method and Meaning*. London: Cambridge University Press, 1975, pp. 53-81.
An analysis of the play that discovers irony on two levels: Euripides' choice of a theme just before he left Athens that describes the immorality and depravity of the city after twenty-three years of war (through the actions of Orestes), and Euripides' decision to show wicked actions justified by specious arguments such as Orestes' murder of Helen, explained through Pylades' fanatical speech to the audience as though to the Assembly of the Athenians (lines 1134-1145). Euripides deliberately leaves ambiguous the question of whether Orestes killed Helen.

Wolff, Christian. "*Orestes.*" In *Euripides: A Collection of Critical Essays*, edited by Erich Segal. Englewood Cliffs, N.J.: Prentice-Hall, 1968, pp. 132-149.
Notes the chronological period with which the play deals, between Orestes' return to avenge the death of Agamemnon and Orestes' purgation, trial, and acquittal at Athens. The play is thus poised between the events of Aeschylus' *Libation Bearers* and the *Electra* of Sophocles and partially repeats Euripides' own *Electra*. Each of these echoes creates effects of dislocation, and Euripides intentionally creates verbal dissonances and contradictions with these other dramas.

Phoenician Women

Bates, William Nickerson. "The Extant Plays: The *Phoenissae.*" In his *Euripides: A Student of Human Nature*. New York: Atheneum, 1930. Reprint. New York: Russell and Russell, 1969, pp. 176-189.
Observes that the play is one of Euripides' two extant treatments of the Oedipus myths, the other being the *Suppliants*. A simple plot summary follows, after which Bates notes the two parallel plots: the strife between Eteocles and Polyneices and the struggle between the Argives and the Thebans. He

follows with a general comparison of Aeschylus' *Seven Against Thebes*, but does not note the allegorical applications to the Peloponnesian War, which most contemporary criticism accepts.

Conacher, D. J. "*Tragédie Manquée*: The *Phoenissae*." In his *Euripidean Drama: Myth, Theme, and Structure*. Toronto: University of Toronto Press, 1967, pp. 227-248.
Conacher argues that the play presents a series of deterministic curse fulfillments that paradoxically illustrate the disastrous results of human passion. He sees the play as a series of confrontations between the world of myth, in which events occur through some external and supernatural force, and the real world of Euripidean drama, where events unfold as a result of human passions and human folly.

Foley, Helene P. "The *Phoenissae*." In her *Ritual Irony: Poetry and Sacrifice in Euripides*. Ithaca, N.Y.: Cornell University Press, 1985, pp. 106-146.
Considers ways to interpret the sacrifice of Mendeceus: as the positive climax of a play in which many of the characters show inappropriate or untraditional attitudes to family and city; or as another example of Euripidean irony, an act of selflessness wasted upon those for whom performed. Foley argues that both views are partially correct, for the action means one thing in the light of the choral odes and Teiresias' speech, another from the perspective of the rest of the stage action.

Grube, G. M. A. "The *Phoenician Women*." In his *The Drama of Euripides*. London: Bradford and Dickens, 1941. Reprint. New York: Barnes and Noble books, 1961, pp. 353-371.
Notes the bold changes Euripides makes in the myth, specifically that both Oedipus and Jocasta are alive and in Thebes when the siege of the seven heroes begins. Grube considers each scene, observing that the corrupt text indicates ancient tampering.

Rhesus

Bates, William Nickerson. "The Extant Plays: The *Rhesus*." In his *Euripides: A Student of Human Nature*. New York: Atheneum, 1930. Reprint. New York: Russell and Russell, 1969, pp. 186-193.
Though Euripides wrote a play with the title *Rhesus*, many would argue that the extant play with that name is not his work. Bates recounts the story of Rhesus as told by Homer in the *Iliad* 10 and in the plot of the extant play. He notes non-Euripidean features, such as the lack of a prologue and the presence of twenty-nine words not found elsewhere in Euripides' works, but finally accepts Euripidean authorship based on the underlying thought, the presence

of double entendre, and Aristophanes' playful imitation of *Rhesus* 674-685 in his *Acharnians* 280ff.

Burnett, Anne Pippin. "*Rhesus*: Are Smiles Allowed?" In *Directions in Euripidean Criticism: A Collection of Essays*, edited by Peter Burian. Durham, N.C.: Duke University Press, 1985, pp. 13-51.
Burnett notes that concern about who the author of the play may be has inhibited criticism of the text that exists. Critics are also uncomfortable because of the discrepancies between poetic intention and poetic performance. Burnett's summary analysis singles out the play's farcical elements and cautions that the play should not be judged against the commonplace elements of tragedy or even tragicomedy.

Grube, G. M. A. "*Rhesus*." In his *The Drama of Euripides*. London: Bradford and Dickens, 1941. Reprint. New York: Barnes and Noble Books, 1961, pp. 439-447.
Grube does not settle the question of authenticity, merely noting that Euripides did write a play with this title; he does, however, accept it as an early work of Euripides and recounts the arguments for and against Euripidean authorship. The discussion notes elements in the character portraits that Grube holds are Euripidean.

Kitto, H. D. F. "The *Rhesus* and Related Matters." In *Yale Classical Studies, Volume XXV: Greek Tragedy*, edited by T. F. Gould and C. J. Herington. New York: Cambridge University Press, 1977, pp. 317-350.
An internal examination of the play which suggests that despite Euripidean features, there is more to argue against Euripides' authorship than for it. Kitto considers Ritchie's study (cited below) and provides a discussion of scenes; he concludes that the play is a fourth rather than fifth century drama of generally inferior quality.

Ritchie, William. *The Authenticity of the Rhesus of Euripides*. Cambridge, England: Cambridge University Press, 1964.
Considers that the *Rhesus* may be an authentically Euripidean play, though he assembles considerable evidence against Euripidean authorship. Ritchie argues that even if it had been composed later than the fifth century the question would remain important since the *Rhesus* would then become the single extant specimen of later Greek drama. Ritchie's arguments, especially those based upon vocabulary, syntax, and meter, necessarily become technical; nevertheless, all readers can follow his arguments on external evidence, plot and characters, and dramatic technique. The study is equally valuable for its observations on style and methods, developed through comparisons with the dramas of certain Euripidean authorship.

Suppliants

Bates, William Nickerson. "The Extant Plays: The *Suppliants*." In his *Euripides: A Student of Human Nature*. New York: Atheneum, 1930. Reprint. New York: Russell and Russell, 1969, pp. 194-197.

Accepts the play as a glorification of Athens. Bates sets the scene and provides a simple plot summary, noting its episodic nature. He provides no meaningful discussion of the play's historical implications, merely noting that it was written during strife between Argos and Sparta.

Conacher, D. J. "Political Tragedy: The *Suppliants*." In his *Euripidean Drama: Myth, Theme, and Structure*. Toronto: University of Toronto Press, 1967, pp. 93-108.

The play undergoes a curious disintegration of theme after the triumph of Theseus over the Thebans. Conacher argues against the view that Euripides presents an orthodox view of the myth and notes that the conclusion of the play, especially, rests on a series of jarring oppositions: The chorus feels pure grief and wants only to be left alone; yet, it is interrupted twice, first by the intrusive and banal funeral speech and then by the promise of vengeance, which Athena's pronouncements reinforce.

Decharme, Paul. "Foreign Policy: The *Children of Heracles* and the *Suppliants*." In his *Euripides and the Spirit of His Dramas*, translated by J. Loeb. London: Macmillan, 1906. Reprint. Port Washington, N.Y.: Kennikat Press, 1968, pp. 128-142.

Discusses both these plays against the Peloponnesian War, with which they are contemporary. Observing that Euripides is less impressed by the glories of war than its cruelties, Decharme notes that Euripides speaks through the character of Adrastus in the *Suppliants*, who delivers a funeral homily while standing beside the bodies of the Argive leaders who had fallen before Thebes. Decharme argues that Euripides cherished the ideal of Greek unity, even as he criticized Athenian political policy and detested Spartan institutions.

Grube, G. M. A. "The *Suppliants*." In his *The Drama of Euripides*. London: Bradford and Dickens. Reprint. New York: Barnes and Noble Books, 1961, pp. 229-243.

Praises the effectiveness of the introductory tableau, the Chorus grouped in prayer before Aethra, mother of Theseus. Grube's summary notes applications to Greece during the Peloponnesian War, citing Adrastus' outburst on the folly of preferring war to a reasonable settlement. He criticizes weaknesses in the speeches of the play, especially those of Theseus.

Norwood, Gilbert. "The *Supplices*." In his *Essays on Euripidean Drama*. Berkeley: University of California Press, 1954, pp. 112-181.

An analysis of the *Suppliants* that focuses on its odd and unusual features. He deals with such matters as the number of suppliants in the Chorus, the tableau of the beginning, in which the crucial supplication of Aethra has already taken place, and what women could possibly have to do with the alliance of Argos and Athens. Norwood discusses the entire play in this manner, citing difficulties, suggesting solutions, and making comparisons with other plays of Euripides.

Zuntz, Gunther. *The Political Plays of Euripides*. Manchester, England: Manchester University Press, 1963.
An integrated discussion of the political implications of the *Suppliants* and the *Heracleidae*. Cited above among works on *The Children of Heracles (Heracleidae)*.

Trojan Women

Bates, William Nickerson. "The Extant Plays: The *Troades*." In his *Euripides: A Student of Human Nature*. New York: Atheneum, 1930. Reprint. New York: Russell and Russell, 1969, pp. 197-201.
Cites mention in Aelian that the *Trojan Women* was originally the third play of a trilogy, then provides a basic plot summary. Bates notes the absence of a catharsis, that its plot is one of unrelieved tension. He cites Gilbert Murray's defence of the pattern through which a series of hopes for the women are raised only to be dashed one after the next. Bates concludes by considering the strength of the character portraits of Hecuba, Cassandra, and Andromache against the dull weakness of that of Talthybius.

Burnett, Anne. "*Trojan Women* and the Ganymede Ode." In *Yale Classical Studies, Volume XXV: Greek Tragedy*, edited by T. F. Gould and C. J. Herington. New York: Cambridge University Press, 1977, pp. 291-316.
Defends the play against the accusation that it is essentially a work in which nothing happens. Burnett notes a formal likeness to Aeschylus' *Prometheus Bound*. She argues that the play portends a coming disaster for the Greeks as much as it expresses the accomplished destruction of Troy.

Conacher, D. J. "War and Its Aftermath: The *Trojan Women*." In his *Euripidean Drama: Myth, Theme, and Structure*. Toronto: University of Toronto Press, 1967, pp. 127-145.
Cites evidence that the play was once part of a connected trilogy as its third constituent, then reviews what is known of the lost *Alexander* and *Palamedes*. Conacher discusses objections that the *Trojan Women* is essentially plotless and argues for its dramatic structure based on its brilliant episodes: the Cassandra scene, the choral description of the Trojan Horse debacle, and the final lamentation of the women. He argues that the play is essentially about a

tragedy that has already happened, that the time for action that could meaningfully change conditions has passed.

Grube, G. M. A. "The *Trojan Women*." In his *The Drama of Euripides*. London: Bradford and Dickens, 1941. Reprint. New York: Barnes and Noble Books, 1961, pp. 280- 296.
Notes that despite the horrors the Trojan women face, the play is far from a veiled criticism of Athens, that, indeed, the women hope they will be taken to that city (the land of Theseus) rather than Sparta. Grube's analysis maintains that the play is a resigned recognition of the horrors of war that skillfully combines profound sorrow with desires for vengeance.

Havelock, Eric A. "Watching the *Trojan Women*." In *Euripides: A Collection of Critical Essays*, edited by Erich Segal. Englewood Cliffs, N.J.: Prentice-Hall, 1968, pp. 115-131.
An examination of the visual impression the play makes that considers the interplay of emotions between the chorus and Hecuba and how these interchanges produce an existential hopelessness in the audience. Havelock emphasizes the recurring element of nothingness in the scenes he analyzes.

Sartre, Jean-Paul. "Why the *Trojan Women*?" In *Euripides: A Collection of Critical Essays*, edited by Erich Segal. Englewood Cliffs, N.J.: Prentice-Hall, 1968, pp. 128-131.
Contends that the play indicates Euripides', and by extension Athenian, willingness to contest the value of the old myths. Drama retains its ritual value, but the audience is more interested in the manner of speaking rather than in what is being said. Sartre compares the effect produced on ancient and contemporary audiences, concluding it is much the same: The gods of the play are both powerful and ridiculous; the Trojan War is their work, but observed closely they are as petty and grudge-filled as most of humanity.

General Criticism on Euripides

Bates, William Nickerson. *Euripides: A Student of Human Nature*. New York: Atheneum, 1930. Reprint. New York: Russell and Russell, 1969.
Though first published in 1930, this work remains a good introduction for the general reader and is readily available. There is a brief life of Euripides, which cites ancient sources for what is known, and a discussion of technique that considers Euripides' use of the *deus ex machina* and stage machinery. Good observations on the playwright's use of humor follow. The final two chapters analyze first the extant plays, then the lost or fragmentary plays. The volume concludes with a brief appendix on the appearance of Euripides' works in the

papyri. There are ten photographic plates and fifteen line drawings of mythic themes treated by Euripides.

Burian, Peter, ed. *Directions in Euripidean Criticism: A Collection of Essays.* Durham, N.C.: Duke University Press, 1985.

The essays, by various authors, illustrate a number of ways of reading Euripides, and the collection includes thoughts on both the early and late plays, including the disputed *Rhesus.* Some of the selections have been incorporated into subsequent larger studies, such as Pietro Pucci's essay on the *Medea* and Charles Segal's discussion of the *Bacchae* (both cited herein). Bernard Knox explores Euripides as rhetorician, iconoclast, and precursor of Menandrean comedy. Anne Pippin Burnett examines similes in the *Rhesus*; Fromma I. Zeitlin discusses Aphrodite in the *Hippolytus*; Kenneth J. Reckford considers demoralization in the *Hecuba*; and Peter Burian reflects on *logos* and *pathos* in the *Suppliant Women.* There is a good selection of articles, including foreign language works on Euripides, in the selected bibliography at the end of the volume. These cover the years 1945-1985.

Burnett, Anne Pippin. *Catastrophe Survived: Euripides' Plays of Mixed Reversal.* Oxford, England: Clarendon Press, 1971.

Burnett bases her study on the observation that the myths, through persistent retelling, had assumed a predictable form when fragmented for stage presentation. Euripides sought to vary their expected outcomes through reversals not entirely tragic. The result is that his tragic dramas often resemble satyr plays in their resolutions and juxtapose both tragic terror and fulfilled joy. She begins by outlining the general nature of mixed and multiple levels of action in Euripides and then discusses the *Alcestis*, *Iphigenia*, *Helen*, *Ion*, *Andromache*, the *Madness of Heracles*, and *Orestes*, each in separate chapters. The discussion is straightforward and nontechnical. All cited Greek passages appear in English translation.

Conacher, D. J. *Euripidean Drama: Myth, Theme, and Structure.* Toronto: University of Toronto Press, 1967.

A good general discussion of each of the extant plays. Conacher discusses them thematically in pairs and triads. For example, he considers the *Hippolytus*, *Bacchae*, and *Heracles* "mythological tragedy," and he notes Euripides' modifications and variations in the myths. The *Suppliants* and *Heracleidae* (*Children of Heracles*) are "political tragedy," and Conacher examines how they represent social and ethical positions. *Trojan Women*, *Hecuba*, and *Andromache* are classified as commentaries on war, *Medea*, *Electra*, and *Orestes* as studies in realism. The *Phoenician Women* and the *Iphigenia in Aulis*, sometimes dismissed as failures, are examined and defended as presenting a series of dramatic encounters. The *Ion*, *Helen*, and *Iphigenia in Tauris* are related as aspects of romance. In a final section, Conacher analyzes the *Cyclops* and *Alcestis* as imitative of the satyr play.

Decharme, Paul. *Euripides and the Spirit of His Dramas.* Translated by J. Loeb. London: Macmillan, 1906. Reprint. Port Washington, N.Y.: Kennikat Press, 1968.
A good overview of Euripides' influences and background, this volume remains a standard and often-cited work. Decharme discusses Euripides' relations with philosophers and the Sophists, Euripides' criticism of myth and religion, women and slaves; he examines Euripides' unusual subject matter, dramatic situations, his choruses, the mixed outcomes of his plays. General readers will profit by the author's frequent citations from each of the extant plays and the excellent analytical index, which includes names and identification of all Euripidean characters as well as of all technical terms used in the study.

Diggle, James. *Studies on the Text of Euripides.* Oxford, England: Clarendon Press, 1981.
Discusses a large number of passages from the plays, rather technically but in terms not beyond the interested reader. Though Diggle includes textual and metrical problems of primary interest to scholars, there are good observations on style and interpretation that are of general interest.

Foley, Helene P. *Ritual Irony: Poetry and Sacrifice in Euripides.* Ithaca, N.Y.: Cornell University Press, 1985.
Analyzes the apparent discontinuities of Euripidean drama, seeing them not as polemical inconsistencies but as the poet's reaction to tensions within his own culture. Foley discusses the most unfavorably criticized plays: *Iphigenia in Aulis, Phoenician Women, Heracles,* and the controversial *Bacchae.* She defines ritual as the point at which communication occurs between the divine and human realms, between public and private worlds, between past and present, between myth and a more secular interpretation of events. The timelessness of sacrifice is often placed in the disorder of political or social events, causing surface inconsistency, which Foley sees as essential to Euripides. All Greek citations are translated. Though derived from the author's dissertation, Foley has adapted the study for general readers.

Grube, G. M. A. *The Drama of Euripides.* London: Bradford and Dickens, 1941. Reprint. New York: Barnes and Noble Books, 1961.
Remains an often-cited introduction to Euripides written for the nonspecialist. Grube discusses obstacles that contemporary readers of Euripides face, from obvious problems of translation and historical background to more subtle differences, such as audience tastes. He next discusses the prologues and

epilogues of the surviving plays, then considers their structural unity, episodic scenes, and philosophic passages. There is a good discussion of lyric choral poetry and the role of the chorus in Euripides' plays. The entire second half of the book contains basic discussions and summaries of each of the plays, including the *Rhesus*, a play attributed to Euripides. These analyses, however, display marked impatience with plays written in a tragicomic or farcical mode. They are inclined to dismiss plays in which later critics discern Euripides' distinctive genius. Grube's dismissal of the *Cyclops* in hardly more than a one-paragraph discussion is particularly unfortunate.

Jaeger, Werner. "Euripides and His Age." In his *Paideia: The Ideals of Greek Culture*, translated by Gilbert Highet. 2d ed. Vol. 1. New York: Oxford University Press, 1949, pp. 332-357.
Examines the style of Euripides as a by-product of sophism and the collapse of Athenian society that followed the Peloponnesian War. These factors caused radical changes in the nature of drama and in its production and brought elements of comedy and parody into the tragic form.

Kovacs, David. *The Heroic Muse: Studies in the Hippolytus and Hecuba of Euripides*. Baltimore: Johns Hopkins University Press, 1987.
Kovacs seeks to avoid three suppositions normally held for all Euripides' works: that he is skeptical and antitraditionalist in matters of religion and morality; that his subject matter is markedly different from that of his predecessors; that he did not expect his audience to fully understand the radical reassessment of tragedy which he offered. The author holds that such preconceptions have caused a blindness to what is actually in the text and argues that traditional themes of tragedy, such as heroism, divine justice and inscrutability, and mutability of the human condition do appear. He compares the frequently interpreted *Hippolytus* and the less-discussed *Hecuba* in close readings and without these preconceptions. The arguments and language are straightforward and suitable for general readers, though the passages discussed, while quoted with line numberings, appear only in Greek.

Lucas, F. L. *Euripides and His Influence*. Our Debt to Greece and Rome Series. New York: Cooper Square, 1963.
Useful for comparative studies in literature and following the regular format of this series. There are chapters on Euripides and his work, on his influence in antiquity, on the Middle Ages and Renaissance, the neoclassical period, on nineteenth and twentieth century literature. The volume neither presents much detail nor discusses unusual interpretations, though it does give direction to those pursuing comparative literature studies.

Macurdy, Grace Harriet. *The Chronology of the Extant Plays of Euripides*. New York: Columbia University Press, 1905. Reprint. New York: Haskell House, 1966.

Only eight of Euripides' extant plays have firm datings by ancient testimony; yet, proximate datings are possible through allusions to contemporaneous events, parodies of Euripides' plays in Aristophanes' comedies, Euripides' attitude toward religion and politics, and by the character of a given play in relation to other works of known date. Macurdy's study, revised from a 1903 Columbia University dissertation, is still cited and uses these techniques against the plays of known date (*Alcestis, Medea, Hippolytus, Trojan Women, Helen,* and *Orestes*). She does not dwell on overly technical questions, and the study can be followed by interested general readers. The texts cited appear in Greek, though always with line numberings.

Melchinger, Siegfried. *Euripides.* Translated by Samuel R. Rosenbaum. World Dramatists Series. New York: Frederick Ungar, 1973.
This very basic volume contains few insights on Euripides, though it is a satisfactory introduction for first-time readers of the plays. It offers a chronology, brief essays on the life and times of Euripides, on the theater at Athens, and on Euripides' treatment of gods, heroes, and mortals. It concludes with plot summaries of each of the extant plays; these informally recount stage action but make no attempt at interpretation. The volume contains several photographs of famous contemporary productions.

Murray, Gilbert. *Euripides and His Age.* London: Oxford University Press, 1918, reprint, 1946. Reprints with new introduction by H. D. F. Kitto, 1965; Westport, Conn.: Greenwood Press, 1979.
This volume is often cited for its discussion of Euripides' life as considered against the political and social background of the fifth century. There are good comments on Athens after the Persian War and on the Sophists at Athens. The plays are each discussed, always parallel to the political, social, or personal events that inspired them. There are two concluding essays on the art of Euripides with comments on his prologues and use of messengers and the *deus ex machina*; the second of these deals with the role of the chorus in his plays. Kitto's introduction is brief and does nothing to change, update, or improve the earlier printing.

Norwood, Gilbert. *Essays on Euripidean Drama.* Berkeley: University of California Press, 1954.
This often-cited study contains a general essay on understanding Euripides in the context of his predecessors, then considers at length the *Bacchae*, discussing its apparent contradictions, the relationship between deities and mortals in the *Hippolytus*, and arguments relating to the *Suppliant Women*, such as the role of the chorus and its discussion of war and politics. Norwood rejects the argument that the *Suppliant Women* is merely a failed play. He cites the Greek texts without translation, though he provides line numberings.

Segal, Erich, ed. *Euripides: A Collection of Critical Essays.* Englewood Cliffs, N.J.: Prentice-Hall, 1968.

Follows the *Twentieth Century Views* format and contains a brief introduction by Segal followed by essays and articles by various critics. William Arrowsmith argues that Euripides presents a "theatre of ideas" that constitutes the playwright's distinctive way of perceiving his world. G. M. A. Grube discusses Euripides' view of the gods. The volume also contains essays on the *Alcestis*, the *Medea*, the *Hippolytus*, the *Trojan Women*, the *Orestes*, and the *Bacchae*. All cited passages appear in translation, and there is a short bibliography that includes articles and foreign criticism.

Vellacott, Philip. *Ironic Drama: A Study of Euripides' Method and Meaning.* London: Cambridge University Press, 1975.

Vellacott argues that perceiving irony in Euripides' plays yields new meaning for all the dramas, those dismissed as failed or uneven as well as those generally considered masterpieces. He holds that Euripidean irony is neither the *eironeía* (pretense of ignorance) that Plato applies to Socrates' method in philosophical discussion, nor is it dramatic irony in the accepted sense. It is, on the one hand, irony of characterization (discussed with reference to the *Suppliant Women, Andromache,* and *Iphigenia in Aulis*) and, on the other, of situation (discussed in terms of the *Orestes*). There are two good chapters on the ironic characterizations of women, with extended discussion of Helen in the Trojan War plays, and four concluding chapters: on war, sacrifice, freedom, and anger as ironic motifs.

MENANDER

Recommended Translations and Commentaries

The Arbitration (Epitrepontes)
Murray, Gilbert, trans. *The Arbitration: The Epitrepontes of Menander.* London: Allen and Unwin, 1945.
An often-cited verse translation, though disconcerting for its use of Victorian idiom. Nevertheless, it is valuable as a discrete edition of the play and for its brief introduction.

The Bad-Tempered Man (Dyskolos)
Blake, Warren E., ed., trans. *Dyscolus.* New York: American Philological Association, 1966.
An edition of the Greek text with English translation on facing pages and a commentary that considers both interpretative and textual difficulties. Prepared six years after discovery of the *Dyskolos* papyrus, this volume combines a lively translation, a text with primary apparatus, and a commentary that, though designed for readers of Greek, also contains insights on staging and characterization.

Handley, E. W., ed. *The Dyskolos of Menander.* Cambridge, Mass.: Harvard University Press, 1965.
Provides the Greek text without translation but includes an introductory essay on Menander and Greek drama and a line-by-line commentary that are more substantive than those of the Blake text, cited above. There is a good treatment in the introduction on Menander's relationship to Aristophanes and Middle Comedy, a second part on staging the *Dyskolos*, and more technical subsequent sections on constituting the text and Menander's meter. The commentary pays equal attention to questions of interpretation and to language and textual difficulties.

Vellacott, Philip, trans. *The Bad-Tempered Man (or The Misanthrope).* New York: Oxford University Press, 1960.
A satisfactory translation, though more in the comic idiom of Molière than Menander. The short introduction to the literary tradition by Christopher Fry makes the volume worth noting, as does its discrete format.

The Girl from Samos (Samia)
Bain, D. M., ed., trans. *Samia.* Wauconda, Ill.: Bolchazy-Carducci, 1983.
A Greek text, translation, and brief commentary designed both for students of the language and for readers interested in further study in New Comedy. There is a very brief outline of Menander's life and of the *Samia*, his second best

preserved play. Short sections follow on the plot, the genre, characters and morals, dramatic form, establishing the text, the *Samia* papyrus, and identification of speakers. The translation (neither overly literal nor excessively idiomatic) appears on pages facing the Greek text. There is a short list of further readings; most of the English language criticism cited by Bain is annotated in this bibliography.

Turner, Eric, trans. *Menander: The Girl from Samos*. London: Athlone Press, 1972.
A good translation, though with only a short introduction and bare supporting notes, its principle virtue is its separate format. It remains one of the few discrete translations of this play.

The Girl Who Was Shorn (Perikeiromene)
Murray, Gilbert, trans. *The Rape of the Locks*. London: Allen and Unwin, 1942. Reprint. Winchester, Mass.: Unwin Hyman, 1984.
The Murray translations of Greek plays were much praised when they began to appear in the early years of the century. By contemporary standards, however, their idiom makes them stiff and awkward. This volume's title, attempting to convey something of Menander's parodic style in the *Perikeiromene* by adapting the title of Alexander Pope's *The Rape of the Lock*, gives some idea of the precious tone the translation maintains. Brief notes and introduction with verse translation.

Complete Collections
Allinson, Francis G., trans. *Menander*. Loeb Classical Library. Cambridge, Mass.: Harvard University Press, 1921. Reprint. Westport, Conn.: Greenwood Press, 1970.
This one-volume translation of the plays with Greek text on facing pages has been replaced by the three-volume Arnott translation, cited below. Nevertheless, Allinson's translation remains in many college and public libraries. The essential difference is that the Arnott volume contains all the fragments published since 1945, important since all the plays of Menander require considerable reconstruction of their texts. Allinson's translations include only *The Arbitrants*, *The Girl from Samos*, *The Girl Who Was Shorn*, and the badly mutilated fragment of the *Hero*. It lacks the *Dyskolos* (*The Bad-Tempered Man*), which was discovered in a relatively complete papyrus in 1960, though it does contain an introduction and a number of miscellaneous fragments with translations (many of which have since been identified).

Arnott, W. G., trans. *Menander*. 3 vols. Loeb Classical Library. Cambridge, Mass.: Harvard University Press, 1980.
This expanded edition of Menander contains the fragments published since 1945, an introduction to Menander's works in volume 1, and Greek text with

English translation on facing pages. It effectively replaces the one-volume edition of F. C. Allinson (1921) and provides both a smoother translation and a survey of recent developments in Menandrean scholarship. Arnott's is also, for these reasons, clearly superior to the earliest Loeb edition, that of T. E. Page (1912). Both of the earlier Loeb editions remain available in many libraries.

Casson, Lionel, trans. *Masters of Ancient Comedy: Selections from Aristophanes, Menander, Plautus, Terence*. New York: Macmillan, 1960. Reprint. New York: Minerva Press, 1967.

Includes the four most complete and most often read plays of Menander (*The Bad-Tempered Man*, *The Girl from Samos*, *The Arbitration*, and *The Girl Who Was Shorn*) in addition to Aristophanes' *Acharnians*, Plautus' *The Haunted House* and *The Rope*, and Terence's *Phormio* and *The Brothers*. The translations are uniformly excellent. Casson provides notes with his translation of Aristophanes, though the book contains no other notes or explanatory material except a brief introduction to ancient comedy and an epilogue on comedy's decline after Terence. The Menander translations appear discretely in the volume cited below.

——————. *The Plays of Menander*. New York: New York University Press, 1971.

A convenient anthology, ideal for school use. Casson's translations are accurate and colloquial without straying from the tone of Menander's Greek. This work is one of the few complete translations of Menander intended for general readers, and it shows the playwright's brilliance to good advantage. The translations appear with selected plays of Aristophanes, Plautus, and Terence in the volume cited above.

Gomme, A. W., and F. H. Sandbach. *Menander: A Commentary*. London: Oxford University Press, 1973.

Gomme's major commentary on all the plays, revised, extended, and completed by Sandbach; includes line analyses of every extant text assigned to Menander as well as discussion of fragments cited by other ancient sources and attributed to Menander, fragments from unnamed plays that the editors consider Menandrean, and pseudo-Menandrean fragments from the papyri. General readers will find the scene discussions useful, as well as the volume's introduction, which surveys Menander's life and works, the Latin adaptations, Menander's theater, the life of his time, and men and women in Athenian society.

Miller, Norma, trans. *Menander: Plays and Fragments*. New York: Penguin Books, 1988.

More colloquial and spritely than Vellacott's translation (cited below), which it is intended to replace in this series. Miller's introduction is good, particularly so on the character types in Menander's plays. The volume also includes pseudo-Menandrean texts translated from the papyri and a basic set of notes, designed for general readers.

Vellacott, Philip, trans. *Menander: Plays and Fragments with Theophrastus*. New York: Penguin Books, 1971.

A good translation of the plays, though British in its idiom, it also includes the *Characters* of Theophrastus, pupil of Aristotle and teacher of Menander. Vellacott's introduction discusses the relationship of Theophrastus and Menander. Norma Miller's translation for the Penguin Classics series (1988), cited above, is more colloquial though it lacks Theophrastus.

Recommended Criticism on Menander

The Arbitration (Epitrepontes)

Bain, David. "Asides in New Comedy: I, Men. *Epitr.*" and "Asides in New Comedy: II, Men. *Epitr.*" In his *Actors and Audience: A Study of Asides and Related Conventions in Greek Drama*. Oxford, England: Oxford University Press, 1977, pp. 110-112; 129-130.

Having established that there are two varieties of sudden audience address in Menander's comedies, that in which the victim is either unaware of or does not acknowledge the comment made and that in which the victim's address, monologue, or dialogue is disturbed by the interruption, Bain provides a complete list of these occurrences, in two complementary chapters, for *The Arbitration* as well as for a number of other Menander plays.

Goldberg, Sander M. "*Epitrepontes* (*The Arbitrants*): The Refashioned Recognition." In *The Making of Menander's Comedy*. Berkeley: University of California Press, 1980, pp. 59-71.

Demonstrates how the recognition scene of this play differs from the predictable comic pattern. The recognition comes early, with Onesimos' discovery of a ring in act 2. The abandoned child of Charisios is scarcely more animate than the ring; indeed, the child is not central to the play at all, and the arbitration to which the play's title refers is not crucial to its theme. Goldberg examines the diverse elements that give the play its real interest and shows how, by refashioning the recognition motif, Menander unites these elements into a coherent whole.

Long, Timothy. "Barbarian - Hellene Antithesis." In his *Barbarians in Greek Comedy*. Carbondale: Southern Illinois University Press, 1986, pp. 153-156.

In the context of his study on the conflict between Greeks and non-Greeks as portrayed in Greek comedy, Long cites the scene in *The Arbitration* in which Charisius blames himself as that he has shown no forgiveness to Pamphile for bearing an illegitimate child. Charisius denounces himself as a "barbarian and pitiless" (lines 898-924). Long notes that in New Comedy the word *barbaros* (literally "barbarian" but implying any non-Greek) is only marginally thought of in a national or ethnic sense. See complete description of Long's book, cited with general entries, below.

Webster, T. B. L. *"Epitrepontes* (after 305)." In his *An Introduction to Menander*. New York: Barnes and Noble Books, 1974.
A scene-by-scene summary of *The Arbitration*, part of the appendix that summarizes relatively complete plays and describes the major fragments. All interpretation occurs at length within the context of Webster's book. See description under general entries, cited below.

——————— . "Restorations in Menander: *Epitrepontes.*" In his *Studies in Menander*, 2d ed. Manchester, England: Manchester University Press, 1960, pp. 34-40.
This play has serious textual gaps in its first act. Using a papyrus fragment and seven brief quotations conventionally ascribed to the play, Webster estimates the original length of the act by simple arithmetic, using the first acts of other Menander plays to determine average length. He then reconstructs the action by placing the fragments against the extant sections of the play. The author explains the procedure in a straightforward way and without technical language.

The Bad-Tempered Man (*Dyskolos*)

Bain, David. "Asides in New Comedy: I, Men. *Dysc.*" and "Asides in New Comedy: II, Men. *Dysc.*" In his *Actors and Audience: A Study of Asides and Related Conventions in Greek Drama*. Oxford, England: Oxford University Press, 1977, pp. 109-110; 127-129.
Discusses the several varieties of audience address in *The Bad-Tempered Man*: Cnemon's entrance monologue interrupted twice by comments from Sostratus (lines 168 and 171); the entrance speech of Cnemon's daughter interrupted by an aside from Sostratus (191), who remains unseen until he addresses her at line 199; Daos' two asides (212-213 and 215); Cnemon's aside comments (431-432 and 435); and Getas' malicious interruptions of Simiche's entrance speech (575). Bain offers these as illustrations of eavesdropping asides (when the victim takes no notice) and interruption asides (when the victim must stop speaking to acknowledge the remark). He provides many others from selected Menander plays.

Goldberg, Sander M. *"Dyskolos* (*The Grouch*): A Play of Combinations." In his *The Making of Menander's Comedy*. Berkeley: University of California Press, 1980, pp. 72-91.

Notes that Pan's introduction of Knemon adds the implication of rustication to the comic stereotype of the misanthrope. Knemon's complaints sometimes turn to self-pity, and beneath his bluster are hints of an inability to cope; this vulnerability peaks in the long monologue upon which both the play's romantic interest and its resolution depend. This combination of elements allows Menander to portray what might have been a mere stock character with greater depth and dimension than otherwise possible and to build his entire play around this misanthrope, who has only two major scenes on stage, in acts 4 and 5.

Keuls, Eva. "Mystery Elements in Menander's *Dyscolus*." *Transactions of the American Philological Association* 100 (1969): 209-220.
Argues for veiled allusions to mystic ritual in the play. Cnemon is socially humiliated by dung-shoveling, falls into a well, and is tormented by a slave and a hired cook. A comparable ordeal, of Sostratus, is foretold to his mother in a dream in which she sees the god Pan chaining her son's feet, handing him a pick and goatskin jacket, and ordering him to dig, as though a slave. Kuels discusses ordeal imagery, shackles, and the well as possible allusions to the preliminary Eleusinian initiations at Agrai and considers the tradition that Menander was himself an Eleusinian initiate.

Webster, T. B. L. "Appendix." In his *Studies in Menander*, 2d ed. Manchester, England: Manchester University Press, 1960, pp. 220-234.
Webster notes discoveries of Menander's works in the papyri from 1953 to 1960, among them the *Dyskolos* papyrus in 1959; he uses it to date the play at 316 B.C., provides a brief plot summary, and makes comparisons with other Menander plays. Webster wrote this appendix immediately following discovery of the *Dyskolos* papyrus. For definitive information on this play, see the translation and commentary by Blake or the commentary by Handley, both cited above.

_____ . "*Dyskolos* (317/16)." In his *An Introduction to Menander*. New York: Barnes and Noble Books, 1974, pp. 132-135.
A plot summary by act and scene of *The Bad-Tempered Man* (317-316 B.C.), part of the appendices to this volume. Webster provides all interpretation in the context of general discussions that appear throughout the volume. See entry cited under "General Criticism on Menander," below.

The Girl from Samos (Samia)

Arnott, W. G. "A Note on the Motif of Eavesdropping Behind the Door in Comedy." *Rheinisches Museum* 108 (1965): 371-376.
Shows how the familiar device of the overheard conversation both advances the action and alters its focus. In *The Girl from Samos*, Moschion leaves the stage

at line 162 and does not reappear until act 4. Since Moschion can have little effect on plot, Demeas' discoveries further the plot, and emphasis rests increasingly with him. Menander thus combines the function of the eavesdropper and the soliloquist in a single monologue.

Bader, E. "The *Psophos* of the House-Door in Greek New Comedy." *Antichthon* 5 (1971): 35-48.

Euripides occasionally uses the cue of some sound (*psophos*), articulate or inarticulate, to reduce the formality of entrances; for example, *Bacchae* 638-639; *Orestes* 1311-1312 (footsteps); *Ion* 515, *Helen* 858-860 (doors). Menander varies the technique to fit the context and enhance realism, as in *The Girl from Samos* 280-281 (announcement), 567 (creaking door). Bader examines announced arrivals and those indicated by stage noises as a technique of Menander's comedies.

Bain, David. "Roman Comedy." In his *Actors and Audience: A Study of Asides and Related Conventions in Greek Drama*. Oxford, England: Oxford University Press, 1977, pp. 168-171.

In the context of a chapter on Plautine and Terentian adaptations of the aside and audience address techniques of Greek New Comedy, Bain notes the presence of dual stage action in *The Girl from Samos*, following Niceratus' interrupted words of line 439. There is nothing, despite the broken dialogue, to show that Niceratus and Moschion register Demeas' presence. Bain uses the passage against similar interrupted conversations in Roman comedy.

Dedoussi, Christina. "The *Samia*." In *Menandre: Sept exposés suivis de discussions*. Geneva: Fondation Hardt, 1970, pp. 157-180.

An analysis of the play, written straightforwardly in English, and considering plot, language, and Menander's versification. Delivered as a paper in a symposium on Menander in 1969, it is followed by comments from the other symposium participants. See the general entry below under Handley for complete contents of the volume.

Goldberg, Sander M. "*Samia (The Samian Woman)*: A Play of Successful Combinations." In his *The Making of Menander's Comedy*. Berkeley: University of California Press, 1980, pp. 92-108.

Goldberg notes that the play's action combines the obstructed marriage found in *The Bad-Tempered Man (Dyskolos)* with the disrupted union of *The Girl Who Was Shorn (Perikeiromene)* and *The Hated Man (Misoumenos)*. He demonstrates the similarity of the father-son relationships in Aristophanes' *Clouds* and *Wasps*; conflict between the generations remains the basic thematic motif. Old Strepsiades of the *Clouds* complains about sophisticated living; young Moschion's prologue in the *Samia* shows he prizes urbane virtues. Moschion is sexually indiscreet and has fathered a child by Chrysis, a neighbor's daughter; yet, a sense of shame colors his narrative. Similarly, contrasts appear in Demeas and Nikeratos, the former being dominant in the scenes in which he appears, the latter comic. Goldberg's analysis shows how Menander always provides some element that alters the expected comic type or offers some element already familiar through Old Comedy, though combining it with another, fresh, unexpected, and new.

Long, Timothy. "Travelers and Intruders." In his *Barbarians in Greek Comedy*. Carbondale: Southern Illinois University Press, 1986, pp. 118-119.
In *The Girl from Samos*, Demeas and Niceratus have traveled to Pontus and the region around the Black Sea; they have not enjoyed it. Demeas immediately observes the salutary change of being back in Athens, while Niceratus verbally attacks the inhabitants of Pontus as slow-witted old men. A variation on this invective occurs when Moschion (lines 623-629) asserts that he might have become a mercenary in Bactria or Caria rather than accept abuse and dishonor at home and that if Demeas or Niceratus believe that he has behaved like a barbarian, perhaps he should go to one or the other of these places. Long discusses this passage as example of a motif of New Comedy, that of the Greek who goes, or threatens to go, to a barbarian land. See complete description of Long's book, cited with general entries, below.

Webster, T. B. L. "Restorations in Menander: *Samia*." In his *Studies in Menander*, 2d ed. Manchester, England: Manchester University Press, 1960, pp. 40-47.
Considers how to reconstruct the action contained in approximately 575 missing lines. The argument is written entirely for general readers and uses information known from the lines preceding and following the gap as well as conventions of New Comedy (such as that acts often begin with a monologue).

_____ . "*Samia* (321-319)." In his *An Introduction to Menander*. New York: Barnes and Noble Books, 1974, pp. 179-182.
A plot summary, by act and scene, which includes line references to passages mentioned. Webster interprets elements of *The Girl from Samos* (321-319 B.C.) at length throughout this study. The volume contains an index of passages cited but no discrete discussion of the play. See description of the volume's contents, cited under general entries below.

The Girl Who Was Shorn (Perikeiromene)

Bain, David. "Excursus: The Movements and Reactions of Doris in Men. *Per.* 331ff." In his *Actors and Audience: A Study of Asides and Related Conventions in Greek Drama*. Oxford, England: Oxford University Press, 1977, pp. 121-123.
This excursus depends upon Bain's discussion of the recognition scene of *The Girl Who Was Shorn* (*Perikeiromene*), pp. 113-117. The author considers the

possibility that it is not Doris who produces Glycera's tokens of recognition; rather, that Pataecus happens to be carrying on his person Glycera's ornate robe, having picked it up from the finery Polemon had earlier shown him. Bain then considers the reason for Doris' tears (line 335), that they come about through her distress at Glycera's condition. Finally, Bain questions Pataecus' sudden personal involvement after he hears Glycera mention the tokens of recognition (following line 335), concluding that Pataecus is surprised rather than that he hears the object in his pocket being mentioned by a person he assumes to be its owner.

Goldberg, Sander M. *"Perikeiromene (The Shorn Girl)*: Plot and Situation." In his *The Making of Menander's Comedy.* Berkeley: University of California Press, 1980, pp. 44-58.
Uses the play to illustrate Menander's ability to inject variety into a plot that by itself has very narrow scope. Polemon, the stock type of the comic soldier, appears recast sympathetically as a lover intent on winning Glykera. Sosias, the typical wily slave of New Comedy, interrupts his predictable complaint regarding the many duties that burden him with an outburst of sympathy for his master, Polemon. Pataikos, friend of Polemon, appears to be the stock messenger who informs Glykera of Polemon's desperate love; he emerges, however, as the father reunited with his long-lost daughter after a delightful recognition scene.

Webster, T. B. L. "Menander's Plays of Reconciliation: *Perikeiromene*." In his *Studies in Menander*, 2d ed. Manchester, England: University of Manchester Press, 1960, pp. 5-25.
Begins with a plot summary by act and scene, rather more thorough than in this author's *Introduction to Menander*, cited above. Footnotes provide comparisons with Aristophanes, Plautus, and Terence. Webster then analyzes the characters as types, making frequent comparisons to other characters in Menander as well as to adaptations in Plautus and Terence. A final section notes Charisius' self-indictment as "barbarian" (that is, un-Greek) for failing to forgive Pamphile and discusses this antithesis with references to passages from Aeschylus' *Suppliants* and *Persians*, Sophocles' *Antigone*, and Euripides' *Suppliants*, *Orestes*, and *Alcestis*.

_____ . *"Perikeiromene* (314/13)." In his *An Introduction to Menander*. New York: Barnes and Noble Books, 1974, pp. 169-171.
Summarizes the plot of *The Girl Who Was Shorn* (314-313 B.C.) by scene and with references to line numbers. There is no discrete interpretation of the play, other than what appears in Webster's general discussions of Menander's style and types of plots, all at length in the volume cited under general entries, below.

The Shield (Aspis)

Goldberg, Sander M. "*Aspis (The Shield)*: The Mixture of Modes." In his *The Making of Menander's Comedy*. Berkeley: University of California Press, 1980, pp. 29-43.

Analyzes the play through two prevailing motifs: tragic parody (which appears in entire scenes as well as in isolated words or through allusions) and the use of recognizably serious and light elements juxtaposed for the effect achieved by blending them. For example, Daos' initial appearance, as he reports a military catastrophe in Lycia and apostrophizes the lost Kleostrates, evokes the tone of Sophocles' Teucer over the dead Ajax; the first nine lines of Daos' speech conform to tragic meter, and his diction is in tragic style. Despite this, Smikrines, also on stage with Daos, emerges as soon as his name is mentioned as the miserly old man of New Comedy. Daos and Smikrines thus provide dialogue which is tragic-comic counterpoint, and set the tone for the rest of the play.

General Criticism on Menander

Arnott, W. G. "From Aristophanes to Menander." *Greece and Rome* 19 (1972): 65-80.

This article, appearing in a periodical designed for general readers, considers the changed emphasis on stock characters and formula plots characteristic of Menander's New Comedy and how such changes came about through the economic and social conditions after the Peloponnesian War and because of the changed nature of Athenian democracy.

_____ . *Menander, Plautus, and Terence*. Oxford, England: Oxford University Press, 1975.

Starting with a general essay on New Comedy, this study traces its evolution in the plays of three very different playwrights. Menander's plays, descended from Middle Comedy, consign social and political statements to a secondary role to privilege comic types. These types appear in Plautus' Latin adaptations, though devoid of Roman ethos or philosophical level of development. Terence, also using Greek originals, presents New Comedy in its most refined form, emphasizing speeches and characterization at the expense of broad humor. Arnott's study is scholarly, yet an excellent work for general readers interested in the development of New Comedy.

_____ . "Menander, *qui vitae ostendit vitam*." *Greece and Rome* 15 (1968): 1-17.

An article that considers realism in Menander's works and examines, in terms intended for general readers, how the stereotypes of his comedies show reality through their hyperbole.

Bain, David. "From Aristophanes to Menander." In his *Actors and Audience: A Study of Asides and Related Conventions in Greek Drama.* Oxford, England: Oxford University Press, 1977, pp. 100-104.

Bain notes that New Comedy first appears with an apparently well-developed range of conventions unlike those of either tragedy or Old Comedy. The evidence in Aristophanes' late plays is slight, but the *Plutus* (*Wealth*) has certain affinities with Menander's plays. The author cites two fragments, from Alexis' *Milesia* and from that playwright's *Odysseus Weaving* to show that these scenes resemble New Comedy more closely than Middle Comedy.

Casson, Lionel. "The Athenian Upper Class and New Comedy." *Transactions of the American Philological Association* 106 (1976): 29-59.

Focuses on references within New Comedy that indicate great amounts of discretionary wealth: numbers of slaves owned, business interests, money loaned, horses stabled, dowries bestowed. Since only the rich could afford such luxuries, Greek New Comedy, contrary to what is generally thought, concentrates on this particular class, hence the size of dowries mentioned in the plays. Casson supports this argument with references to Menander and to the adaptations of Plautus and Terence and references to currency rates in the speeches of Demosthenes.

Dover, K. J. "Greek Comedy." In *Fifty Years (and Twelve) of Classical Scholarship.* New York: Barnes and Noble Books, 1968, pp. 123-158.

A survey of trends in scholarship, texts, editions, and commentaries to the mid-1960's, this section prepared by Arnott. See complete description, listed by title under "General Works on Classical Drama," above.

Fantham, Elaine. "Sex, Status, and Survival in Hellenistic Athens: A Study of Women in New Comedy." *Phoenix* 29 (1975): 44-74.

Women's roles in New Comedy are predictable; either these women are young and eligible daughters denied the love they seek, or they suddenly become wise, though no less hopeless, through a moment of sexual indiscretion. Fantham shows how the plots of New Comedy depend upon their female characters, that while women have secondary parts, they often are the focus of the plays and provide the basis of the plots.

Goldberg, Sander M. *The Making of Menander's Comedy.* Berkeley: University of California Press, 1980.

Begins with a chapter that traces the transition from Old to New Comedy and views New Comedy as the culmination of dramatic development at Athens. Goldberg then analyzes the variety of subject matter of the surviving plays and makes reasonable conjectures on the nature of the works no longer extant. Analyses of each extant comedy follow in separate chapters: the *Aspis* (*The*

Shield), *Perikeiromene* (*The Girl Who Was Shorn*), *Epitrepontes* (*The Arbitration*), *Dyskolos* (*The Bad-Tempered Man*), and the *Samia* (*The Girl from Samos*). The volume concludes with a life of Menander and a short bibliography. All Greek citations are translated for the convenience of general readers.

Gomme, A. W. "Menander." In his *Essays in Greek History and Literature*. Oxford, England: Clarendon Press, 1937, pp. 249-295.
A survey that includes what is known of Menander's life, the nature and variety of his plots, characteristics of New Comedy, actors, costumes, and stock characters.

Handley, E. W. "From Aristophanes to Menander" and "Menander and the New Comedy." In *The Cambridge History of Classical Literature: Volume I, Greek Literature*, edited by P. E. Easterling and B. M. W. Knox. Cambridge, England: Cambridge University Press, 1985, pp. 398-414; 414-425.
The first of these sections, which appears as part of Handley's survey of Greek comedy, discusses the seventy years of Greek comedy between Aristophanes' *Plutus* (*Wealth*) and Menander's *Dyskolos* (*The Bad-Tempered Man*). Handley considers the relationship of the tragicomic plays of Euripides to Aristophanic parody, notes the decline of parody and satire, observes connections in Aristophanes to Plato (*Ecclesiazusae* and *Republic*), then, in the related section that follows, discusses the appearance of New Comedy and the plots of Menander's surviving plays. Handley notes the discovery of the Cairo codex and its contents (*The Arbitration*, *The Girl Who Was Shorn*, and *The Girl from Samos*) and comments on the adaptations of Menander by Plautus and Terence.

_____ . *Menander and Plautus: A Study in Comparison*. London: Methuen, 1968.
Suitable for general readers as well as for specialists, this volume surveys Plautus' adaptations of Greek originals, concentrating on his use of Menander's plays. There is a good discussion of *contaminatio* (contamination), the combining of plots from two or more original plays, also analyses of specific adapted sections, an introduction to New Comedy and its scenic conventions as well as a selected bibliography.

Handley, E. W., Walther Ludwig, F. H. Sandbach, et al. *Ménandre: Sept exposés suivis de discussions*. Geneva: Fondation Hardt, 1970.
Papers by seven scholars on various aspects of Menandrean studies, followed by discussions of each presentation. Handley considers the conventions of the comic stage, Sandbach examines Menander's manipulation of language for dramatic purposes, and Christina Dedoussi analyzes the *Samia*. The other papers are in German (Walther Ludwig's comparison of the treatment of

deities in Plautus and Menander, Fritz Wehrli on Menander and philosophy), French (Lilly Kahil on the iconography of Menander's plays), and Italian (Cesare Questa on scenic structure on Plautus and Menander).

Harsh, Philip Whaley. "The Intriguing Slave in Greek Comedy." *Transactions of the American Philological Association* 86 (1955): 135-142.
Considers the device of the slave's trick, both for good and evil purposes, and how it becomes a staple element in Menander's comedies. Menander refines and develops the slave characters of Old Comedy, making their personalities and tricks the elements upon which his plots turn.

Legrand, P. E. *The New Greek Comedy*. Translated by James Loeb. New York: G. P. Putnam's Sons, 1917. Reprint. Westport, Conn.: Greenwood Press, 1970.
Massive and old-fashioned though it is, the nontechnical, readable style allows this volume to remain a good introduction for general readers, the audience for whom it was originally written. Legrand defines New Comedy, its subject matter, and what it rejected (invective, myth, the supernatural); he also examines sources for knowledge of New Comedy, its stock characters, plots, and realistic themes. Part 2 considers Plautus' and Terence's translations of Menander, the five-act law and rule of three actors, conventions regarding openings, soliloquies and asides, length of plays, use of interludes, stage settings, rule of unity of place, prologues, and devices for clarifying plot. Part 3 notes the use of moral precepts, bawdy humor, and pathetic elements. Though there are no individual discussions of Menander's plays, an excellent index cites passages and fragments considered in context of the topics noted above.

Lever, Katherine. "Athenian New Comedy." In her *The Art of Greek Comedy*. London: Methuen, 1956, pp. 186-205.
Considers the advent of New Comedy at Athens, starting with anticipations of the form in the later works of Aristophanes and with particular focus on Menander, the only playwright whose works survive complete enough to make generalizations about the form. The discussion is general, however, and does not concentrate on particular plays.

Long, Timothy. *Barbarians in Greek Comedy*. Carbondale: Southern Illinois University Press, 1986.
Examines the role the firm distinction made by the Greeks between Hellenes and non-Hellenes (hence, barbarians) plays in comedy and concludes that Menander's works pose greater problems in using this convention than those of Aristophanes, in which satire or parody are more pronounced. Long's first chapter defines the Greek understanding of the word "barbarian" both by geography and ethnography. He then considers, in three separate chapters, barbarian religion as portrayed in Greek comedy; barbarian figures from litera-

ture and myth; barbarian music, food, perfume, and clothing. There is a chapter on barbarian travelers and intruders, and one on the barbarian-Hellene antithesis. See his comments on Menander's *The Arbitration*, and *The Girl from Samos*, cited above. See parallel study by Helen H. Bacon, *Barbarians in Greek Tragedy*, cited under "General Studies," above.

MacCary, W. Thomas. "Menander's Old Men." *Transactions of the American Philological Association* 102 (1971): 303-326.
Three types of old men appear in Menander's comedies: the barrier type, who opposes the movement of the play toward its goal (most interesting when he tries to thwart the plans of young lovers); the friend and confidant type (usually in the position of advice-giver to the young male lover); the *deus ex machina* type (who suddenly alters the course of the play's action). MacCary illustrates all these with references both to the generally complete plays and to the fragments.

_____ . "Menander's Slaves: Their Names, Roles, and Masks." *Transactions of the American Philological Association* 100 (1969): 278-286.
Uses the *Perinthia* fragment to deduce characteristics of slaves as stock characters of Greek New Comedy; considers the recurring stock name "Daos," and Terence's modifications of both personality and name change to "Davus," the slave of his *Andria*. MacCary frequently alludes to Menander's other plays and concludes there were about ten slaves named Daos in Menander's works, that they all had leading roles, and that they probably wore the same mask.

Mette, H. J. "Bibliography of Criticism on Menander: 1955-1973." *Lustrum* 10 (1965): 5-211; 11 (1966): 139-143; (1968): 535-568; 16 (1971-1972): 5-80.
Most general readers will discover that this bibliography includes material beyond their immediate interest. There is much foreign language criticism, as well as technical articles on prosody and manuscript tradition and transmission and a large number of dissertations. Nevertheless, Mette's is one of the few complete bibliographies of Menander criticism.

Murray, Gilbert. "Menander, and the Transformation of Comedy." In his *Aristophanes: A Study*. Oxford, England: Clarendon Press, 1933. Reprint. New York: Russell and Russell, 1964, pp. 221-263.
This final chapter of Murray's study of Aristophanes discusses Menander's importance as a dramatist who once and for all changed comedy's appearance and provided both texts and inspiration for the plays of Plautus and Terence. Murray considers reasons why Menander's approach became so popular and analyzes it rather severely as appealing to a society that had lost its sense of freedom, religion, and public duty.

Webster, T. B. L. *An Introduction to Menander*. New York: Barnes and Noble Books, 1974.

A sequel to Webster's *Studies in Menander*, 2d ed. (1960), cited below, this study includes summaries of the major extant plays as well as the papyri fragments published since the second edition of that volume. Webster concentrates on the way Menander worked, discussing typology and the "codes" implicit in the plays; these are social (the relative wealth of their characters), ethical, tragic (misfortunes they undergo), and professional (their appearance, names, language). The first appendix summarizes, scene by scene, what is known about each play that is relatively complete and provides what one can conjecture about the plays that survive only in scattered fragments. The second appendix lists and describes the papyri used in the study.

——————————— . *Studies in Later Greek Comedy*. Manchester, England: Manchester University Press, 1953.

Designed as a companion volume to the author's *Studies in Menander*, cited below. Webster shows how the late comedies of Aristophanes give rise to New Comedy, discusses the role of politics and philosophy in the themes of the new form, and considers ideas, types, and use of myth. The author also examines changed production techniques, costumes and masks, settings, characters, and characterization. The last four chapters explore what is known of the lives and styles of Philemon, Diphilos, Apollodorus of Gela, and Apollodorus of Karystos and discuss Menandrean and pseudo-Menandrean fragments. A useful chronological table lists the names of late Greek comic playwrights, titles of their plays, and approximate dates of these comedies.

——————————— . *Studies in Menander*, 2d ed. Manchester, England: Manchester University Press, 1960.

Designed as a general discussion of Menander and his comedies. The first edition (1950) lacks the appendix on Menander papyri discovered or published since World War II. Webster presents a short life of Menander, considers historical and social background, and summarizes the major plays scene by scene, providing his own commentary throughout the volume. He considers that one can read social criticism, satire, and philosophical positions in Menander's comedies and makes appropriate comparisons with Plautus' and Terence's adaptations of Menandrean themes.

PLAUTUS

Recommended Translations and Commentaries

Amphitryon

Casson, Lionel, trans. *Plautus' Amphitryon*. New York: W. W. Norton, 1971.
An excellent and inexpensive translation, with a short introduction but no notes.

Mantinband, James H., ed. *Amphitryon: Three Plays in New Verse Translation*. Chapel Hill: University of North Carolina Press, 1974.
A good translation of three plays that use the legend of Amphitryon. There are texts of the *Amphitryon* of Plautus, Molière, and Heinrich von Kleist (the Kleist play translated by Charles E. Passage). The introduction traces the origins and development of the myths concerning the births of Hercules and his half-brother Iphicles, explores the comic situation implicit in the deception of Alcmena and Amphitryon, and notes the modifications of the French and German plays.

Sedgwick, W. B., ed. *Amphitruo*. Manchester, England: University Press, 1960.
A school edition of the Latin text with accompanying commentary. General readers will find the introduction of interest; it considers the questions of date, sources, production history, meter, manuscripts, acrostic and non-acrostic argument-summaries originally appended to all Plautus' plays, prologues, and *didascaliae* (which provide title, author, Greek original and its author, date of production, and the nature and composer of musical accompaniment).

The Braggart Warrior (Miles Gloriosus)

Hammond, Mason, Arthur M. Mack, and Walter Moskalew, eds. *Plautus: Miles Gloriosus*. Cambridge, Mass.: Harvard University Press, 1963, reprint 1968.
Contains much that is valuable for general readers; specifically, an introduction that discusses Roman comedy's relationship to Greek drama, a comparison of Plautus and Terence, the staging and production of Roman comedy with comparison to Greek production methods, specific discussion of the staging of *Miles Gloriosus*, theater music in Roman comedy, manuscript contamination in the play, and its influence on English comedy. Latin text with line-by-line commentary and good notes on meter.

The Captives (Captivi)

Lindsay, W. M., ed. *The Captivi of Plautus*. London: Methuen, 1900. Reprint. Salem, N.H.: Ayer, 1979.
Remains the major scholarly commentary on this play. Though it contains

much more than general readers will likely want to know about manuscript tradition, prosody, and meter, it also clarifies the text with line-by-line notes. These stress grammar and manuscript problems rather than staging or inter-pretation, but they also frequently provide citations to parallel texts, similar scenes in other Plautine comedies, as well as comments from Latin authors who discuss or quote Plautus. A reader of the *Captivi* in translation who is willing to sort out this material will learn much about Plautus, his adaptations from Greek sources, and his importance in later Latin literature. Contains Latin text and full apparatus. A minor edition of this play, based on this longer edition, is kept in print. See item below.

_____ . *The Captivi of Plautus*. London: Methuen, 1900. Reprints. Ox-ford, England: Oxford University Press, 1930; Cambridge, Mass.: Bristol Clas-sical Press, 1981.
A simplified commentary, designed for school use and based on Lindsay's major edition, cited above. Those reading the play in translation will find more thorough exegetical notes in the major edition.

Casina
MacCary, W. Thomas, and M. M. Willcock, eds. *Plautus: Casina*. Cambridge Greek and Latin Classics. New York: Cambridge University Press, 1976.
Contains Latin text and English commentary. The exegetical sections of the commentary are suitable for those reading the play in translation. There is a short introduction to Terence and to the play.

Epidicus
Duckworth, George E., ed. *Plautus: Epidicus*. Princeton, N.J.: Princeton University Press; London: Oxford University Press, 1940. Reprint. Salem, N.H.: Ayer, 1979.
A scholar's commentary with full apparatus and notes. This remains the most thorough analysis of the *Epidicus*, illuminating the text and stage action through grammatical analyses and parallel citations of ancient authors. A general reader will find it useful for specific questions relating to this under-discussed play. Duckworth's remains the major commentary on this play, con-tinued from the preliminary work of Arthur Wheeler.

The Haunted House (*Mostellaria*)
Sturtevant, Edgar H., ed. *T. Macci Plauti Mostellaria*. New Haven, Conn.: Yale University Press, 1925.
The introduction to this edition of Plautus' play is far-ranging and of interest to all readers of Roman comedy. Sturtevant sketches the development of tragedy, tracing it through special comic elements in Euripides' *Helen*. He then exam-ines the methods of Greek Old Comedy through passages from Aristophanes'

Clouds and Greek New Comedy through the *Epitrepontes* (*Arbitration*) of Menander. This section is background for his discussion of Plautus and the *Mostellaria*. The second half of the volume consists of a Latin text and student commentary on the play.

The Merchant (*Mercator*)

Enk, P. J., ed. *Plauti Mercator*. Leiden, Netherlands: E. J. Brill, 1932. Reprint. Salem, N.H.: Ayer, 1979.

A Latin text bound with major commentary in English, the standard commentary on the play with complete apparatus and parallel passages in Menander and other plays of Plautus cited. The commentary is exegetical as well as critical and thus may be used to elucidate stage action and problems of interpretation as well as questions regarding language and text.

The Pot of Gold (*Aulularia*)

Wagner, Wilhelm, ed. *T. Macci Plauti Aulularia*. 2d ed. Cambridge, England: Cambridge University Press, 1876. Reprint. Salem, N.H.: Ayer, 1979.

Latin text and student commentary in English. Those reading the play in translation will find the exegetical portions of the commentary useful. There is also a worthwhile introduction that covers the life of Plautus, the action of the play, and production history.

Pseudolus

Sonnenschein, Edward A., ed. *T. Macci Plauti Pseudolus*. Oxford, England: Clarendon Press, 1932. Reprint. Salem, N.H.: Ayer, 1979.

Despite its age, this remains the best available English commentary on the play. The exegetical notes are suitable for all readers. Contains a brief introductory essay and a Latin text of the play with short apparatus.

The Rope (*Rudens*)

Fay, H. C., ed. *Plautus: Rudens*. New Rochelle, N.Y.: Caratzas, 1984.

The English commentary that accompanies the Latin text contains references to recent Plautine scholarship. The commentary is both exegetical and critical, making it suitable for all readers of the play.

Sonnenschein, Edward A., ed. *Plautus, Rudens: Editio Minor for the Use of Schools*. Oxford, England: Clarendon Press, 1901.

This edition of the Latin text with student commentary is an abridgment of Sonnenschein's major edition, originally published in 1891. It is valuable for students of the language in that it incorporates stress markings in its text and provides a simple commentary on both language problems and staging as well as problems of interpretation. The appendix on scansion explains all Plautus' meters in simple terms and with copious examples. The volume is kept in print; it remains the most often used school edition. The major edition, upon which this volume is based, appears below.

_____ . *T. Macci Plauti Rudens*. Oxford, England: Clarendon Press, 1891. Reprint. Salem, N.H.: Ayer, 1979.
Remains the standard major edition of this play. A minor edition, based on this volume is cited above. This larger volume includes Latin text, short apparatus, and English commentary. The commentary is particularly strong on Plautine idiom; a critical appendix focuses on some of the major textual problems.

Truculentus
Enk, P. J., ed. *Plauti Truculentus*. Leiden, Netherlands: E. J. Brill, 1953. Reprint. Salem, N.H.: Ayer, 1979.
Latin text with major English commentary. This volume remains one of the few commentaries on this play; notes are exegetical as well as critical and thus may be used with a translation to elucidate stage action. The volume includes prolegomena on the life of Plautus, production history, and manuscript tradition.

The Twin Menaechmi
Casson, Lionel, trans. *Plautus' The Twins Menaechmus*. New York: W. W. Norton, 1971.
Complements Casson's translation of the *Amphitryon*, as excellent as the former. Brief introduction but no notes.

Copley, Frank O., trans. *Plautus: Menaechmi*. Library of Liberal Arts. Indianapolis: Bobbs-Merrill, 1956.
A fast-paced popular translation of the play, containing a brief introduction but no notes. Despite its date of original publication, the volume remains in print as part of the Library of Liberal Arts series.

Muecke, Frances. *Plautus, Menaechmi: A Companion to the Penguin Translation*. Cambridge, Mass.: Bristol Classical Press, 1987.
This ninety-six-page volume is a general reader's commentary, based on the English translation by E. F. Watling, cited below. It makes no emendations of the Penguin text but focuses on a discussion of the dramatic and literary characteristics of Plautine comedy with special emphasis on the *Menaechmi* as a play with the mistaken identity theme. This emphasis makes it especially worthwhile for students of comparative literature and as a commentary to be read against Shakespeare's *The Two Gentlemen of Verona*, which is a variation on the Plautus play.

The Two Bacchides

Barsby, John, ed., trans. *Bacchides of Plautus*. Wauconda, Ill.: Bolchazy-Carducci, 1986.

Parallel Latin and English texts on facing pages; the ictus is marked for easy scansion, an unusual and welcome feature. The editors have designed this edition for the widest possible variety of readers. There is an introduction that discusses background and Plautus' life, Plautus and Greek New Comedy, native Italian influences on his work, theatrical conditions, and language, style, and meter. A short bibliography includes peripheral and foreign language works. The translation is literal, though well paced and readable.

Complete Collections

Casson, Lionel, trans. *Masters of Modern Comedy: Selections from Aristophanes, Menander, Plautus, Terence*. New York: Macmillan, 1960. Reprint. New York: Minerva Press, 1967.

Excellent translations of Plautus' *The Haunted House* (*Mostellaria*) and *The Rope* (*Rudens*), though without notes. There is a short but good introduction to Roman comedy and essential information on the life of Plautus. See above under Menander, "Complete Collections."

Harsh, Philip Whaley, ed. *An Anthology of Roman Drama*. New York: Holt, Rinehart and Winston, 1960.

Translations of Plautus' *Menaechmi* and *Rudens*, Terence's *Phormio* and *Brothers*, and Seneca's *Medea*, *Phaedra*, and *Thyestes*. The advantage of the volume is its excellent selection of plays, designed to illustrate each playwright's style. There is also an excellent introduction to Roman drama by Harsh. Disadvantages include the lack of notes and the uneven quality of the translations, all by various hands.

Nixon, Paul, ed. *Plautus*. 5 vols. Loeb Classical Library. Cambridge, Mass.: Harvard University Press, 1912-1938.

This complete collection, kept in print as part of the Loeb Classical Library series, contains a translation of each play with the Latin text on facing pages. The first volume contains a brief life and introduction to Plautus, the last includes the larger fragments. Though the translation is overly literal and stiff, inclusion of less often translated material combined with easy availability make this set worth noting.

Segal, Erich, trans. *Plautus, Three Comedies: The Braggart Soldier, The Brothers Menaechmus, The Haunted House*. New York: Harper and Row, 1978.

Delightful popular translations of three often-read plays. Contains a brief introduction but no notes.

Stace, Christopher, trans. *Rudens, Curculio, Casina of Plautus*. New York: Cambridge University Press, 1981.

This fast-paced translation of three of Plautus' comedies is available in paperback and features a brief introduction to Roman comedy, tracing its origins in Aristophanes and Menander and considering Plautus' portrait of Roman society as well as performance and staging in Greece and Rome. There are very brief notes appended to each play that explain allusions not obvious for general readers as well as wordplay difficult to render in translation.

Tatum, James, ed., trans. *Plautus, The Darker Comedies: Bacchides, Casina, and Truculentus*. Baltimore: Johns Hopkins University Press, 1983.

Contains good translations of three less-often read plays. All three plays are uncompromisingly derisive of family and conventional love; unlike Plautus' earlier plays, they suggest no easy return to the social order. In *Truculentus*, the courtesan Phronesium and her maid successfully ensnare four men and take their money. The final scene of *Bacchides* has the two sisters persuading two fathers to join their own sons in the same bed. The *Casina* contains unambiguous scenes of transvestitism and homosexuality; indeed, it scandalized ancient audiences. All three plays contain gaps and numerous difficulties of translation. Tatum's translation includes a brief introduction and notes.

Watling, E. F., trans. *The Rope and Other Plays* and *The Pot of Gold and Other Plays*. Harmondsworth, Middlesex, England: Penguin Books, 1965.

These two volumes, part of the Penguin Classics series, provide good translations of the best-known extant plays. The first volume contains an introduction that discusses the life and work of Plautus, noting his influence on Elizabethan comedy and Molière. It also includes translations of *The Rope (Rudens)*, *Amphitryo*, *The Ghost (Mostellaria)*, and *A Three-Dollar Day (Trinummus)*. The second volume has translations of *The Pot of Gold (Aulularia)*, *The Prisoners (Captivi)*, *The Brothers Menaechmus*, *The Swaggering Soldier (Miles Gloriosus)* and the *Pseudolus*. A companion by Muecke to the *Menaechmi* translation is cited above.

Recommended Criticism on Plautus

Amphitryon
Segal, Erich. "Why Plautus Chose *Amphitruo*." In his *Roman Laughter*, 2d ed. New York: Oxford University Press, 1987, pp. 171-191.

Notes the wide variety of modern writers who have adapted the Amphitryon myth, then concludes its popularity rests on the fundamental theme of faithlessness and marital infidelity, not the birth of Heracles. He examines the humor of Plautus' play, illustrating that much of it relates directly to the social constraints marriage imposes.

The Captives (*Captivi*)

Konstan, David. "*Captivi*: City-State and Nation." In his *Roman Comedy*. Ithaca, N.Y.: Cornell University Press, 1983, pp. 57-72.

Considers the play as one of discovery rather than action. The two-stage revelation of the identity of Tyndarus is its fundamental feature, though Plautus never explains why Tyndarus and Philocrates change identities in the first place. The manner in which Hegio discovers his long-lost son is just as implausible; Philocrates just happens to appear on the scene with the very slave who had abducted Tyndarus in infancy, and the slave reveals this crucial fact under cross-examination. Konstan then examines arguments that the play is a dramatic failure or an example of moral instruction and a classic discovery play.

Segal, Erich. "Is the *Captivi* Plautine?" In his *Roman Laughter*, 2d ed. New York: Oxford University Press, 1987, pp. 191-214.

Critics often contend that the play inhabits a special province on the frontier of tragedy, that both Hegio and Tyndarus are sometimes seen as tragic figures. Segal considers this view an overliteral misreading that derives from lines 60-62 of the prologue. He continues with an analysis of the play that illustrates its consistently Plautine features.

Casina

Forehand, Walter E. "Plautus' *Casina*: An Explication." *Arethusa* 6 (1973): 233-256.

Outlines the plot, making comparisons with the *Mercator*. The author sees the *Casina* as making important departures from stock plots and characters generally associated with New Comedy. This deviation is most apparent in the delay of its recognition scene and in its variation on the expected father-son encounter, which becomes a husband-wife contest. Forehand examines each of these elements in some detail, though in terms appropriate for general readers.

Frank, Tenney. "On the Dates of Plautus' *Casina* and Its Revival." *American Journal of Philology* 54 (1933): 368-372.

Critics generally maintain that there is no certain date for the play's first production; however, there are indications in the prologue and in several other sections of the *Casina* that the text as extant is that of a revival. Internal evidence suggests a twenty-five-year period between the first production and the revival; a first production about 185 B.C. with the revival between 160 and 150 B.C. seems likely, though others argue for a first production as early as 210 B.C. or a revival as late as 155 B.C.

Slater, Niall W. "The Pilots of Penance—or—The Slave of Lust." In his *Plautus in Performance: The Theatre of the Mind*. Princeton, N.J.: Princeton University Press, 1985, pp. 70-93.

Having noted that the play indicates a conflation of its Greek sources, Slater illustrates how it shows shiftings of plot: from Lysidamus' plan to win Casina for himself to his wife Cleostrata's counterplot, and multiple role reversals in which old man becomes ardent lover, master becomes slave, and slave becomes pompous slave. There are sexual reversals in the transformation of dignified matron to servant and in Cleostrata's personality transition from passive to aggressive.

The Casket (Cistellaria)

Konstan, David. "*Cistellaria*: Noncitizen Order." In his *Roman Comedy*. Ithaca, N.Y.: Cornell University Press, 1983, pp. 96-114.

Examines the play as illustrating the political view of marriage held by parents and sees the plot as producing the dramatic revelation by which the interests of father and son may coincide. Konstan alludes to possible social and political interpretations, especially that the Latin allies held ambiguous rights regarding citizenship. He also notes Plautus' exhortation to the audience encouraging punishment of the conquered Phoenicians and reads the play as Plautus' injunction to his fellow citizens to resolve their own internal differences.

The Comedy of Asses (Asinaria)

Konstan, David. "*Asinaria*: The Family." In his *Roman Comedy*. Ithaca, N.Y.: Cornell University Press, 1983, pp. 47-56.

Though the play opens with the characteristic situation involving father, son, and beautiful but ineligible girl and suggests the paradigm of deceived and irate old man and intriguing slave, Demaenetus sheds the persona of patriarch, intrigues to win the courtesan Philaenium for Argyrippus, but then imposes the stipulation that he have the privilege of a night with the girl. Konstan examines these unexpected reversions from type as a distinctive function of the play's plot and as demonstrating an implicit structure of values.

Slater, Niall W. "Six Authors in Search of a Character—*Asinaria* as Guerilla Theatre." In his *Plautus in Performance: The Theatre of the Mind*. Princeton, N.J.: Princeton University Press, 1985, pp. 55-69.

Contends that the speaker of the Plautine prologue, unlike his Menandrean or Terentian counterparts, can speak from within and from without the world of the play, that he comments on his own past and future as lines in the script, that this practice holds not only for the speaker of the prologue in this play but also for the actor pairs of Demaenetus and his slave Libanus, Argyrippus (Demaenetus' son) and Cleareta (mother of Argyrippus' mistress), and Leonida (Libanus' fellow slave) all of whom self-consciously comment on their actions and motivations.

Epidicus

Goldberg, Sander M. "Plautus' *Epidicus* and the Case of the Missing Original." *Transactions of the American Philological Association* 108 (1978): 81-91.

The *Epidicus* is one of the few Plautine comedies for which the ancient critics suggest no Greek original; nevertheless, internal contradictions, as for example, identification of a soldier as Euboean (in line 153) then subsequently as Rhodian (299), indicate the possibility of two originals combined. Goldberg assembles similar problem passages and considers other explanations for their contradictions as well, such as the playwright's retractions and dramatic reasons for inconsistencies.

Slater, Niall W. "*Epidicus*." In his *Plautus in Performance: The Theatre of the Mind*. Princeton, N.J.: Princeton University Press, 1985, pp. 19-36.

An analysis of the title character's role, analyzing the play as Plautus' most unified work. Slater emphasizes the challenge an actor faces in playing the role of Epidicus and notes the distinctive character of the play itself through an analysis of its scenes. He argues that there is no alternation of plot and slapstick, though this pattern is common in many of Plautus' other comedies.

The Merchant (Mercator)

Norwood, Gilbert. "Plautus: *Mercator*." In his *Plautus and Terence*. Our Debt to Greece and Rome. New York: Cooper Square, 1931, reprint 1963, pp. 29-53.

One of the few discrete analyses of this play, examining each scene as the play the author considers most representatively Plautine. Norwood discusses it against the nineteen other extant comedies, noting formulaic elements in its plot, stock characters, and modern adaptations.

The Persian (Persa)

Slater, Niall W. "The Ruse of Persia—or—The Story-Telling Slaves." In his *Plautus in Performance: The Theatre of the Mind*. Princeton, N.J.: Princeton University Press, 1985, pp. 37-54.

Slater believes the play rests on paradox, established from its beginning through the monologue of a slave who speaks like a disappointed lover. It presents two theatrical modes: that of Toxilus and his fellow revelers, which is the world of comedy; that of Dordalus, which is the world of tragedy. Plautus successfully mixes these modes to produce a play that contains two varieties of comedy.

The Pot of Gold (Aulularia)

Konstan, David. "*Aulularia*: City-State and Individual." In his *Roman Comedy*. Ithaca, N.Y.: Cornell University Press, 1983, pp. 33-46.

Konstan analyzes the play in terms of Euclio's relationship to his social environment. The theft of the miser's gold is a function of succession from society. At the same time, it exposes Euclio's lack of self-sufficiency and establishes the conditions under which the audience may elect to be reintegrated into the community and thus satisfy the dramatic demands of comedy. The rape of Phaedria is, on another level, also an assault on Euclio; both are violations of the sanctity of contract.

Pseudolus

Slater, Niall W. "Words, Words, Words." In his *Plautus in Performance: The Theatre of the Mind*. Princeton, N.J.: Princeton University Press, 1985, pp. 118-146.

Considers the *Pseudolus* as an example of a play that moves spectators from a serious to a nobly comic world. Pseudolus controls the action and creates his own fantastic environment; yet, before the end of the play, he drops the farce. This change is accomplished through the introduction of Simia, who offers a strong challenge to Pseudolus' dominance. Slater notes that Plautus may have seen the character of Pseudolus as his own actor's persona and conjectures on similarities to Prospero in Shakespeare's *The Tempest*.

The Rope (Rudens)

Konstan, David. "*Rudens*: City-State Utopia." In his *Roman Comedy*. Ithaca, N.Y.: Cornell University Press, 1983, pp. 73-95.

Konstan contends that the rope of the title locates the theme as one that concerns the metaphysics of ownership, symbolized in the tug-of-war between the two slaves for a chest tossed up by the sea. The analysis compares a passage from Herman Melville's *Moby-Dick* on possession of a whale caught, escaped through some external occurrence, than retaken by another crew. Konstan focuses on Palaestra's identification of the chest and discusses the play's question of moral ownership and physical possession.

The Three-Penny Day (Trinummus)

Segal, Erich. "Morality and Money" The Purpose of the *Trinummus*." In his *Roman Laughter*, 2d ed. New York: Oxford University Press, 1987, pp. 214-226.

Segal notes the play's unique features: It has neither cunning slave, harsh father, scheming villain, nor sweet courtesan, though it does have a cast of eight members. No one is pleasure-loving or vainglorious, though the stage teems with senior citizens indistinguishable in their conservatism. He argues that Plautus made the most of this unusual mix to write a secular comedy of morals and illustrates his thesis with selected passages and discussion.

Truculentus

Konstan, David. "*Truculentus*: Satiric Comedy." In his *Roman Comedy*. Ithaca, N.Y.: Cornell University Press, 1983, pp. 142-164.

Konstan considers objections critics have raised: that the play is plotless, incoherent, even obscene. He concludes that it aims to demonstrate the consequences of greed and lust unchecked. He notes its numerous conflicts, reversals, and intrigues, concluding that the play is comic satire, not merely satiric comedy, that Phronesium anticipates the Rabelaisian courtesan.

The Twin Menaechmi

Quinn, Kenneth. "Comedy as Entertainment: Plautus' *The Brothers Menaechmus*." In his *Texts and Contexts: The Roman Writers and Their Audience*. London: Routledge and Kegan Paul, 1979, pp. 94-100.

Examines the plot of the play as representative of Plautine comedy. Quinn compares the narrative technique with that of Euripides, noting that both Euripides and Plautus privilege narrative line. Plautus was a practical man of the theater whose aim was to entertain rather than instruct.

The Two Bacchides

Jocelyn, H. D. "Chrysalus and the Fall of Troy." *Harvard Studies in Classical Philology* 73 (1969): 135-152.

Deals with the omission of the monody spoken by Chrysalus in *Bacchides* 925-978, in which, as a typically crafty slave of Plautine comedy, he compares his talents to the Greek strategists who conquered Troy. (Chrysalus means to devise a scheme to rob an old man named Nicobulus.) Jocelyn would strike the lines and offers valuable and intriguing information on staging and iconography for doing so. In all, the article is worthwhile for its consideration of the stage "aside," for its contrasts with scenes in Menander, and for its references to ancient art that portrays stage details. The *Bacchides* is the least critically examined play of Plautus, and easy availability combined with interesting content make this article worth consulting.

Lacey, Douglas N. "Like Father, Like Son: Comic Themes in Plautus' *Bacchides*." *Classical Journal* 74 (1978/1979): 132-135.

A brief article of interest to generalists. Lacey examines the play's double plot and complexity, the character of the two fathers and two sons, the two love affairs, and the two courtesans (both named Bacchis). The double plot lines of the *Bacchides* allow a double deception of Nicobulus, one of fathers of the play, but also a reversal in which both fathers (the second named Philoxenus) show that they are as vulnerable to the blandishments of the courtesan Bacchides as their sons.

Slater, Niall W. "The Double-Dealer—or—The Skin Changer." In his *Plautus in Performance: The Theatre of the Mind*. Princeton, N.J.: Princeton University Press, 1985, pp. 94-117.

Notes the duality of the play: two old men, two youths, and twin Bacchides. Slater shows how these pairs run in tandem throughout the play. He observes that it is also a Chrysalus play within the Bacchides play. During Chrysalus' time on stage, he is playwright and controls all action. The outer play is controlled by Bacchis. Discussion of representative scenes illustrates this thesis.

General Criticism on Plautus

Bain, David. "Roman Comedy." In his *Actors and Audience: A Study of Asides and Related Conventions in Greek Drama*. Oxford, England: Oxford University Press, 1977, pp. 154-184.
Examines aside and audience address conventions in several plays of Plautus and Terence as a means of judging to what degree these playwrights used the formulations they inherited from Greek new comedy. Bain considers the spoken thought, failure to notice the presence of a newly entered speaking character, simultaneous but independent stage actions, and pretended unawareness of another character's presence.

Gratwick, A. S. "Drama." In *The Cambridge History of Classical Literature: Volume II, Latin Literature*. Edited by E. J. Kenney and W. V. Clausen. Cambridge, England: Cambridge University Press, 1983, pp. 77-138.
A good essay on Plautus, Terence, and Roman drama, suitable for general readers. There are short biographies, a survey of titles, types of plots and characters, and brief discussions of the plays.

Handley, E. W. "Plautus and His Public: Some Thoughts on New Comedy in Latin." *Dioniso* 46 (1975): 117-132.
An examination of Roman New Comedy as popular entertainment. Plautus' plays feature broad, bawdy character-types and situations, allowing a basis for comparison with many members of the audience. By staging his plays in Greek dress with exotic locations, Plautus comfortably removed explicitly satiric implications yet allowed the audience to laugh at itself. Handley also notes the largely secular and political character of the Roman theatre festivals, as contrasted with the specifically religious purposes for which the Greek festivals had been founded.

Hanson, John Arthur. "Scholarship on Plautus Since 1950." *Classical World* 59 (1965-1966): 103-109, 126-129, 141-148.
The standard survey of Plautine criticism. It includes general books on the Roman theater, analyses of Plautus' plays, and a concluding section that consists primarily of non-English studies on Plautine chronology, meter, and text transmission. The list is designed for teachers and extends only to the early

1960's; nevertheless, it does contain worthwhile entries suitable for specialized interest. This survey continues with the list gathered by Erich Segal, cited below.

Harsh, Philip Whaley. *Iambic Words and Regard for Accent in Plautus*. Stanford, Calif.: Stanford University Press, 1949. Reprint. New York: AMS Press, 1967.
A specialized study for those reading Plautus in Latin. Harsh considers the problem of ictus (metrical stress) and accent clash, the use of trochaic septinarii in Plautus (contrasting the tetrameter catalectic of Menander), and Plautine modifications of the septinarius with changes of speaker. He then follows a similar procedure to examine Plautus' use of iambic senarii. He concludes with statistics on the appearance of iambic words and an appendix of words of iambic measure that are not final words in the line but which bear an ictus. Though too technical for general readers, students of Latin will find this work helpful in perfecting their skill in reading Plautus' verse.

Hughes, J. David. *A Bibliography of Scholarship on Plautus*. Amsterdam: Hakkert, 1975.
A scholar's bibliography of Plautine criticism that features major and minor editions of the Latin texts, more specialized and more esoteric material than the bibliographies for teachers by Hanson and Segal, cited herein. Entries consist primarily of postwar criticism; they include a large number of articles and non-English works published to the early 1970's; the entries are briefly annotated.

McLeish, Kenneth. *Roman Comedy*. Reprint. Cambridge, Mass.: Bristol Classical Press, 1986.
This small volume is an introduction to the plays of Plautus and Terence designed for first-time readers of the plays. It considers differences in style and variety of humor and examines the ways in which Plautus and Terence "Romanized" their Greek originals. It is valuable, also, for its insights on daily life. There are chapters on the playwrights' sources, both Greek and native Italian, on production, and on theaters and actors.

Norwood, Gilbert. *Plautus and Terence*. Our Debt to Greece and Rome. New York: Cooper Square, 1931, reprint 1963.
Most valuable as an introduction to Plautus and Terence that emphasizes their contrasting styles. Norwood provides separate chapters with general remarks on their lives. Focusing first on Plautus, he uses the play *Mercator* (*The Merchant*), based on the lost play *Emporos* (*The Merchant*) by Philemon, to isolate the Greek elements and show how Plautus' play was, in turn, utilized by subsequent writers. It is oddly amusing that Norwood devotes but a single chapter to Plautus' nineteen other surviving plays, though he justifies this

through his belief that *Mercator*, a play not often analyzed in detail, best illustrates what is distinctive in Plautine comedy. Norwood includes separate chapters on moralizing, characterization, plot structure, and thought in Terence. As with all the volumes of this series, there is considerable attention to influence, in this case an appendix on English plays influenced by Plautus and Terence. The bibliography is short and outdated.

Segal, Erich. *Roman Laughter: The Comedy of Plautus*. Cambridge, Mass.: Harvard University Press, 1968. 2d ed. New York: Oxford University Press, 1987.
   Segal's gift for popular writing, reflected in his best-selling novels, emerges in this introduction to Plautine comedy. Rather than recount the often discussed questions of influence from the Greek originals, Segal investigates what made Plautus' plays particularly Roman. His analyses are social and historical, and he translates all the Latin he quotes, thus broadening the appeal of his work. Beginning with an overview of the social atmosphere of the middle Republic, he turns to discussion of Roman holiday festivals and how these differed from the context in which Greek comedy was presented. There are cross references to Shakespeare's use of Plautus as well as a chapter on how the bawdy nature of Plautine comedy can be seen against the sober republican stereotype. He notes how the plays feature stock personalities such as the wise slave and the foolish master, how they were, essentially, the "situation" comedies of the period. There is a good appendix on staging problems in Plautus, an informative set of notes, and a new preface and new essays on the *Amphitryon*, *Captivi*, and *Trinummus* in the revised edition. Segal also provides integrated, comparative discussions of passages from all Plautus' plays throughout the volume.

———— . "Scholarship on Plautus 1965-1976." *Classical World* 74 (1981): 353-433.
   An extension of the bibliography by Hanson, cited above. It follows the same format, written in paragraphed sections that feature general books on the Roman theater, studies of Plautus' plays, and a final section of more specialized criticism on chronology, meter, and text transmission. Though designed primarily for teachers, it is valuable for its broad inclusion of more specialized material. It is also more readily available than the bibliography by Hughes, cited above.

Slater, Niall W. *Plautus in Performance: The Theatre of the Mind*. Princeton, N.J.: Princeton University Press, 1985.
   This volume is a cheerful, intelligently written, and decidedly nontraditional examination of Plautine comedy. It is worthwhile both for specialists in Latin literature and for those interested in theater history. Slater has intentionally stressed comedies not often examined and has considered only six from the

corpus: *Epidicus*, *Persa*, *Asinaria*, *Casina*, *Bacchides*, and *Pseudolus*. Slater's primary concern is to examine how these plays function within the theater. He extrapolates from their texts to make generally plausible conjectures on the nature of the Roman audience, ancient theatrical conventions, and on Plautus himself of whose background much is mere conjecture. The author's general approach resembles that of Erich Segal and is generally unconcerned with Plautus' use of nonextant Greek originals and manuscript transmission problems. There is a short but useful bibliography (not annotated) that lists important works on theater history.

Wright, F. A. *Three Roman Poets: Plautus, Catullus, Ovid, Their Lives, Times, and Works*. London: Routledge, 1938.

Contains popular appreciations of these three poets and is good as an evocative introduction to each. Wright describes in considerable detail the native regions of Plautus, Catullus, and Ovid. In the case of Plautus, he describes early influences that led him to drama and provides integrated discussions of elements of the surviving plays. About one-third of the volume is devoted to each author; its tone remains popular but factually reliable throughout.

SENECA

Recommended Translations and Commentaries

Agamemnon

Tarrant, R. J., ed. *The Agamemnon of Seneca*. Cambridge, England: Cambridge
University Press, 1976.

A Latin text of the play and English commentary follows a general essay on
Seneca and the *Agamemnon*. The volume includes a selected bibliography of
criticism on Seneca published to 1975. This bibliography extends the two-part
listing by Coffey and Mette, cited with general criticism, below.

The Madness of Hercules (Hercules Furens)

Fitch, John G. *Seneca's Hercules Furens: A Critical Text with Introduction and
Commentary*. Ithaca, N.Y.: Cornell University Press, 1987.

General readers will find the first half of Fitch's introduction of considerable
interest. He provides an excellent overview of Hercules as portrayed by Sophocles and Euripides, then notes how Seneca understood Hercules as an ambivalent hero, as sane and insane and functioning in the worlds of the living
and the dead. Fitch also reads the play against Senecan Stoicism and Neronian
Rome, then considers Seneca's sources. Primarily though, this work is a major
edition, presenting both Latin text and line-by-line commentary. The volume
concludes with a substantial bibliography, listing major Latin editions and
scholarly criticism.

Medea

Ahl, Frederick, trans. *Seneca: Medea*. Masters of Latin Literature. Ithaca, N.Y.:
Cornell University Press, 1986.

A separately printed translation of the play, also available as a single volume
with the *Trojan Women* and the *Phaedra*. It contains an introduction to the play
and a glossary, and is published in inexpensive paperbound format. See entry
under complete collections, below.

Costa, C. D. N., ed. *Seneca: Medea*. Oxford, England: Oxford University Press,
1973.

A full-scale edition that includes an introduction, Latin text, apparatus, and
English commentary. Costa's commentary elucidates problems of text and
staging. Students of comparative literature will welcome its substantial references to Euripides and to modern dramatists. A selected bibliography lists
other editions, earlier commentaries, and specialized criticism.

Oedipus

Hughes, Ted, trans. *Seneca's Oedipus*. London: Faber and Faber, 1969, reprint 1983.
An effective verse adaptation of Seneca's play by one of Great Britain's outstanding contemporary poets. It is valuable as Hughes's conception of the play rather than as a literal representation of Seneca's verse. There is a brief introduction by the translator that notes Seneca's distinctive treatment of the Oedipus legend.

Phaedra

Ahl, Frederick, trans. *Seneca: Phaedra*. Masters of Latin Literature. Ithaca, N.Y.: Cornell University Press, 1986.
A separately printed translation of the play, also available as a single volume with the *Trojan Women* and the *Phaedra*. It contains an introduction to the play and a glossary. It is published in an inexpensive paperbound format. See entry under complete collections, below.

Thyestes

Elder, Jane, trans. *Seneca: Thyestes*. Northumberland, England: Northumberland Press, 1982.
The excellence of the translation combined with the fact that the play rarely appears in a discrete volume makes this item worth noting, though it is difficult to obtain in the United States. Elder aims to reproduce the effect of Seneca's poetry in her verse translation, but her translation retains a contemporary tone throughout.

Trojan Women (Troades)

Ahl, Frederick, trans. *Seneca: Trojan Women*. Masters of Latin Literature. Ithaca, N.Y.: Cornell University Press, 1986.
A separately printed translation of the play, also available as a single volume with the *Medea* and the *Phaedra*. It contains an introduction to the play and a glossary and is published in an inexpensive paperbound format. See entry under complete collections, below.

Fantham, E., ed. *The Troades of Seneca*. Princeton, N.J.: Princeton University Press, 1982.
A Latin text with English commentary. There is a brief introduction on Seneca's drama compared with that of Euripides. The commentary is especially strong on rhetorical elements in the play and may be used to elucidate a good English translation, such as that of E. F. Watling, cited below.

Complete Collections

Ahl, Frederick, trans. *Three Tragedies of Seneca: Trojan Women, Medea, Phaedra*. Ithaca, N.Y.: Cornell University Press, 1986.

A good translation, designed for use in schools as an introduction to Seneca. An important feature is its introduction, which includes biographical information, a survey of Seneca's philosophic and dramatic works, generally accepted dates for the plays, varieties of criticism (both favorable and unfavorable) of Seneca as dramatist, questions relating to the plays as staged or declaimed works, difficulties relating to translating the plays, and common problems encountered by readers of Seneca's plays in translation. A complete glossary of names accompanies the translation.

Miller, Frank Justus, trans. *Seneca's Tragedies*. 2 vols. Cambridge, Mass.: Harvard University Press, 1960-1961.
This two-volume set from the Loeb Classical Library provides the Latin text with English translation on facing pages. It provides the generally attributed plays as well as the *Octavia* with an introductory note and selected bibliography of older Latin editions in its first volume. An unusual and worthwhile feature are the parallel analyses of Seneca's plays and comparable Greek dramas.

Newton, Thomas, ed. *Seneca: His Tenne Tragedies*. Introduction by T. S. Eliot. 2 vols. New York: Alfred A. Knopf, 1927 (1581). Reprint. New York: AMS Press, 1967.
Newton's edition of Seneca's plays, dating from 1581 (the translations by various hands), was read widely in Elizabethan England and was influential in shaping the Elizabethan understanding of classical drama. It is likely that these translations inspired Shakespeare as well. This set reprints the ten attributed Senecan plays; the texts appear in modern typeface with T. S. Eliot's essays "Seneca in Elizabethan Translation" (1927) appended in volume 1.

Sherburne, Edward, trans. *The Tragedies of L. Annaeus Seneca the Philosopher*. London: S. Smith and B. Walford, 1702. Reprint. New York: AMS Press, 1976.
A facsimile reprinting of Sherburne's translations of the *Medea*, *Phaedra*, *Hippolytus*, *Helen*, and *Troades* (the last with the title *The Royal Captives*). Sherburne's was the most widely read English verse translation during the neoclassic period, when all Seneca's works experienced a renascence, primarily because Seneca came to represent enlightened thought attempting to function in the midst of political tyranny. This unusual reprint, photographically reproduced from an original copy in the University of Minnesota Library, also contains Sherburne's biography of Seneca, the translator's notes to the plays, and the frontispiece engravings that appear in the eighteenth century editions.

Watling, E. F., trans. *Seneca: Four Tragedies and Octavia*. Harmondsworth, Middlesex, England: Penguin Books, 1966.

This translation, kept in print as part of the Penguin Classics series, includes a good introduction that emphasizes Seneca's influence on Elizabethan drama. The translations of *Thyestes*, *Phaedra*, *The Trojan Women*, *Oedipus*, and the historical drama *Octavia* are uniformly excellent. Two useful appendices, selections from Elizabethan translations and from Seneca's prose works, conclude the volume.

Recommended Criticism on Seneca

Agamemnon

Henry, Denis, and B. Walker. "Seneca's *Agamemnon*: Some Thoughts on Tragic Doom." *Classical Philology* 58 (1963): 1-10.
Considers the conflicts in the play as abstract rather than personal antagonisms. The dominant images of the *Agamemnon* (fire and storm) are universal rather than original, though their use is far from conventional, and they provide the basis for the play's moral and intellectual themes.

Shelton, J. A. "The Dramatisation of Inner Experience: The Opening Scene of Seneca's *Agamemnon*." *Ramus* 6 (1977): 33-43.
The first chorus notes Fortuna's random treatment of humanity; the goddess leaves fear and disarray behind her, and she destroys the good and the bad alike. The magnitude of disaster causes Fortuna to use all of her strength to the point at which she holds no fear. Shelton traces the Stoic pattern of resignation here.

The Madness of Hercules (Hercules Furens)

Hadas, Moses. "The Roman Stamp of Seneca's Tragedies." *American Journal of Philology* 60 (1939): 220-231.
Discusses elements within the plays that derive from the social and cultural milieu of the early Roman Empire. The approach is historical rather than linguistic, emphasizing the importance of public occasions in Julio-Claudian Rome. Hadas considers how the city of nearly a million people, grandly and densely built, with regular spectacles, whether military, sporting, or ceremonial, manifests itself in the plays. He discusses *Hercules Furens* 939-1048, the slaughter of Megara and her children; the killings, onstage, become a gruesome parody of these spectacles.

Motto, Anna Lydia, and John R. Clark. "*Maxima Virtus* in Seneca's *Hercules Furens*." *Classical Philology* 76 (1981): 101-117.
Discusses the personality of Seneca's Hercules, noting that he does not conform to the hubristic pattern of most tragic heroes. Since Jupiter is Hercules' father, the grandiose claims the hero makes about himself have a basis in truth.

Shelton, J. A. *Seneca's Hercules Furens: Theme, Structure, and Style*. Göttingen, West Germany: Universität Göttingen, 1978.

Particularly good in its analysis of the speeches as successions of pictorial images that describe heroic action. In his analysis of *Hercules Furens* 205-308, Shelton notes that Amphitryon's seventy-three-line speech followed by one half that length from Megara provide two interpretations of Hercules' heroic actions. These are contrasting and describe the speakers' characters: Amphitryon as devoted father, Megara as passionate, defiant wife. Shelton calls the rhetorical elaboration "shorthand" by which formulas express specific emotions and varieties of character.

Medea

Bishop, J. D. "The Choral Odes of Seneca's *Medea*." *Classical Quarterly* 60 (1965): 313-316.

Illustrates the ways in which Seneca's choral odes follow a distinctly Latin tradition rather than merely imitate the odes of Euripides' *Medea*. The second chorus in Seneca's play elaborates one of the themes in Horace's *Odes*. The chorus' description of Medea (lines 849-869) finds a parallel in Seneca's treatise *On Anger*, and Bishop traces patterns of Stoic thought here.

Fantham, Elaine. "Virgil's Dido and Seneca's Tragic Heroines." *Greece and Rome* 22 (1975): 1-10.

Cites adaptations of Dido passages as applied to Seneca's heroines. Fantham notes several of these in the case of Medea and suggests that Seneca wishes to identify the passion and exotic qualities both women share.

Octavia

Walker, B. "The *Octavia*." *Classical Philology* 52 (1957): 163-173.

Considers the boat image as associated with Styx, death, and the underworld. Walker discusses the play in the context of this review article and traces its death imagery through its references to water as life-death symbol.

Phaedra

Henry, Denis, and B. Walker. "Phantasmagoria and Idyll: An Element of Seneca's *Phaedra*." *Greece and Rome* 13 (1966): 223-239.

Examines the patterns of tranquillity and fevered fantasy, rationality and irrationality in Phaedra's speeches. She discards her royal robes and desires to look like Hippolytus' Amazon mother, the illicit love of the stepmother becoming the incestuous love of the mother.

Segal, Charles. *Language and Desire in Seneca's Phaedra*. Princeton, N.J.: Princeton University Press, 1986.

A provocative psychoanalytic study of Seneca's most influential play. Segal draws heavily on the structuralist techniques of Jacques Lacan and to a lesser extent on the Freudian concepts of the unconscious, repression, and displacement. His primary concern is to analyze how such elements manifest themselves in Seneca's deliberately artificial rhetoric. The derivative qualities inherent in Senecan drama thus become an asset in Segal's study. The author avoids jargon and aims his study at the widest possible audience. He provides a useful selected bibliography, including article-length works on the psychoanalytic study of ancient drama.

Thyestes

Poe, John Park. "An Analysis of Seneca's *Thyestes*." *Transactions of the American Philological Association* 100 (1969): 355-376.

An excellent analysis of the entire play, the author having noted the insufficient critical attention the play has received. Poe considers the unusual structure of the drama, that 424 of 1112 lines are devoted to the prologue and choral odes, that another 166 contain the messenger's speech; yet, none of these constituents add to either the portraits of Atreus or Thyestes.

Trojan Women (Troades)

Calder, W. M., III. "Originality in Seneca's *Troades*." *Classical Philology* 65 (1970): 75-82.

Compares the play with Euripides' *Trojan Women*, noting the degree to which Seneca shows his independence from the Greek drama. Calder concentrates on what, primarily in the Latinity of Seneca's choruses, makes this play a product of imperial Rome as well as of Seneca's own philosophic outlook.

Haywood, Richard Mansfield. "The Poetry of the Choruses of Seneca's *Troades*." *Latomus* 101 (1969): 415-420.

Analyzes Horatian elements in the play's choral odes, noting their debt to Latin literature and contrasts them with the choral odes of Euripides' *Trojan Women*.

Herington, C. J. "Senecan Tragedy." *Arion* 5 (1966): 422-471. Reprint. In *Essays in Classical Literature*, edited by N. Rudd. Cambridge, England: Cambridge University Press, 1972.

Contains a good analysis of the *Trojan Women*, considering it a fantasy on the Stoic view of death as liberator. Herington examines the variety of ways death appears in the play and notes the strangeness of these passages.

Knight, W. F. Jackson. "Magical Motives in Seneca's *Troades*." *Transactions of the American Philological Association* 63 (1932): 20-33.

Hector, mourned by Hecuba and the Trojan women, is called the *columen patriae* (pillar of his country). Knight links this with the walls that protect the city. The fall of Hector's son Astyanax becomes a sacrifice to the walls and represents the final death of the city's future.

General Criticism on Seneca

Braden, G. "The Rhetoric and Psychology of Power in the Dramas of Seneca." *Arion* 9 (1970): 5-41.

As literary advisor and philosopher at the courts of Gaius (Caligula), Claudius, and Nero, Seneca daily witnessed the results of abuse of power and civic corruption. One could read the themes of his plays as Seneca's philosophic insights into the nature and abuse of power and see the reversals of their tragic figures come about as a result of failure to provide moral examples for civic life; considers *Oedipus*, *Medea*, *Thyestes*.

Canter, H. V. *Rhetorical Elements in the Tragedies of Seneca.* Urbana: University of Illinois Press, 1925, reprint 1970.

Discusses the appearance of words, phrases, and motifs that show that Senecan drama privileges rhetorical techniques. Among these, Canter considers Seneca's use of the *adynaton* (impossibility) scene in which a speaker, having noted some natural phenomenon (tides, night and day, countless stars in the sky, grains of sand on a beach), shows the strength of an emotion by noting that it is as impossible to measure as changing, measuring, or halting any of these phenomena. He cites and discusses eighteen examples from Seneca's plays.

Coffey, M., and H. J. Mette. "A Bibliography of Criticism on Seneca." *Lustrum* 2 (1957): 113-186; *Lustrum* 9 (1964): 5-213.

This survey covers scholarship on Seneca from 1922 to 1955 (by Coffey) with an overlapping second half (by Mette) from 1945 to 1964. It considers works on Senecan philosophy as well as drama, includes Latin editions of Seneca's works, non-English and specialized criticism, and is intended for teachers and specialists. The list is extended to 1975 in Tarrant's commentary on the *Agamemnon*, cited above.

Duff, J. Wight. "Senecan Satire and Poetry: Drama of the Age." In *A Literary History of Rome*, edited by A. M. Duff, vol. 2. New York: Barnes and Noble Books, 1953, rev. ed. 1959.

Summarizes and discusses the nine extant plays plus the historical drama *Octavia*. See description of this two- volume set, listed above under general works on classical drama.

Eliot, T. S. "Seneca in Elizabethan Translation." In his *Selected Essays*. New York: Harcourt, Brace and World, 1932, reprint 1964.

Prints Eliot's essay to Newton's edition of Seneca's plays, cited with collected translations above. The Eliot volume also contains essays on a variety of literary subjects and figures.

Garton, Charles. "The Background to Character Portrayal in Seneca." *Classical Philology* 54 (1959): 1-9.

Argues that the subjects as treated and the distinctive personalities of the plays cannot be related as imitations of their counterparts in the Greek dramas.

Griffin, Miriam T. *Seneca: A Philosopher in Politics*. Oxford, England: Oxford University Press, 1976.

This study of Roman imperial history focuses on the conflict inherent in Seneca's role as Nero's former tutor and advisor and Senecan philosophy. It concentrates on the prose works and provides good explications of these. Though it does not deal specifically with Seneca as playwright, it provides useful information on Senecan thought.

Gummere, R. M. *Seneca the Philosopher and His Modern Message*. New York: Cooper Square, 1963.

A volume from the Our Debt to Greece and Rome series that is useful as an introductory study for students of comparative literature. Gummere follows the regular format, discussing Seneca's relationship to Rome's Republican past, then his influence in imperial Rome, upon the emerging Christian religion, then the Middle Ages and Renaissance. Two good chapters concentrate on Senecan philosophy, how it was interpreted by Montaigne and Bacon with concluding remarks on Stoicism's survivals in twentieth century thought. Though specifically concerned with Seneca's philosophical works, this volume serves as a useful introduction to Stoicism, which one may also discern in the dramas.

Henry, Denis, and Elizabeth Henry. *The Mask of Power: Seneca's Tragedies and Imperial Rome*. Chicago, Ill.: Bolchazy-Carducci, 1985.

The authors consider Seneca as dramatist in his own right, rather than as an imitator of Greek tragedy, and apart from Aristotelian norms. They contrast Seneca's understanding of *adynaton*, or impossibility, with that of other classical authors, and in subsequent chapters examine his portrayal of fear and ruin, tyrants and evil will, nature and human nature, personal identity, and imperial power. There is a separate chapter on patterns of imagery as well as two appendices, the first on *adynaton* in classical tragedy, the second on destruction and reversal. The book's best feature is the authors' emphasis on Seneca's independent understanding of what Roman tragedy should be; they emphasize that he did not feel bound by the norms of his predecessors, and they contrast his political understanding of Roman drama with the prevailing social and religious concerns of various Greek and other imperial Roman authors. All Greek and Latin quotations appear in the original and in translation.

Kenney, E. J., and W. V. Clausen, eds. "Seneca." In *The Cambridge History of Classical Literature: Volume II, Latin Literature*, 77-137. Cambridge, England: Cambridge University Press, 1985.
Contains full biographical information, discussion of Seneca's philosophical works, letters, and the eleven extant plays. The article also surveys trends in Senecan scholarship and considers the role of Stoic philosophy in first century A.D. Rome.

Kingery, Hugh MacMaster, ed. *Seneca, Three Tragedies: Hercules Furens, Troades, Medea*. Norman: University of Oklahoma Press, 1966.
Provides a Latin text and English commentary on the three plays. An introduction considers the nature of tragic drama at Rome before Seneca, briefly surveys the nine extant plays ascribed to Seneca (viewing the *Octavia* as of later date though reflecting Senecan thought and style), and considers Greek models (relating the *Hercules* and *Medea* most directly to Euripides' plays and the *Troades* as a contamination of two Euripidean dramas with elements of a lost Latin tragedy). Kingery argues that Seneca's plays were staged and considers ways several of the problematic scenes might have been treated. He also cites arguments for and against Seneca's authorship, though without a firm position of his own, except in the case of the *Octavia*. There is a brief biography of Seneca, some general remarks on language and style, and a very good introduction to his prosody.

Lucas, Frank Laurence. *Seneca and Elizabethan Tragedy*. Cambridge, England: Cambridge University Press, 1922. Reprint. New York: Haskell House, 1966.
A sound study, designed for general readers and published originally in 1921. Lucas outlines the nature of Roman drama as it was understood before Seneca, then notes the modifications in form and language that Seneca introduced. A second chapter considers the two Senecas, Elder and Younger, the father as symbol of Republican Rome, the son as a primary example of imperial Stoicism. Subsequent chapters survey Seneca's extant tragedies, and the last sets Seneca's plays against the Elizabethan dramatists most influenced by them, specifically Samuel Daniel, Fulke Greville, Thomas Kyd, and Shakespeare.

Marti, Berthe M. "Seneca's Tragedies: A New Interpretation." *Transactions of the American Philological Association* 76 (1945): 216-245.
Argues that Seneca was influenced by Posidonius (fl. first century B.C.), who

claimed that the irrational medium of drama best conveys a message to irrational humanity. Marti thus contends that Seneca's plays present moral lessons. Clytemnestra and Medea are examples of the consequences of fury in the soul; Pyrrhus and Agamemnon, when they quarrel in the *Troades*, are like the heroes of Homeric epic debating an ethical question. See also the author's "The Prototypes of Seneca's Tragedies" *Classical Philology* 42 (1947): 1-16, which continues this study.

Mendell, Clarence W. *Our Seneca*. New Haven, Conn.: Yale University Press; London: Oxford University Press, 1941.
A standard of Senecan criticism, still readily available, which concentrates on his dramas and their philosophic content. Especially noteworthy is Mendell's comparison of Sophocles' and Seneca's treatments of the Oedipus myths. There are also two good chapters that compare the declamatory style of the longer speeches with the dramatic elements of the shorter ones and the dialogue. Mendell considers the virtual disappearance of the chorus in the Senecan plays an important foreshadowing of Elizabethan techniques, allowing the creation of superhuman protagonists. All quotations appear in English translation, and the volume concludes with Mendell's own translations of Sophocles' and Seneca's *Oedipus*.

Pratt, Norman T. "Major Systems of Figurative Language in Senecan Melodrama." *Transactions of the American Philological Association* 94 (1963): 199-234.
Considers imagery that uses the language of physical experience: dazzling light, smoke that stifles, the smell of death, and how Seneca juxtaposes these descriptions with ideas of the most general kind. Pratt discusses such image patterns in the *Medea*, the *Agamemnon*, the *Thyestes*, and the *Orestes*.

——————— . *Seneca's Drama*. Chapel Hill: University of North Carolina Press, 1983.
Pratt's study focuses on three areas: Stoicism and its relationship to Senecan drama, Seneca's use of declamatory rhetoric, and imperial Rome's influence on Seneca as a dramatist. There are excellent chapters on Stoic philosophy within the plays, on philosophic drama as pioneered by Seneca, on declamation and rhetorical drama, on the place of reality in Senecan drama, and on Senecan tragedy as melodrama.

——————— . "The Stoic Base of Senecan Drama." *Transactions of the American Philological Association* 79 (1948): 1-11.
Considers that Seneca's choral odes best demonstrate the elements of Stoicism in his plays and that the choruses stand as didactic elements within his dramas.

Quinn, Kenneth. "Rhetorical Tragedy: Seneca." In his *Texts and Contexts: The Roman Writers and Their Audience*. London: Routledge and Kegan Paul, 1979, pp. 112-119.
Considers that the atmosphere of Julio-Claudian Rome fostered development of rhetorical drama. Quinn provides a brief sketch of Seneca's career and discusses his emphasis on language in the *Madness of Hercules* and *Thyestes* as examples.

Rees, B. R. "English Seneca: A Preamble." *Greece and Rome* 16 (1969): 119-133.
Rees surveys the large number of Restoration translations into English of Seneca's plays and accounts for Seneca's immense popularity in Restoration England from the degree to which Senecan drama admits political allegory.

Sevenster, Jan Nicolaas. *Paul and Seneca*. Leiden, Netherlands: E. J. Brill, 1961.
Though concerned with Seneca's Stoicism rather than his plays, this volume has become a standard work, readily available, which considers the degree to which Seneca's possible acquaintance with his Christian contemporary might have influenced Seneca's philosophy. In all, it is useful in setting the conflict between secular and Christian Rome that began to be felt in Nero's Rome. Parallels between various philosophical works of Seneca and Paul's Epistle to the Romans reveal the similar educational background of both men.

Sørensen, Villy. *Seneca, the Humanist at the Court of Nero*. Translated by W. Glyn Jones. Chicago: University of Chicago Press, 1984.
Sorensen bases his study on the historical accidents of Seneca's contemporaneity with Jesus Christ and Nero, as one who lived in the midst of the contradictory standards they represented yet was himself educated in the values of classical Greece. There are good chapters on Seneca's philosophy, on imperial morals, on Seneca's view of imperial tyranny, and on his relationship to Nero. There is a separate chapter on the tragedies that examines them historically and focuses on the *Agamemnon*, the *Oedipus*, the *Hercules*, the *Medea*, the *Thyestes*, the *Trojan Women*, and the *Octavia* (which the author accepts as by Seneca).

Strem, George G. *The Life and Teaching of Lucius Annaeus Seneca*. New York: Vantage Press, 1981.
This study provides no special insights on Seneca's life or philosophy; still, it offers a good historical treatment of his milieu: his provincial birth, his service to the imperial family, his period of exile on Corsica, and his relationship to Nero. The second half of the volume is an explication of Seneca's Stoicism, in simple terms for general readers.

Tobin, Ronald W. *Racine and Seneca*. University of North Carolina Studies in the Romance Languages and Literatures 96. Chapel Hill: University of North Carolina Press, 1971.

The first third of this monograph, in two chapters, sets forth the structure and themes of Senecan drama, then considers a variety of Senecan characters. A second part discusses the relationship of Senecan tragedy and French drama of the sixteenth and seventeenth century. Discussion of Jean Racine's *La Thébïade*, *Andromaque*, *Bajazet*, *Mithridate*, and *Phèdre* relates these plays to similar themes, characters, and structure in Seneca's plays. There is also a selected bibliography of works on the Senecan tradition in French literature.

SOPHOCLES

Recommended Translations and Commentaries

Ajax
Stanford, W. B., ed. *Sophocles: Ajax*. London: Macmillan, 1963. Reprint. Cambridge, Mass.: Bristol Classical Press, 1981.
A Greek text with English commentary, with an introduction to the play and essays on Ajax, the other characters, the structure of the play, meter, style, dating, and themes. The introduction and essays are worthwhile for all readers, as are those portions of the commentary that elucidate stage action.

Antigone
Braun, Richard, trans. *Sophocles: Antigone*. New York: Oxford University Press, 1973.
Reliable translation with brief introduction and short notes following the text. The introduction discusses mythic background and sets the *Antigone* into both its chronological context as the first of the Theban plays and its mythic context as following events described in the *Oedipus Tyrannus* and *Oedipus at Colonus*.

Brown, Andrew, ed., trans. *Sophocles: Antigone*. Wauconda, Ill.: Bolchazy-Carducci, 1987.
Suitable for a wide variety of readers since it contains a good translation of the play, a commentary on both the Greek text, which it includes, and on problematic sections of the play. The volume includes an introduction to the *Antigone* that discusses Sophocles' treatment of the myth, his conception of Antigone, and the conflict between Creon and Antigone. There is also a selected bibliography that covers editions and commentaries and lists general and more specialized article-length works on the Greek theater and on Sophocles.

Jebb, Richard C., and E. S. Shuckburgh, eds. *The Antigone of Sophocles*. Cambridge, England: Cambridge University Press, 1902, reprints 1963, 1971.
A well-known school edition of the play adapted from Jebb's major edition of Sophocles' plays, cited below. Contains a short introduction to the play, a metrical analysis, a Greek index, a grammatical index, and Jebb's Greek text with short apparatus. The commentary, in English, contains short discussions of each scene that clarify stage action.

O'Brien, Joan V. *Guide to Sophocles' Antigone: A Student Edition with Commentary, Grammatical Notes, and Vocabulary*. Carbondale: Southern Illinois University Press, 1978.

An excellent undergraduate Greek text that includes a vocabulary list appropriate for the intermediate level as well as a commentary that elucidates stage
action and dramatic questions in addition to grammatical questions.

Sophocles. *Antigone*. New York: Caedmon Records, 1960.
An excellent English-language recording of the entire play with an all-British
cast. Dorothy Tutin plays Antigone; Max Adrian, Creon; Jeremy Brett,
Haimon; and Geoffrey Dunn, Teiresias. The text used is based on the elegant
(though not entirely literal) translation by Dudley Fitts and Robert Fitzgerald.

_____ . *Antigone*. New York: Folkways Records, 1957.
This unusual recording offers a reading in Attic Greek of Sophocles' play by
members of the Columbia University Classic Society. The album contains the
play's major scenes and includes the *parados* (entrance of the Chorus) and
several of the choral odes. It is useful as an introduction to iambic trimeter and
lyric meters for students of the language but also worthwhile for those who
wish to hear Sophocles' Greek in a manner that at least approximates the
sound of an actual performance. A text leaflet accompanies the record.

Wilkins, J., and M. Macleod, eds. *Antigone and Oedipus the King: A Companion to
the Penguin Translation*. Cambridge, Mass.: Bristol Classical Press, 1987.
An excellent commentary on the two plays, keyed to the Watling translation,
cited below. Also contains an introduction discussing Sophocles and tragic
drama in terms appropriate for a reader new to Sophocles' works.

Electra
Kells, J. H., ed. *Sophocles: Electra*. London: Cambridge University Press, 1973.
Several parts of this volume can be useful to general readers. Its introduction
offers a good summary and discussion of the play, focusing on the character of
Orestes and making comparisons with Euripides' *Electra* and with Sophocles'
treatment of Electra and Antigone. There is also a good note on the style of
Sophocles, written nontechnically, and a section on stage production of the
Electra. The commentary that accompanies the Greek text focuses on the play
as a study in revenge and stresses Sophocles' use of irony, noting, as well, the
political and social subtext that relates to Sophocles' own times. There are
appendices on the lyric meters, an excursus on lines 1087-1097 (which one can
read against the social conflicts of fifth century Athens), and a note by P. E.
Easterling on text transmission.

Theobald, Lewis, trans. *Electra: A Tragedy, Translated from Sophocles with Notes*.
London: Bernard Lintott, 1714. Reprint. New York: AMS Press, 1979.
Theobald's translations of ancient dramas were widely read in the early eighteenth century and reflect the same spirit of popularizing culture that one finds
in the essays of Joseph Addison. Addison was Theobald's patron, and this

volume contains the translator's dedication to him. This reprint is one of a series of similar early English translations. The original from which it was photographed is from the University of Illinois, Urbana-Champaign. The volume, as reproduced, contains the original frontispiece engraving and woodcuts; the translation is British idiom of the period. Like other volumes in this series (Theobald's *Oedipus* and Sheridan's *Philoctetes*, both cited below), it is useful for students of comparative literature and theater history.

Watling, E. F., trans. *Sophocles: Electra and Other Plays*. New York: Penguin Books, 1953.
   The companion volume to Watling's translation of the Theban plays of Sophocles. It includes the *Women of Trachis*, *Philoctetes*, and *Ajax*, as well as a brief introduction.

Oedipus Tyrannus

Berg, Stephen, and Diskin Clay, trans. *Sophocles: Oedipus the King*. New York: Oxford University Press, 1978.
   An excellent translation with brief notes following the text and an introduction that sets the play in its mythic and chronological context.

Berkowitz, Luci, and Theodore F. Gunner, eds., trans. *Sophocles: Oedipus Tyrannus*. Norton Critical Edition. New York: W. W. Norton, 1970.
   An excellent translation with introductory material, notes, and essays on the play. The volume is ideal as an introduction to the play.

Burgess, Anthony, trans. *Sophocles: Oedipus the King*. Minneapolis: University of Minnesota Press, 1972.
   More an adaptation than a translation and more Burgess than Sophocles, this volume offers a very modern reading of the play and a short introduction by Burgess.

Dawe, R. D., ed. *Sophocles: Oedipus Rex*. Cambridge, England: Cambridge University Press, 1982.
   A Greek text with commentary that also contains material useful for general readers. The introduction provides a survey of content and analysis of structure and is straightforwardly written. It also contains a good note that discusses how manuscript transmission affects the relationship between playwright and play. The commentary includes comments on staging and interpretation in addition to elucidation of textual and grammatical problems. There is an appendix on lyric meters.

Jebb, Richard C., ed. *Sophocles: Oedipus Tyrannus*. Cambridge, England: Cambridge University Press, 1885. Reprint. Cambridge, Mass.: Bristol Classical Press, 1981.

This school edition has a shortened, less technical commentary than Jebb's major edition of the complete plays, cited below. It contains the Greek text with reduced apparatus, an essay on metrics, and others on textual tradition, treatments of the Oedipus legend before Sophocles, and Aristotle's criticism of the play from the *Poetics*. Summaries precede each section of the commentary.

Theobald, Lewis, trans. *Oedipus, King of Thebes: A Tragedy*. London: Bernard Lintott, 1715. Reprint. New York: AMS Press, 1976.
A facsimile reprinting, with original notes and engravings, of a popular eighteenth century translation. This volume will appeal to students of theater history and comparative literature. Theobald divides the play into five acts and provides a verse translation that transforms Sophocles' play into an example of Augustan drama. The translation illustrates the taste for classical revivals characteristic of early eighteenth century England.

Wilkins, J., and M. Macleod, eds. *Antigone and Oedipus the King: A Companion to the Penguin Translation*. Cambridge, Mass.: Bristol Classical Press, 1987.
An excellent commentary on the two plays, keyed to the Watling translation, cited below. Also contains an introduction discussing Sophocles and tragic drama in terms appropriate for a reader new to Sophocles' works.

Philoctetes
Sheridan, Thomas, trans. *The Philoctetes of Sophocles*. Dublin, Ireland: J. Hyde and E. Dobson, 1725. Reprint. New York: AMS Press, 1980.
A translation of Sophocles' play by the eighteenth century dramatist Thomas Sheridan. The reprint is in reduced-size facsimile and contains Sheridan's notes as well as his dedication to his patron Lady Carteret. It is another in the AMS series of early English translations of classical drama, and, like the Newton and Sherburne translations of Seneca, cited above, is of interest to students of comparative literature and theater history. See also, the Theobald translations of *Oedipus Tyrannus* and *Electra*, cited above.

Webster, T. B. L., ed. *Sophocles: Philoctetes*. Cambridge, England: Cambridge University Press, 1970.
A Greek text of the play with apparatus. The commentary emphasizes literary rather than textual problems. An introduction traces development of the Philoctetes myth and considers how it appears in the context of Sophocles' play. It includes a note on staging and a brief bibliography. There are two good appendices, on meters used in the play and on text transmission (the latter written by P. E. Easterling).

Women of Trachis (Trachiniae)
Easterling, P. E., ed. *Sophocles: Trachiniae*. New York: Cambridge University Press, 1982.

This volume includes a Greek text with English commentary and introduction. The introduction is completely suitable for all readers; it outlines plot and discusses stage action, the Heracles myths, and the dating of Sophocles' play. The commentary is subdivided by scene, and each subdivision begins with a brief and clear essay on imagery, stage action, and references to parallel passages in other works. Notes feature problems relating to the Greek text but also discuss matters relating to stage action and interpretation.

Pound, Ezra, trans. *Sophocles, Women of Trachis: A Version*. New York: New Directions, 1957.

A version rather than a translation, it caused considerable controversy when it appeared because it reflects Pound's own lean and inflexible style. Pound, in effect, creates his own play, the only published example of his poetry in drama form. Students of comparative literature as well as readers of Pound's poetry, itself rooted in classical allusions, should be aware of this volume. It appears with two concluding essays: an "Editorial Declaration," by Denis Goacher and Peter Whigham on the relationship of Pound and the modernist poets he championed, and "Why Pound Liked Italy," on the poet's love of Dante, Rapallo (his summer home near Pisa), and his antipathy for the "usurocracy" of the West's monetary system.

Williams, C. K., and Gregory W. Dickerson, trans. *Women of Trachis*. New York: Oxford University Press, 1978.

An excellent translation, one of the few discrete English translations of the play. It contains an introduction to the myth of Heracles and Deianira, to the action of the play, and brief notes.

Complete Collections

Banks, Theodore H., trans. *Sophocles: Three Theban Plays*. New York: Oxford University Press, 1956.

Good verse translations of the *Oedipus Tyrannus*, *Oedipus at Colonus*, and *Antigone* with short notes. The volume remains in print. Less literal than the newer Oxford translations, it retains a certain attractiveness for its elegance and greater modernity than the Jebb translations cited below. It is available in inexpensive paperbound format.

Fagles, Robert, trans., and B. M. W. Knox, ed. *Sophocles: The Three Theban Plays*. New York: Viking Press, 1982; New York: Penguin Books, 1984.

The best translation of the *Antigone*, *Oedipus Tyrannus*, and *Oedipus at Colonus* available. The translations are good, and there are excellent introductions and notes written by Knox. Available in inexpensive paperbound edition and in hardcover.

Grene, David, and Richmond Lattimore, eds., trans. *Sophocles*. 2 vols. The Complete Greek Tragedies. Chicago: University of Chicago Press, 1954, 1957.

These two volumes, part of a series of translations of all the extant Greek tragedies, offer translations of uniformly high quality, though without notes. The first volume contains Grene's brief introduction to the Theban plays and translations of the *Oedipus Tyrannus*, *Oedipus at Colonus*, and *Antigone*. The second offers brief individual introductions and translations of the *Ajax*, *Women of Trachis*, *Electra*, and *Philoctetes*. The volumes remain in print and are available individually.

Hadas, Moses, ed. *Complete Plays of Sophocles*. New York: Bantam Books, 1982.

Hadas has revised and modernized the Jebb translations, written a general introduction to Sophoclean drama, and included prefatory comments on each play. See citation on the Jebb translations, below.

Jebb, Richard C., ed., trans. *Sophocles: The Plays and Fragments with Critical Notes, Commentary, and Translation in English Prose*. 7 vols. Cambridge, England: Cambridge University Press, 1883-1900. Reprint. Amsterdam: Hakkert, 1967.

Though the translations are in stiff Victorian idiom, the set remains a standard. General readers will find the introductions filled with valuable insights on the plays and their staging. Volume 1 contains the *Oedipus Tyrannus*; volume 2, the *Oedipus Coloneus*; volume 3, the *Antigone*; volume 4, the *Philoctetes*; volume 5, the *Trachiniae*; volume 6, the *Electra*; and volume 7, the *Ajax*. Though the commentaries are primarily concerned with language and textual problems, they also deal with questions of staging and production, and they provide valuable cross-references to parallel ancient texts. The commentaries on the extant plays of Sophocles by J. C. Kamerbeck (Leiden, Netherlands: E. J. Brill, 1963-1975), though they contain more recent scholarship, are exclusively for scholarly use.

_____ . *The Tragedies of Sophocles*. Cambridge, England: Cambridge University Press, 1904. Reprint. Salem, N.H.: Ayer, 1987.

These Victorian translations of the extant plays depart from the Greek and are not the best for a reader new to the works of Sophocles because of their stiff idiomatic style; still, they retain a British elegance that some readers find attractive, and for many they remain the classic English translation of the plays. They were originally planned to accompany Jebb's major commentary, cited above. Hadas has modernized these translations and written prefatory comments to each of the plays in the volume cited above.

Kitto, H. D. F., trans. *Sophocles: Three Tragedies*. New York: Oxford University Press, 1962.

Verse translations of the *Antigone*, *Oedipus Tyrannus*, and *Electra*; with brief notes and available in inexpensive paperbound format. The volume remains in print.

McLeish, Kenneth, trans. *Sophocles: Electra, Antigone, Philoctetes*. New York: Cambridge University Press, 1979.
A good translation of the plays with a short introduction and essential notes.

Storr, F., ed., trans. *Sophocles*. 2 vols. Loeb Classical Library. Cambridge, Mass.: Harvard University Press, 1912, 1913.
These two volumes are kept in print as part of the Loeb Classical Library. They offer the convenience of Greek text and English translation on facing pages, though no notes and only the barest introductory material. The translations themselves are antiquated and depart considerably from the Greek.

Watling, E. F., trans. *Sophocles: The Theban Plays*. New York: Penguin Books, 1950.
Good translations of the *Oedipus Tyrannus*, *Oedipus at Colonus*, and *Antigone*, though without commentary or meaningful notes. Can be read with the companion keyed to this translation by Wilkins and Macleod, cited with *Antigone* entries above.

Recommended Criticism on Sophocles

Ajax
Blundell, Mary Whitlock. "*Ajax*." In her *Helping Friends and Harming Enemies: A Study in Sophocles and Greek Ethics*. New York: Cambridge University Press, 1989, pp. 60-105.
A thorough analysis of the play's alliances and antagonisms. Teucer's alliance with his brother Ajax continues even after that hero's suicide when he discovers that Zeus, an Erinys, and Justice may destroy Ajax's enemies. Agamemnon, like Ajax himself, refuses to abandon his hatred. Ajax's friends finally unite to give him burial, symbolizing both the unity and the exclusiveness of his supporters. Though Odysseus says he is a friend, he leaves the stage before the final choral ode. These friendships and frictions lend unity, allowing Ajax to influence the action of the play, even after his death.

Bowra, C. M. "*Ajax*." In his *Sophoclean Tragedy*. Oxford, England: Clarendon Press, 1944, reprint 1965, pp. 16-62.
Discusses the paradoxical nature of the hero, his prowess and long, heroic career ended in madness and suicide. Having cited the Ajax allusions in Homer and Pindar, Bowra provides a complete analysis of the play, noting how

the last scenes emphasize Ajax's mobility and strength. That Ajax's final encomium comes from Odysseus shows the profound degree to which Ajax achieves heroic status.

Burton, R. W. B. *"Ajax."* In his *The Chorus in Sophocles' Tragedies*. Oxford, England: Clarendon Press, 1980, pp. 6-40.
The choral odes reflect the mutual devotion and interdependence of Ajax and his sailors. The loyalty of the sailors, mirrored in the lyrics, is a powerful means of revealing the pathos inherent in the myth and in the setting of the play.

Davis, Michael. "Politics and Madness." In *Greek Tragedy and Political Theory*, edited by J. Peter Euben. Berkeley: University of California Press, 1986, pp. 142-161.
Relates the disintegration of Ajax's personality to the unraveling of the civic process, providing a close reading of the scenes with Odysseus (illustrating the latter's brutality), Agamemnon and Menelaus (mutual dependence in unholy alliance), and Teucer (the defense of Ajax's corpse). Davis concludes that the play is about the problem of politics, that Ajax's slaughter of the animals amounts almost to a caricature of a tragic action.

Gardiner, Cynthia P. *"Ajax."* In her *The Sophoclean Chorus: A Study of Character and Function*. Iowa City: University of Iowa Press, 1987, pp. 50-78.
The Chorus here is a passive instrument, men who undeservedly suffer the consequences of Ajax's actions, but they also have an active role in reinforcing the dramatic impressions that Ajax's madness, slaughter of the animals, and suicide create.

Gellie, G. H. *"Ajax."* In his *Sophocles: A Reading*. Carlton, Victoria, Australia: Melbourne University Press, 1972, pp. 3-28.
Argues that the play contrasts the isolated heroism of Ajax, a man perceived as unable to recognize life as it is, and the collaborative heroism of Odysseus. Odysseus can respect individual heroism but has no place for it in his world. Agamemnon retains a patronizing sense of office through and beyond the play; he finally concedes Ajax's burial as a friendly gesture to Odysseus but dissociates himself from the act of burial.

Knox, Bernard M. W. "The *Ajax* of Sophocles." *Harvard Studies in Classical Philology*, 65 (1961): 1-37. Reprint. In *Sophocles: A Collection of Critical Essays*, edited by Thomas Woodard. Twentieth Century Views. Englewood Cliffs, N.J.: Prentice-Hall, 1966, pp. 29-61.
A full analysis of the play, focusing on the puzzling nature of the maddened hero, seemingly small-minded and contentious when quarreling for the arms of

the dead Achilles, yet magnanimous and eloquent in the final scene of the play. Having considered the nature of the mythic hero, in general and with application to Sophocles' Ajax, Knox concludes that Ajax died as he had lived: hating his enemies. Ajax would rather die than acknowledge Odysseus as a friend. Ajax's brother Teucer recognizes this and so will not let Odysseus take part in the burial.

Lucas, D. W. "The Plays of Sophocles: The *Ajax.*" In his *The Greek Tragic Poets*, 2d ed. London: Cohen and West, 1950, rev. ed. 1959, pp. 133-139.
Considers Ajax Sophocles' most didactic play and a study in the prideful arrogance of its hero. Ajax's outrage at being denied the armor of Achilles knows no bounds. Lucas provides a plot summary and notes that the emphasis is on the magnificence of Ajax rather than on the punishment his blasphemies merit.

Moore, John. "The Dissembling-Speech of Ajax." In *Yale Classical Studies, Volume XXV: Greek Tragedy*, edited by T. F. Gould and C. J. Herington. New York: Cambridge University Press, 1977, pp. 47-66.
Considers the controversy concerning the meaning of Ajax's speech (lines 646-692). Moore notes examples of its verbal ambiguity, specifically Ajax's sudden pity for Tecmessa and his allusions to what could be either ritual purification or suicide. Moore argues that Ajax must deceive those he loves, precisely because he pities them; conscience will not allow actual falsehood, so he must hit upon words that in some interpretation contain truth.

Seale, David. "The *Ajax*: The Shame of Revelation." In his *Vision and Stagecraft in Sophocles*. Chicago: University of Chicago Press, 1982, pp. 144-180.
Notes that a sword is the play's key visual element, relating to Ajax's having been denied the arms of Achilles, to Ajax's mad slaughter of the animals, and ultimately to Ajax's suicide. The title character remains the center of attention throughout, developed until Ajax learns what he has done in a fit of madness.

Segal, Charles. "*Ajax.*" In his *Tragedy and Civilization: An Interpretation of Sophocles*. Cambridge, Mass.: Harvard University Press, 1981, pp. 109-151.
The funerary ritual at play's end implies a civilized community that can affirm the heroism of Ajax, just as the tragic performance can enclose and frame the sufferings and negations of order the play contains in its plot. Segal reads the play as a series of tensions and resolutions that ultimately affirm order and civilization.

Sicherl, M. "The Tragic Issue in Sophocles' *Ajax.*" In *Yale Classical Studies, Volume XXV: Greek Tragedy*, edited by T. F. Gould and C. J. Herington. New York: Cambridge University Press, 1977, pp. 67-98.

Sicherl examines the deception speech (lines 646-692) as illustrative of Sophocles' conception of the tragic world-order. The major question of the play is the status of the central character. By sacrificing himself voluntarily, Ajax purges himself of pollution and becomes reconciled with Athena, submitting, and thereby taking his place beside Athens' protectress. The chief issue is Ajax's burial, effected despite the opposition of his enemies. His tomb becomes his shrine, and the unity of the play rests on his consecration as a hero. The latter part of the play is not, therefore, an arbitrary addition to the earlier section but a necessary development of it.

Whitman, Cedric H. "The Matrix of Heroism: *Ajax*." In his *Sophocles: A Study of Heroic Humanism*. Cambridge, Mass.: Harvard University Press, 1951, pp. 59-80.
Whitman notes the self-destructive qualities often found in Greek heroes. A second element that often appears in their personalities is intimacy with the gods. Sophocles' play begins in the middle of Ajax's fit of madness, continues with Ajax's suicide, and ends with Ajax's burial. Formally, it is imperfect because of the long final section, played after the hero's death; still, the greatness of Ajax is vindicated by play's end over any nominal authority or personal animosity.

Winnington-Ingram, R. P. "The Mind of Ajax" and "The Burial of Ajax." In his *Sophocles: An Interpretation*. Cambridge, England: Cambridge University Press, 1980, pp. 11-56; 57-72.
These complementary essays provide a thorough study of Sophocles' Ajax. The first is a good examination of the range of Ajax's emotions; from haughty, angry warrior denied the arms of Achilles, he becomes madman and ultimately reconciled hero who faces death bravely. There is a good analysis of the choral odes which punctuate these transitions in Ajax's behavior. The second essay considers the lament of Tecmessa and the chorus after Ajax's suicide, considering the ways in which Sophocles sustains interest in the play when the major action is presumably complete.

Antigone

Benardete, Seth. "A Reading of Sophocles' *Antigone*." *Interpretation: A Journal of Political Philosophy* 4 (1975): 148-196; 5 (1975): 1-55; 5 (1975): 148-184.
A close reading of every scene and element of the play that uses its language and its dramatic action to construe it as a work of political philosophy. Benardete explores the outer conflict of the protagonist and the external political environment that requires investigation of Laius' murder, a situation that resembles the tension between the old oligarchy and charismatic individuals in fifth century Athenian politics. The *demos* (people) and its power is a subtextual

element in Sophocles' play, for it is the group the plague most immediately affects. Benardete considers allusions to the people as well, and, in addition, examines the plague as a metaphor of social miasma.

Blundell, Mary Whitlock. "*Antigone.*" In her *Helping Friends and Harming Enemies: A Study in Sophocles and Greek Ethics*. New York: Cambridge University Press, 1989, pp. 106-148.
Observes that Antigone is the only character in Sophocles who explicitly purports to honor brotherly love above hatred. The play's themes are bound up in the exchange of Antigone and Creon; they concern the proper objects of honor and reverence, the nature of law and custom, and the clash between two opposing views of *philia* (friendship and love of those who are related).

Bowra, C. M. "*Antigone.*" In his *Sophoclean Tragedy*. Oxford, England: Clarendon Press, 1944, reprint 1965, pp. 63-115.
Outlines the play in terms of its essential conflict: divine law as represented by Antigone and human law as represented by Creon. Bowra notes the essential originality of the dramatic conflict Sophocles sets and provides a complete analysis of the play by scene.

Burton, R. W. B. "*Antigone.*" In his *The Chorus in Sophocles' Tragedies*. Oxford, England: Clarendon Press, 1980, pp. 85-137.
The content of the choral odes is the most far-ranging of any of Sophocles' plays. Burton's analysis of each ode shows how they become increasingly more expressive of the feelings of the entire community and ever more tied to Antigone's plight.

Gardiner, Cynthia P. "*Antigone, Oedipus Tyrannus, Oedipus Coloneus.*" In her *The Sophoclean Chorus: A Study of Character and Function*. Iowa City: University of Iowa Press, 1987, pp. 81-116.
Considers the Theban plays as a group because each has a chorus of elders: mature, conservative men of responsible position who function as citizens and are involved in events that affect not only their own lives but the welfare of their cities. They are not isolated; the subject matter of each play relates directly to their personal welfare. The chorus in the *Antigone* is most patently concerned with the topic of political morality, with philosophies of governance, and the conflict of religion and law.

Gellie, G. H. "*Antigone.*" In his *Sophocles: A Reading*. Carlton, Victoria, Australia: Melbourne University Press, 1972, pp. 29-52.
Considers the sympathetic and unsympathetic aspects of Antigone, contending that the audience is asked to consider only Creon's tragedy at the play's end. Ismene's compliant character makes Antigone's tough-minded rejoinders

sound false. While Antigone asks that the dead be her judges, Creon remains within the world of the living and suffers for his actions.

Goheen, Robert F. *Imagery of Sophocles' Antigone: A Study of Poetic Language and Structure*. Princeton, N.J.: Princeton University Press, 1951.
An excellent general analysis that outlines the tragic form of the *Antigone* then provides unusual analyses of its patterns of images. The author juxtaposes what he identifies as "The Money Sequence" (references to money in speeches of Creon and Teiresias and Antigone's different understanding of "gain") and "The Military Sequence" (references to control and discipline). He also examines marriage, disease, and sea motifs, patterns of imagery in the choral odes, and the conflict of sense and reason, sight and blindness, and nature and law.

Heidegger, Martin. "The Ode on Man in Sophocles' *Antigone*." In *Sophocles: A Collection of Critical Essays*, edited by Thomas Woodard. Twentieth Century Views. Englewood Cliffs, N.J.: Prentice-Hall, 1966, pp. 86-100.
A famous analysis of the play's first choral ode by the German existentialist philosopher. All good and bad shatters against death. Death is an end beyond all consummation. Heidegger examines the structure of the ode; he perceives that it touches upon all realms of the violent and depends upon the conflict between justice (that being should continue) and nature (that it does not).

Lane, Warren J., and Ann M. Lane. "The Politics of *Antigone*." In *Greek Tragedy and Political Theory*, edited by J. Peter Euben. Berkeley: University of California Press, 1986, pp. 162-182.
Argues that Antigone acted rightly and for the right reason. The authors desire to shift the prevailing trend in criticism of the play, which locates the conflict in terms of family and city. They contend that the excesses attributable to Antigone relate to her efforts to overcome the subordinate place she holds because of her gender.

Lucas, D. W. "The Plays of Sophocles: The *Antigone*." In his *The Greek Tragic Poets*, 2d ed. London: Cohen and West, 1950, rev. ed. 1959, pp. 139-148.
Notes that divine agency remains clear throughout the play, even though no deities appear. Lucas believes that Hegel's interpreters have clouded the issue by taking the *Antigone* as a fusion of two partial rights in a higher synthesis, that as far as Sophocles is concerned Creon is wrong and Antigone right. Compare the views of Nussbaum on this play, cited below.

McCall, Marsh. "Divine and Human Action in Sophocles: The Two Burials of the *Antigone*." In *Yale Classical Studies, Volume XXII: Studies in Fifth-Century Thought and Literature*, edited by Adam Parry. Cambridge, England: Cambridge University Press, 1972, pp. 103-118.

Discusses the two burials of Polyneices, only the second of which is clearly assigned as the work of Antigone. If Antigone performed both, it could signify her hubris, that she wants to be caught, that the audience does not notice or question the two visits, that she wishes to restore the work undone by the guards, or that the two burials increase suspense. McCall argues that the last possibility is the strongest, though he lists reservations about even this theory and suggests that the moral rightness of Polyneices' burial, implied by references to Antigone's devotion to family allows the possibility of a burial by the gods.

Nussbaum, Martha C. "Sophocles' *Antigone*: Conflict, Vision, and Simplification." In her *The Fragility of Goodness: Luck and Ethics in Greek Tragedy and Philosophy*. New York: Cambridge University Press, 1986, pp. 51-82.
A philosophical examination of Antigone's moral dilemma considered against Aristotle's *Ethics*, the background of Aeschylus' *Oresteia*, and the philosophical thought of Hegel. Nussbaum views the Guard as symbolic of ordinary practical reason filled with conflict, Creon as representative of one who denies the tension among values by recognizing only one value, Antigone as one who has a narrow value system, flawed, but still superior to that of Creon.

Porter, David H. *"Only Connect": Three Studies in Greek Tragedy*. Lanham, Md.: University Press of America, 1987.
Discusses the *Antigone* against Aeschylus' *Seven Against Thebes* and Euripides' *Heracles*. The study focuses on continuity and discontinuity, unity, connection, and separation both in the thematic structure and in the content of these plays. Close readings of the plays, discussion of thematic similarities, and translated quotations from the Greek texts make this volume suitable for general readers as well as classicists and students of drama.

Seale, David. "The *Antigone*: Concrete Visualization." In *Vision and Stagecraft in Sophocles*. Chicago: University of Chicago Press, 1982, pp. 84-112.
Antigone and Creon are the play's symbols; no properties, special effects, ensemble scenes, or divine apparitions detract from the visual impact of this confrontation. Within this austere conception, Sophocles has made the scheme of this encounter visually significant. Seale examines the connection between theme and visual impact, considering the play as a series of visual and verbal confrontations.

Segal, Charles. "*Antigone*: Death and Love, Hades and Dionysus." In his *Tragedy and Civilization: An Interpretation of Sophocles*. Cambridge, Mass.: Harvard University Press, 1981, pp. 152-206.
The tension of the play is in the darkness of human actions, revealed best

through the character of Creon, and the glimpses of eternal order, seen in the actions of Antigone and in the choral odes. Tragic art enables the polis to confront the contradictions inherent in human nature. Compare Segal's earlier study of this play, cited below.

_____ . "Sophocles' Praise of Man and the Conflicts of the *Antigone*." *Arion* 3.2 (1964): 46-66. Reprint. In *Sophocles: A Collection of Critical Essays*, edited by Thomas Woodard. Twentieth Century Views. Englewood Cliffs, N.J.: Prentice-Hall, 1966, pp. 62-85.
Notes the risk of following the Hegelian interpretation of the play, that the drama becomes merely a set of antithetical principles to be dialectically reconciled. Segal considers that the characters are the issues but that the play also concerns the dignity of humanity. Antigone accepts the unknown consequences of death, while Creon comes to act out the equally tragic consequences of becoming fully human. Compare Segal's more recent thoughts on this play, cited above.

Steiner, George. *Antigones*. New York: Oxford University Press, 1984.
Examines the influence of the figure of Antigone, as transmitted through Sophocles' play, upon a wide variety of dramatists and philosophers. Steiner considers German philosophy and literature extensively, beginning with the Age of Reason and moving through the twentieth century. There is also a thorough survey of the Antigone figure as it appears among the French philosophers, especially Jean-Jacques Rousseau, and the English romanticists, especially Percy Bysshe Shelley and John Keats; nor does the author overlook modern psychology, including frequent references to Sigmund Freud's writings. Though impressive in its breadth and documentation, the style and presentation are straightforward and clear, intended for a wide variety of readers.

Whitman, Cedric H. "Man the Measure: *Antigone*." In his *Sophocles: A Study of Heroic Humanism*. Cambridge, Mass.: Harvard University Press, 1951, pp. 81-99.
Considers that the play is relatively simple. Antigone's perception of divine law faces institutions that have usurped the right to legislate in an area beyond their justifiable authority. Creon's decree represents this tendency of human institutions. Whitman notes that Antigone's unyielding nature risks forfeit of audience sympathy as much as it harms her in the encounter with Creon; nevertheless, Sophocles' heroine sets herself apart from the rest of humanity from the very beginning of the play.

Winnington-Ingram, R. P. "Creon and Antigone." In his *Sophocles: An Interpretation*. Cambridge, England: Cambridge University Press, 1980, pp. 117-149.

Considers the claims Creon has as principal character of the play: a longer part than Antigone, that he is visible to the audience for a longer time, that the second half of the play focuses on him. Even so, Creon lacks the endurance and obstinacy that characterize the Sophoclean hero.

_____ . "Sophocles and the Irrational: Three Odes in *Antigone*." In his *Sophocles: An Interpretation*. Cambridge, England: Cambridge University Press, 1980, pp. 91-116.
Examines the choral songs that follow the confrontation of Creon and Haemon (lines 781-800), of Creon and Antigone as she is led to her entombment (lines 944-987), and preceding the entrance of the Messenger (at line 1153). The analysis notes an increasing number of references to chance, fate, irrationality and irrational actions, and to the god of the irrational, Dionysus, the odes thus mirroring the action of the play and foreshadowing its outcome.

Electra

Blundell, Mary Whitlock. "*Electra*." In her *Helping Friends and Harming Enemies: A Study in Sophocles and Greek Ethics*. New York: Cambridge University Press, 1989, pp. 149-183.
The help-harm pattern is especially clear in this play. Orestes announces his intention for vengeance in line 66. Electra makes similar statements (lines 453-456; 979) and makes loyalty to friends a cardinal principle (lines 345; 367; 395). The two, in effect, conspire to oppose and destroy what they perceive as the conspiracy of Clytemnestra and Aegisthus.

Bowra, C. M. "*Electra*." In his *Sophoclean Tragedy*. Oxford, England: Clarendon Press, 1944, reprint 1965, pp. 212-260.
Parallels the Aeschylean, Sophoclean, and Euripidean treatments of the Electra myth, noting as well that Homer avoids the central dramatic issue of Clytemnestra's death when he mentions Orestes in the *Odyssey* (lines 421-434). Bowra argues that Sophocles exploits the dilemma Orestes faces; Orestes must avenge the murder of his father Agamemnon, yet must face the burden of blood-guilt, indeed matricide, if he kills the murderer. Electra helps Orestes resolve this conflict by pointing out the divine justice they must face if they do not avenge Agamemnon's death.

Burton, R. W. B. "*Electra*." In his *The Chorus in Sophocles' Tragedies*. Oxford, England: Clarendon Press, 1980, pp. 186-225.
The most important feature of the odes here is the stress they lay on the theme of vengeance and justice. Their identification of the two provides a moral basis for the plot.

Gardiner, Cynthia P. "*Electra*." In her *The Sophoclean Chorus: A Study of Character and Function*. Iowa City: University of Iowa Press, 1987, pp. 139-163.

The women of this chorus are not dependents or connections of the family but outsiders. Aegisthus and Clytemnestra are clearly concerned that these outsiders do not hear Electra's complaints. The chorus symbolizes the spirit of the state, though there is no indication of their active involvement in its political process; their reactions constitute an emotional response that implies that Electra's actions are right.

Gellie, G. H. "*Electra.*" In his *Sophocles: A Reading*. Carlton, Victoria, Australia: Melbourne University Press, 1972, pp. 106-130.
Though enjoyment of the play comes in part from the adroitness with which Sophocles distracts the audience from too concentrated a consideration of moral issues, the *Electra* remains a play about matricide. The playwright keeps the audience constantly uneasy, thus aware of his real purpose. Gellie's analysis notes the male and female components of the play, the former involving recognition, intrigue, and practical success, the latter undeserved suffering, the will to endure, and the distortion and ultimate collapse of a loving nature.

Lucas, D. W. "The Plays of Sophocles: The *Electra.*" In his *The Greek Tragic Poets*, 2d ed. London: Cohen and West, 1950, rev. ed. 1959, pp. 152-156.
Sophocles' heroine has a noble nature that Euripides' *Electra* lacks. Lucas argues that Sophocles' play would have been like Aeschylus' *Libation Bearers* were the latter play to have ended at line 972, before Orestes' madness begins. The plot summary focuses on how Sophocles develops the portrait of his central character.

Seale, David. "The *Electra*: Illusion and Suffering." In his *Vision and Stagecraft in Sophocles*. Chicago: University of Chicago Press, 1982, pp. 56-83.
Examines the relation between setting and plot. The austere atmosphere of Electra's surroundings emphasizes her suffering and mirrors the bitter satisfaction of Orestes and Electra at having successfully concluded their vengeance. Sophocles repeatedly involves the audience in verbal illusion and misleading trails that the narrative of the play does not pursue, probably to maintain complete involvement until the foreknown conclusion.

Segal, Charles. "*Electra.*" In his *Tragedy and Civilization: An Interpretation of Sophocles*. Cambridge, Mass.: Harvard University Press, 1981, pp. 249-291.
Contends that the play concerns the destruction of a personality once capable of love, a vengeance gone sour in an embittered world, deceit and misunderstanding between those who should and do love one another, the ambiguities of truth amid the difficulties of communication and deceptiveness of language. Segal traces the pattern of violated civilized order he discerns throughout the play.

Whitman, Cedric H. "Trial by Time: *Electra*." In his *Sophocles: A Study of Heroic Humanism*. Cambridge, Mass.: Harvard University Press, 1951, pp. 149-171.
Whitman notes the apparent religious heterodoxy of the play, uncharacteristic of Sophocles' works, in allowing Orestes to slay Clytemnestra without having to face pursuit of the Furies or judgment by the Areopagus. The author contends that Sophocles intends audience attention be directed at Electra as long-suffering tragic figure. Orestes comes to triumph, to free his sister from her trials.

Winnington-Ingram, R. P. "*Electra*." In his *Sophocles: An Interpretation*. Cambridge, England: Cambridge University Press, 1980, pp. 217-247.
Argues that Sophocles wrote the play with Aeschylus' *Choephoroi* (*Libation Bearers*) in mind, that it contains many reminiscences of the earlier work. The objection that the Furies do not appear in Sophocles' play is not entirely true. The word "Erinys" occurs four times; they also figure importantly in the first choral ode. The analysis continues by citing various Aeschylean echoes of Sophocles' play.

Woodard, Thomas. "The *Electra* of Sophocles." In *Sophocles: A Collection of Critical Essays*, edited by Thomas Woodard. Twentieth Century Views. Englewood Cliffs, N.J.: Prentice-Hall, 1966, pp. 125-145.
An analysis of the character of Electra within the context of the entire play. Electra remains the focus of the work throughout. The play is most profound in uniting *logos* (word, or specifically the way the story is told) and *mythos* (the legend as it is understood in the abstract).

Woolf, Virginia. "On Sophocles' *Electra*." In *Sophocles: A Collection of Critical Essays*, edited by Thomas Woodard. Twentieth Century Views. Englewood Cliffs, N.J.: Prentice-Hall, 1966, pp. 122-124.
An extract from the English novelist's essay "On Not Knowing Greek," published originally in her *The Common Reader* (1925). Instinctive reflections on the character of Electra by one who loves literature rather than by a classicist or other scholar. Woolf's references are far-ranging; she notes Electra's simple character portrait in Sophocles' play, her timeless emotions, her human need for vengeance. Woolf makes comparisons with Jane Austen's *Emma*, with Marcel Proust's characters, and with those of Geoffrey Chaucer.

Oedipus at Colonus

Blundell, Mary Whitlock. "*Oedipus at Colonus*." In her *Helping Friends and Harming Enemies: A Study in Sophocles and Greek Ethics*. New York: Cambridge University Press, 1989, pp. 226-259.
Oedipus enunciates the play's help-friends, harm-enemies theme as early as line 92. He will find rest at Athens and, by dwelling there, benefit those who

welcomed him but bring doom to those who drove him away. Likewise, Oedipus shows love for Antigone and Ismene, who attended him, and curses Eteocles and Polyneices who want his support only to have the throne of Thebes. Theseus, King of Athens, shows his love for Oedipus by allowing him the sanctuary of Apollo's shrine at Colonus, and the play ends with the reconcilement of Oedipus and Apollo.

Bowra, C. M. *"Oedipus at Colonus."* In his *Sophoclean Tragedy*. Oxford, England: Clarendon Press, 1944, reprint, 1965, pp. 307-355.
The central theme is Oedipus' transformation to a hero. Bowra notes that Colonus was Sophocles' own deme and considers that Colonus' position as suburb of Athens probably held some patriotic implications in the generally demoralized fifth century city. The analysis compares the Oedipus of this play with the younger, less mature character of the *Oedipus Tyrannus* and offers a full summary and discussion of plot.

Burton, R. W. B. *"Oedipus at Colonus."* In his *The Chorus in Sophocles' Tragedies*. Oxford, England: Clarendon Press, 1980, pp. 251-295.
The songs of this play are completely consistent with the status and role of the chorus. They develop the many themes suggested by the action: love of country, desire to experience the excitement of battle, the pathos of old age, the hope of an easy death as deliverance from the troubles of life.

Buxton, R. G. A. "Sophokles: *Oidipous at Kolonos*." In his *Persuasion in Greek Tragedy: A Study of Peitho*. New York: Cambridge University Press, 1982, pp. 132-145.
Considers that the ambivalent figure of Oedipus (guilty-innocent; harsh-just; bringer of pollution or good fortune) is at the heart of the play, though *peitho* (persuasion) occupies a place among the subsidiary motifs. Buxton notes the frequent comparisons many have made with Shakespeare's *King Lear* and *The Tempest*, then analyzes the play's use of *peitho* with comparisons to the *Philoctetes*.

Gardiner, Cynthia P. *"Antigone, Oedipus Tyrannus, Oedipus Coloneus."* In her *The Sophoclean Chorus: A Study of Character and Function*. Iowa City: University of Iowa Press, 1987, pp. 81-113.
The *Oedipus at Colonus* has a chorus of civic leaders as does the *Antigone* and *Oedipus Tyrannus*, though they are more involved with the structure of this drama than the choruses of the latter two plays. Their purpose is to provide the pious respect, compassion, and generous forgiveness Oedipus lacked during his exile.

Gellie, G. H. *"Oedipus at Colonus."* In his *Sophocles: A Reading*. Carlton, Victoria, Australia: Melbourne University Press, 1972, pp. 159-183.

Considers that the play lacks the integrated structure characteristic of Sophocles' other dramas. Gellie believes there are close associations with the *Eumenides* of Aeschylus; Athens figures importantly in both works. Oedipus, having suffered, uses a new standard of justice on himself and others. He draws nearer to godhead, and godhead draws nearer to him.

Lucas, D. W. "The Plays of Sophocles: The *Oedipus Coloneus*." In his *The Greek Tragic Poets*, 2d ed. London: Cohen and West, 1950, rev. ed. 1959, pp. 160-167.
Lucas notes the difficulties of the play: To what extent should the prominent associations of Colonus as suburb of Athens imply a patriotic theme; to what extent should one understand Oedipus as hero; to what extent is Oedipus a victim? He discusses these questions in a summary-analysis of the play.

Seale, David. "The *Oedipus at Colonus*: Inner Vision." In his *Vision and Stagecraft in Sophocles*. Chicago: University of Chicago Press, 1982, pp. 113-143.
Shows how the play portrays the attachment of its central character to a single physical location. Oedipus and the play's audience share knowledge of the destiny implied by his having refused support to his sons and by his having been granted right of burial at Colonus. Both Eteocles and Polyneices are denied this insight, and the play gives visual and dramatic expression to this blindness and insight.

Segal, Charles. "*Oedipus at Colonus*: The End of a Vision." In his *Tragedy and Civilization: An Interpretation of Sophocles*. Cambridge, Mass.: Harvard University Press, 1981, pp. 362-408.
As the hero Oedipus receives his final honor of burial at Colonus, tragedy reunites fear and intelligence, human helplessness before the mysteries of the universe, and human confidence in the power of a spiritual vision. The heroization of Oedipus represents the aged Sophocles' insight into the civilizing power of tragic drama.

Slatkin, Laura. "*Oedipus at Colonus*: Exile and Integration." In *Greek Tragedy and Political Theory*, edited by J. Peter Euben. Berkeley: University of California Press, 1986, pp. 210-221.
Contends that Sophocles is as interested in political concerns and their bearing on religious thought as he is in using religion to provide a resolution for the play. Slatkin focuses on the recurring reference to the *onesis* (benefit) that Oedipus possesses; it is never defined, though evidently crucial to the meaning of the drama.

Whitman, Cedric H. "Apocalypse: *Oedipus at Colonus*." In his *Sophocles: A Study of Heroic Humanism*. Cambridge, Mass.: Harvard University Press, 1951, pp. 190-218.

Aside from the scenes with Creon and Polyneices, the play contains forms of conflict less characteristic of Sophocles' works. Most notably, it shows an Oedipus without the self-destructiveness that accompanied his' will in the *Oedipus Tyrannus*. Whitman notes the religious and mystery elements that attend Oedipus' arrival at Colonus, observes the patriotic implications in Oedipus' being received there, and describes the play through summary and analysis.

Winnington-Ingram, R. P. *"Oedipus at Colonus."* In his *Sophocles: An Interpretation*. Cambridge, England: Cambridge University Press, 1980, pp. 248-279.
A general analysis that discerns five movements in the play: entrance of Oedipus and Antigone, entrance of Ismene, the Creon episode, Theseus' allusion to Polyneices, the heroization of Oedipus. The study examines each, showing how the character of Oedipus always remains pivotal to the stage action.

Oedipus Tyrannus
Benardete, Seth. "Sophocles' *Oedipus Tyrannus*." In *Sophocles: A Collection of Critical Essays*, edited by Thomas Woodard. Twentieth Century Views. Englewood Cliffs, N.J.: Prentice-Hall, 1966, pp. 106-121.
An analysis in Hegelian terms that considers that the play reveals Oedipus as possessor of the most profound knowledge about his inner self; yet, this information is masked by colossal ignorance, which the narrative slowly removes as it continues. This knowledge relates directly to Oedipus' perception of self within the political and social environment of his city. Benardete examines closely the language of the play that relates to maturing and maturity.

Bloom, Harold, ed. *Sophocles' Oedipus Rex*. Modern Critical Interpretations. New York: Chelsea House, 1988.
This volume, part of a series of critical works on the masterpieces of world literature, contains essays by various scholars, all of which have appeared earlier in other contexts. Bernard Knox writes on Sophocles' conception of the character of Oedipus, John Jones on the relationship between characterization and deductive plot, and E. R. Dodds on common misreadings of the play. Thomas Gould answers Dodds's essay, discussing the place of fate and personal responsibility and considers the play against Aristotelian definitions. Karl Reinhardt discusses the play's reversal, the point at which the truth and illusion of Oedipus' situation collide. J. P. Vernant continues Reinhardt's theme, discussing the place of ambiguity and reversal in terms of the play's structure. Charles Segal uses the symbol of the Sphinx to argue the place of ambiguity in language, and John Gould continues the discussions of both Dodds and Segal, emphasizing Apollo's role and that of oracular prophecy. ·

Bowra, C. M. *"King Oedipus."* In his *Sophoclean Tragedy*. Oxford, England: Clarendon Press, 1944, reprint 1965, pp. 162-211.
Bowra believes that the play illustrates that the gods ordain horrendous lives for some and that control of destiny is outside of human ability. He considers the idea of inherited guilt characteristic of Aeschylean rather than Sophoclean drama and discounts the argument that Oedipus is punished for his hubris. Bowra provides a complete analysis of the play and considers these arguments in his discussion.

Burton, R. W. B. *"Oedipus Tyrannus."* In his *The Chorus in Sophocles' Tragedies*. Oxford, England: Clarendon Press, 1980, pp. 138-185.
Though they contain references that might be obscure to the modern audience, the odes of the play powerfully underscore its irony. Like the words of Oedipus, they implicitly foresee the play's outcome. The members of the chorus themselves represent the most conservative elements of the community, implied by their identification as Theban elders.

Cameron, Alister. *The Identity of Oedipus the King: Five Essays on the Oedipus Tyrannus*. New York: New York University Press, 1968.
Essays on Sophocles' play that examine it purely as a work of art rather than from Freudian, historical, or anthropological perspectives. Cameron begins with the observation that there were eight ancient and many more modern treatments of the Oedipus myth. This popularity leads him to conclude that the play has all the aspects of the perfect tragedy; specifically, that it concerns an individual's quest for his own identity and that it describes both the external and internal conflicts he has to face to discover an answer to this fundamental human question. Cameron's treatment is, therefore, almost entirely literary and philosophical. His essays treat the evolution of the myth, the self-discovery theme, the role of the gods, the self-blinding, and the play's tragic perspective.

Freud, Sigmund. *"Oedipus Rex."* In *Sophocles: A Collection of Critical Essays*, edited by Thomas Woodard. Twentieth Century Views. Englewood Cliffs, N.J.: Prentice-Hall, 1966, pp. 101-104.
An extract from Freud's *The Interpretation of Dreams* (1899). The appeal of the play lies in the recognition of the compelling force of destiny Oedipus faces. His dream of having lain with his mother corresponds to the first sexual impulse of male children toward their mothers and the murder of his father Laius to the first murderous wish against their fathers. Freud's "Oedipus Complex" theory has become the background against which many twentieth century readers have interpreted the play.

Gardiner, Cynthia P. *"Antigone, Oedipus Tyrannus, Oedipus Coloneus."* In her *The Sophoclean Chorus: A Study of Character and Function*. Iowa City: University of Iowa Press, 1987, pp. 81-116.

Despite their age, the chorus of the *Oedipus Tyrannus* functions as military advisors to Oedipus. They contrast with the passive survivors of *Antigone*. They also present the public aspect of the story of Oedipus.

Gellie, G. H. *"Oedipus the King."* In his *Sophocles: A Reading*. Carlton, Victoria, Australia: Melbourne University Press, 1972, pp. 79-105.

Notes that the play considers the fate of the title character alone and is impelled by his will alone. Gellie provides a straightforward summary and discussion, stressing the importance of fate in the play's outcome. Oedipus is destroyed by the truth, but Apollo, whose oracle foretold the murder of Laius, cannot be blamed for knowing or being the truth.

Kitto, H. D. F. *"The Tyrannus."* In his *Poiesis: Structure and Thought*. Sather Classical Lectures 36. Berkeley: University of California Press, 1966, pp. 200-242.

Carefully examines the play's structure, contending that the play is great because it touches upon universal emotions and fears. Kitto considers the ways in which Sophocles gives dramatic form to the myth and how the play notes the role change and reason play in life, and he examines the effect of its having been produced in Periclean Athens.

Knox, Bernard M. W. *Oedipus at Thebes*. New Haven, Conn.: Yale University Press, 1957.

Addressed to general readers as well as specialists, this study examines the age that produced the *Oedipus Tyrannus* and assesses the play's meaning for modern audiences. Knox emphasizes what he considers the timeless elements of the play, discovering these in the unusual nature of Oedipus as hero, the psychological interpretation popularized through the writings of Sigmund Freud, and the sense in which fate ultimately overwhelms Oedipus. The book is composed of chapters that strikingly juxtapose discussions of man, hero, and god.

Lucas, D. W. "The Plays of Sophocles: The *Oedipus Tyrannus*." In his *The Greek Tragic Poets*, 2d ed. London: Cohen and West, 1950, rev. ed., 1959, pp. 149-452.

Calls this play a drama of fulfillment and notes its popularity with audiences and as a myth that inspired other ancient playwrights. Lucas notes its inconsistencies and impossibilities as well: Oedipus' complete ignorance about details of Laius' death, his failure to respond to plain hints about his parentage, Oedipus' unreasonable pridefulness.

O'Brien, Michael J., ed. *Twentieth Century Interpretations of Oedipus Rex: A Collection of Critical Essays*. Englewood Cliffs, N.J.: Prentice-Hall, 1968.

Follows the format of this series and consists of two parts, the first a series of previously printed essays by outstanding contemporary critics, the second a series of extracts from the writings of individuals as diverse as Plutarch and Sigmund Freud. In part 1, E. R. Dodds examines common misinterpretations of the play, E. T. Owen considers its dramatic devices, Richmond Lattimore offers a general analysis, Francis Fergusson discusses ritual, G. M. Kirkwood dramatic form, Victor Ehrenberg Sophoclean kings, R. P. Winnington-Ingram the play's relationship to archaic Greek thought, and Bernard M. W. Knox the final scene. The "View Points" of part 2 are short, generally not more than a paragraph or two in length. The volume concludes with a chronology of dates related to Sophocles' career and a selected bibliography.

Pollock, George H., and John Munder Ross, eds. *The Oedipus Papers*. Madison, Conn.: International Universities Press, 1988.

This monograph is a compilation of major articles on the Oedipus myth by well-known psychoanalysts and psychologists. Its first section presents material written before 1970 and includes a selection from Sigmund Freud's *The Interpretation of Dreams* (1899), as well as articles by Mark Kanzer on the Oedipus plays, by George Devereux on the Oedipus Complex in Greek drama, and by Erich Fromm on symbolic language in myth, fairy tale, ritual, and the novel. A second section, articles written after 1970, contains worthwhile pieces by Norman B. Atkins on the Oedipus myth, by Henry Rosner on the scars of Oedipus, and by Erik H. Erikson on the generational cycle, as well as by other contributors. A concluding part deals with clinical, developmental, and cultural implications and includes writings by Gertrude Blanck and Melford E. Spiro on the universality of the Oedipus Complex, James M. Herzog on the father-son dialogue, and Robert Michels on Oedipus and insight.

Rudnytsky, Peter L. *Freud and Oedipus*. New York: Columbia University Press, 1987.

This intriguing study, derived from the author's 1979 doctoral dissertation, begins by tracing the origins of Sigmund Freud's interest in the Oedipus myths and continues with an intellectual history that ascribes German preoccupation with the figure of Oedipus to increasing interest in self-consciousness. There are thorough treatments of the Oedipus theme as it appears in the writings of Friedrich Schiller, Friedrich Holderlin, and Heinrich von Kleist. Part 3 explores Sophocles' Theban plays (*Oedipus the King*, *Oedipus at Colonus*, and *Antigone*) against Freud's self-analysis. The book is intended for general readers in classics as well as those interested in psychology and deconstructionist interpretation of literature. A noteworthy element is the book's excellent bibliography on psychology and the Oedipus myths.

Schwartz, Joel D. "Human Action and Political Action in *Oedipus Tyrannos*." In *Greek Tragedy and Political Theory*, edited by J. Peter Euben. Berkeley: University of California Press, 1986, pp. 183-209.
Examines the ironic conception of freedom of the will (human freedom) in the play. The concluding section extends this analysis to clarify the ironic nature of political freedom for the Athenian citizen.

Seale, David. "*Oedipus the King*: Blindness and Insight." In his *Vision and Stagecraft in Sophocles*. Chicago: University of Chicago Press, 1981, pp. 215-260.
Explores the visual impact of the play as a series of scenes built around the solitary standing figure of Oedipus. He thus becomes an individual set apart, not only because he is king and leader of his city but also because he is the polluted one, guilty of patricide and incest. The visual impression underscores the ironic theme of blindness and insight. Oedipus sees the full implications of what he has done only when he is blind; the audience sees from the beginning, and therein lies the tragedy.

Segal, Charles. "*Oedipus Tyrannus*." In his *Tragedy and Civilization: An Interpretation of Sophocles*. Cambridge, Mass.: Harvard University Press, 1981, pp. 207-248.
The play embodies the paradoxes of humanity's civilizing power. What emerges from Oedipus' tragedy is not a sense of total chaos and despair but a quality of heroism in Oedipus' self-knowledge. No other human being, so the hero says, can bear the degree of suffering Oedipus realizes he has the ability to endure.

Vernant, Jean-Pierre, and Pierre Vidal-Naquet. "Ambiguity and Reversal: On the Enigmatic Structure of *Oedipus Rex*." In their *Tragedy and Myth in Ancient Greece*, translated by Janet Lloyd. Atlantic Highlands, N.J.: Humanities Press, 1981, pp. 87-119.
Cites ambiguities and shifts in language that hasten reversal in the play. All the ambiguity involves Oedipus; what he says often implies something other than or even the opposite of what he believes he is saying.

_____ . "Oedipus Without the Complex." In their *Tragedy and Myth in Ancient Greece*, translated by Janet Lloyd. Atlantic Highlands, N.J.: Humanities Press, 1981, pp. 63-86.
Considers to what extent Freudian theory of the early twentieth century rightly applies to a play written in the fifth century B.C. A modern interpreter needs to consider the social context of the time the play was written, and this study reads the play against modern psychological views, concluding that historical methods must be a part of any psychological analysis.

Whitman, Cedric H. "Irrational Evil: *Oedipus Rex.*" In his *Sophocles: A Study of Heroic Humanism.* Cambridge, Mass.: Harvard University Press, 1951, pp. 122-146.

An analysis that argues that Oedipus falls by an external insufficiency in life itself; proverbial Greek wisdom that those who are careful and prudent avoid trouble does not apply in this play. Oedipus' heroism emerges in his ability to confront the unvarnished truth of his past and still feel able to overcome the destruction it has caused.

Winnington-Ingram, R. P. "The Fall of Oedipus." In his *Sophocles: An Interpretation.* Cambridge, England: Cambridge University Press, 1980, pp. 179-204.

Examines the second choral ode as occupying a central position in the play. Its primary function is ironic, suggesting that Apollo's prophecy on Oedipus' murder of his father has failed to come true. Then, at the end of the ode, Jocasta enters and, ironically, prays to Apollo for a solution to the plague. The Messenger enters, following Jocasta's prayer, to report Polybus' death, which causes Jocasta to condemn all oracles as fake. The study analyzes this series of ironies as initiated by the words of the choral song.

Philoctetes

Blundell, Mary Whitlock. "*Philoctetes.*" In her *Helping Friends and Harming Enemies: A Study in Sophocles and Greek Ethics.* New York: Cambridge University Press, 1989, pp. 184-225.

This drama is the most ethically complex of Sophocles' plays. Odysseus and Achilles present models for the young Neoptolemus, who must decide during the course of the play which to emulate. Heracles' arrival underscores the unresolvable nature of the conflicting demands on Neoptolemus and Philoctetes. Philoctetes must choose between help and harm, while Neoptolemus is unable to help all his friends and must choose between them at severe cost to himself; still, Heracles' intervention indirectly ratifies Neoptolemus' decision. Blundell concludes that the play illustrates the worth of shared friendship based on honest values.

Bowra, C. M. "*Philoctetes.*" In his *Sophoclean Tragedy.* Oxford, England: Clarendon Press, 1944, reprint, 1965, pp. 261-306.

An analysis that notes that the play violates the Aristotelian convention that tragedy must move toward a tragic outcome. Bowra emphasizes the theme of destiny. Philoctetes, despite his physical weakness, is destined to take Troy, a task at which strong men had failed. The discussion notes the contrasting personalities of Agamemnon, Odysseus, and Neoptolemus and provides a thorough reading of the play by scene.

Burton, R. W. B. "*Philoctetes.*" In his *The Chorus in Sophocles' Tragedies.* Oxford, England: Clarendon Press, 1980, pp. 226-250.
Most important here is Sophocles' use of lyric conversation between the actors and between actors and chorus, a use of lyric meters that Euripides would subsequently employ to great advantage. Successful attempts are made in this play to bridge the gap between actors and chorus and to make their relationship less formal.

Buxton, R. G. A. "Sophokles: *Philoktetes.*" In his *Persuasion in Greek Tragedy: A Study of Peitho.* New York: Cambridge University Press, 1982, pp. 118-132.
Traces *peitho* (persuasion) as used by Odysseus to persuade Neoptolemus, by Neoptolemus to deceive Philoctetes, by Philoctetes to persuade Neoptolemus, and in the threats of Odysseus, among other examples. Buxton reviews the legend: Philoctetes, abandoned because of his wound, at the margin of human society and with only the bare essentials of life. The Greeks attempt deceptive persuasion and threats of force to bring him to Troy, though the use of threats undermines the operation of *peitho* and allows Philoctetes to assert his preference for a voyage home. Buxton's ensuing chapter makes comparisons with *peitho* as it appears in the *Philoctetes* and the *Oedipus at Colonus.*

Gardiner, Cynthia P. "*Philoctetes.*" In her *The Sophoclean Chorus: A Study of Character and Function.* Iowa City: University of Iowa Press, 1987, pp. 14-49.
The chorus in this play serves a political purpose; its members have a close relationship with Odysseus, who is portrayed as a demagogue in the play. They accept political expediency and are not concerned with higher concepts of honor, only with the immediate gains of their group's interest. Their inclusion allows Sophocles to broaden the scope of the play, to make the Philoctetes incident impinge directly on Greek fortunes at Troy and to illustrate a petty power struggle.

Gellie, G. H. "*Philoctetes.*" In his *Sophocles: A Reading.* Carlton, Victoria, Australia: Melbourne University Press, 1972, pp. 131-158.
The analysis notes that this play is about the single-minded determination of Philoctetes, whom long suffering has not broken. The conflict involves private hatred, political pragmatism, and a young man's sense of honor and hence is triangular, developed through the characters of Neoptolemus, Odysseus, and Philoctetes.

Lucas, D. W. "The Plays of Sophocles: The *Philoctetes.*" In his *The Greek Tragic Poets,* 2d ed. London: Cohen and West, 1950, rev. ed. 1959, pp. 156-160.
Lucas observes that the action develops out of the myth rather than being determined by it. Logically, Philoctetes would have returned home and the Greeks would have continued besieging Troy, but the play emphasizes the stresses to which events give rise in the minds of the participants.

Seale, David. "The *Philoctetes*: Illusion and Surprise." In his *Vision and Stagecraft in Sophocles*. Chicago: University of Chicago Press, 1982, pp. 26-55.
Discusses the way in which the barren setting of Lemnos defines and underscores the abandonment of Philoctetes. The protagonist addresses his surroundings, personalizing them in a way that links himself to the place he has had to make his home. Sophocles makes a conscious effort to nullify the audience's foreknowledge of the myth of Philoctetes' part in the fall of Troy by integrating it with stage action; the result is the audience's surprise at what it already knows.

Segal, Charles. "*Philoctetes*: Society, Language, Friendship." In his *Tragedy and Civilization: An Interpretation of Sophocles*. Cambridge, Mass.: Harvard University Press, 1981, pp. 328-361.
The play is a profound reflection on the nature of the human as civilized being, on the bonds, needs, and obligations that hold people together. Segal discusses these unifying bonds of friendship as developing the theme of the play.

——————— . "*Philoctetes*: The Myth and the Gods." In his *Tragedy and Civilization: An Interpretation of Sophocles*. Cambridge, Mass.: Harvard University Press, 1981, pp. 292-360.
A detailed structuralist analysis of the play that contrasts the play's characters, images, and motifs as representing either savagery or civilization. Thus Chryse and the lame Philoctetes contrast with Hephaestus Heracles, and the cured Philoctetes as mirroring the larger conflict of disorder and order, primitive and civilized.

Vernant, Jean-Pierre, and Pierre Vidal-Naquet. "Sophocles' *Philoctetes* and the *Ephebia*." In their *Tragedy and Myth in Ancient Greece*, translated by Janet Lloyd. Atlantic Highlands, N.J.: Humanities Press, 1981, pp. 175-199.
Reads Sophocles' play against aspects of the Athenian process of military training. This play held special meaning for the ancient audience because at the time of the play's first presentation in 409 B.C. the Peloponnesian War was in progress, and things were going badly for Athens.

Whitman, Cedric H. "The Paradox of Will: *Philoctetes*." In his *Sophocles: A Study of Heroic Humanism*. Cambridge, Mass.: Harvard University Press, 1951, pp. 172-189.
The play describes the unconquerable will of the outcast Philoctetes. Society makes just and sufficient amends, it is ready to do the hero's bidding; then suddenly the world becomes appropriate to Philoctetes again. The play also shows Neoptolemus' sudden wave of moral insight, latent in his character and implying his heroic potentialities.

Winnington-Ingram, R. P. *"Philoctetes."* In his *Sophocles: An Interpretation.*
Cambridge, England: Cambridge University Press, 1980, pp. 280-303.
Analyzes the character portrait of Philoctetes, noting that this hero shares the
pathetic nature, ironic quality, and pitiable nature of other Sophoclean heroes.
Neoptolemus contrasts with the positive elements in Philoctetes' character
portrait, and the study notes how Sophocles uses Neoptolemus to delineate
Philoctetes' personality.

Women of Trachis (Trachiniae)
Bowra, C. M. *"The Women of Trachis."* In his *Sophoclean Tragedy.* Oxford, En-
gland: Clarendon Press, 1944, reprint 1965, pp. 116-161.
The central subject is neither Heracles nor Deianira but the destiny that in-
volves each in the other's ruin. The characters are so intimately connected that
Sophocles can delay the entrance of Heracles for two-thirds of the drama.
Bowra provides a complete analysis that emphasizes the effects of the play's
diptych construction.

Burton, R. W. B. *"Trachiniae."* In his *The Chorus in Sophocles' Tragedies.* Oxford,
England: Clarendon Press, 1980, pp. 41-84.
Notes the untypical youth of this chorus, seen in both its lack of reflection and
absence of intellectual or moral comment. The odes here contrast with those
of the Theban plays. The chorus has the comforting of Deianira as its main
task; it becomes absorbed in her reactions, offering advice in song and through
spoken interventions, thus sharpening the portrait of this heroine.

Gardiner, Cynthia P. *"Trachiniae."* In her *The Sophoclean Chorus: A Study of
Character and Function.* Iowa City: University of Iowa Press, 1987, pp. 119-138.
Notes that this play contains a chorus of women; though unmarried, they need
not be maidens, yet references to costume and hairstyle imply that they are.
They complement the character portrait of the mature Deianira, and their odes
combine theological content with a style that recalls the style of religious
festival and of worship. This blend maintains a strongly consistent religious
mood throughout the play.

Gellie, G. H. *"The Women of Trachis."* In his *Sophocles: A Reading.* Carlton,
Victoria, Australia: Melbourne University Press, 1972, pp. 53-78.
Discusses the dual nature of the play: the tragedies of Deianira and of Heracles. Deianira is swept away two-thirds into the play, and Heracles dominates
the action throughout, yet Heracles himself does not speak until line 983,
fewer than three hundred lines before the play's conclusion. Gellie concludes
that the play emphasizes relationship rather than individuality and that there is,
consequently, no single overwhelming tragic action.

Kitto, H. D. F. "The *Trachiniae.*" In his *Poiesis: Structure and Thought*. Sather Classical Lectures 36. Berkeley: University of California Press, 1966, pp. 154-199.
Examines the play as an untypical example of Sophoclean drama and rejects the arguments of those who would dismiss it as flawed. Kitto reviews representative objections to the play, most of these contending that it is disunified, and finds unity in Deianira's role, then examines the play with the thesis that she infuses every aspect of it, even when she leaves the stage before the drama's conclusion.

Seale, David. "*The Women of Trachis*: The Verge of Truth." In his *Vision and Stagecraft in Sophocles*. Chicago: University of Chicago Press, 1982, pp. 181-214.
The analysis focuses on Deianira as the central visual element as well as the play's primary character. The audience realizes that Deianira knows her life has been unhappy; yet, she requires clarification of her husband Heracles' destiny before she can confirm her fears. It is in the gap between what Deianira knows and what she fears that Sophocles sets the tragedy.

Segal, Charles. "Sophocles' *Trachiniae*: Myth, Poetry, and Heroic Values." In *Yale Classical Studies, Volume XXV: Greek Tragedy*, edited by T. F. Gould and C. J. Herington. New York: Cambridge University Press, 1977, pp. 99-158.
Examines the diversity of the play's wildly colorful mythic structure, considering how mythic symbol conveys realistic meaning. Segal then considers the linkage of metaphorical language to the reality represented by the marriage of Heracles and Deianeira, how the wildness of Heracles' mythic past cannot be confined and tamed in the stable domesticity of Deianeira's house. It is only in death that both achieve their freedom from the bestial, elemental forces that surround their lives.

_____ . "*Trachiniae.*" In his *Tragedy and Civilization: An Interpretation of Sophocles*. Cambridge, Mass.: Harvard University Press, 1981, pp. 60-108.
An extension of this author's earlier study on the play, cited above. The play creates a dialectical tension between the structure that informs and transcends human life and the unstructurable grief of those to whom a notion of deity is only indifference, remote force, and pain. The oracles and Heracles' last speech intimate that some element in the universe may respond to the human need for meaning, but Sophocles constructs the play in such a way that the possibility of this sympathy is not enough.

Whitman, Cedric H. "Late Learning: The *Trachiniae.*" In his *Sophocles: A Study of Heroic Humanism*. Cambridge, Mass.: Harvard University Press, 1951, pp. 103-121.

Whitman notes that the play contains many references to knowledge acquired too late to affect a reversal. Everything relating to Deianira implies the darkness and danger of future events. To Whitman, she resembles a Euripidean heroine. When Heracles does return, Deianira herself unwittingly brings about his death through the gift of the cloak, given originally as a love charm. The irony here takes a new turn; the characters consistently struggle to accomplish what they consistently say cannot be done.

Winnington-Ingram, R. P. "*Trachiniae*." In his *Sophocles: An Interpretation.* Cambridge, England: Cambridge University Press, 1980, pp. 73-90.
While destruction of Heracles conforms to the expected pattern of classical tragedy, that of Deianira does not appear to do so. She is too appealing a woman, unlike an Antigone or Electra, in the kind of strength that also provides the tragic flaw these women possess. The analysis notes the bipartite quality of the play, featuring both the tragedies of Heracles and of Deianira.

General Criticism on Sophocles

Bain, David. "Aeschylus and Sophocles." In his *Actors and Audience: A Study of Asides and Related Conventions in Greek Drama.* Oxford, England: Oxford University Press, 1977, pp. 67-86.
Compares representative asides, monologues, and disregarded or unheard speech in the two playwrights, noting differences in technique as reflecting the development of drama itself. See description of this volume, listed with "General Studies," above.

Blundell, Mary Whitlock. *Helping Friends and Harming Enemies: A Study in Sophocles and Greek Ethics.* New York: Cambridge University Press, 1989.
The author explores Greek *ethos* (which she understands as Aristotelian "moral sense") as reflected in the plays of Sophocles through the parallel themes of "help friends/harm enemies." She considers that this nexus informs much of Greek literature and is an ethical issue particularly important in the *Ajax, Antigone, Electra, Philoctetes,* and *Oedipus at Colonus.* After a general discussion of Greek morality as delineated in Aristotle's *Ethics,* Blundell analyzes each of these plays with the recurring elements of "help-harm" emphasized. She notes that one element or the other at times predominates, that friends sometimes become enemies, and she observes that the antagonism often increases dramatic tension. The study assumes no knowledge of Greek and is written for undergraduate and general readers as well as classicists.

Bowra, C. M. *Sophoclean Tragedy.* Oxford, England: Clarendon Press, 1944, reprint 1965.

Treats Sophocles as a poet of ideas rather than emphasizing his dramatic techniques or literary style. An introductory chapter places Sophocles' works in a historical context appropriate for understanding tragedy as a dramatic form. The seven chapters that follow consider each of the extant plays scene by scene and trace the development of what Bowra considers their most important ideas. A final chapter offers a tentative chronology based on both internal and external evidence and makes general comparisons with Shakespeare's plays as well as with those of Henrik Ibsen.

Burton, R. W. B. *The Chorus in Sophocles' Tragedies*. Oxford, England: Clarendon Press, 1980.
This unusual study examines each of the extant plays of Sophocles through their choruses, both the choral lyrics themselves and the contribution each chorus makes to the play in which it appears. Each chapter contains a detailed analysis of the choral odes and sung dialogues of the play under discussion. These analyses focus on text, meter, vocabulary, imagery, and religious associations. The author frequently cites echoes of earlier lyric poetry and comments on how Sophocles adapts and develops the form. The volume taken as a whole is, in effect, a commentary on each of the plays considered from this worthwhile perspective. Gardiner also considers the Sophoclean chorus, though with different emphases, in a study cited below.

Bushnell, Rebecca. *Prophesying Tragedy: Sign and Voice in Sophocles' Theban Plays*. Ithaca, N.Y.: Cornell University Press, 1988.
Bushnell argues that fate, as reflected in *Oedipus Tyrannus*, *Oedipus at Colonus*, and *Antigone*, appears most often in these plays in the context of prophecy. She presents a unified discussion of the relationship of fate and prophecy, considering that a tragic hero's subjective interpretation of prophecy inevitably leads to its defiance and to political abuse that threatens an entire society. Underpinning Bushnell's arguments on the Theban plays is contention that Greek society as a whole understood abuse of oracular prophecy and omens as a clear foreshadowing of tragedy in daily social and political life, that tragic drama was thus directly tied to the milieu of the audience.

Campbell, Lewis. *Tragic Drama in Aeschylus, Sophocles, and Shakespeare: An Essay*. New York: Russell and Russell, 1904, reprint 1965.
This study isolates those elements of Aeschylean and Sophoclean drama that Shakespeare found most congenial as influences for his own plays. Part 1 traces the growth of tragic fable in the ancient world and examines historically the rise and decline of tragic drama in the ancient world, important motifs that ancient and Shakespearean tragedy share, characterization and types of tragic protagonists, construction and tragic diction. Part 2 begins with separate chap-

ters on Aeschylus, Sophocles, and Shakespeare and concludes with discrete chapter analyses of *Hamlet, Macbeth, Othello, King Lear*, and, treated in one chapter, *Cymbeline, A Winter's Tale*, and *The Tempest*, discovering elements in these romances that the author finds akin to classical tragedy.

Earp, Frank Russell. *The Style of Sophocles*. New York: Russell and Russell, 1944, reprint 1972.
Earp examines the elements that he believes account for the general excellence of Sophocles' plays. The study is more technical than readers without some knowledge of Greek may desire. Though such readers may find its documentation intimidating, they will discover its arguments straightforward. The author considers three areas of Sophoclean distinctiveness: vocabulary (words that Sophocles uses in one play only and classical Greek that appears only in Sophocles' works), language (specifically figures of speech and how Sophocles modifies or extends their meaning), and prosody (distinctive features in Sophoclean meter).

Easterling, P. E. "Sophocles." In *The Cambridge History of Classical Literature, Volume 1: Greek Literature*, edited by P. E. Easterling and B. M. W. Knox. Cambridge, England: Cambridge University Press, 1985, pp. 295-316.
Provides a life of Sophocles, discusses his contribution to tragic drama, and cites the distinctive nature of his works. Easterling provides capsule discussions of all the extant plays, considering Sophocles' relationship to Aeschylus and to the intellectual climate of fifth century Athens.

Gardiner, Cynthia P. *The Sophoclean Chorus: A Study of Character and Function*. Iowa City: University of Iowa Press, 1987.
This work focuses on what the chorus of each of the extant plays contributes to their dramatic character. It emphasizes that the Sophoclean chorus is a group of individuals rather than merely a nondescript group. Sophoclean choruses often display an intimate acquaintance with the inner life of protagonists, knowing far more about their inner lives than do even the characters to whom these protagonists are closely related. This text is a less technical, less detailed study than that of Burton cited above, though sound and appropriate for general readers. There is a substantial analysis of the *Philoctetes*, which the author uses as a model for her thesis, and shorter examinations of each of the remaining plays. The Theban plays (*Antigone, Oedipus Tyrannus*, and *Oedipus Coloneus*) appear discussed in one chapter and as a unity.

Gellie, G. H. *Sophocles: A Reading*. Carlton, Victoria, Australia: Melbourne University Press, 1972.
A sound, basic discussion of each play, designed for those interested in theater

performance and for students with an interest in the Greek theater but with no knowledge of Greek. The first part of the study contains discrete analyses of each play focusing on five areas: plot, characterization, chorus, gods, and poetry. The second part considers these five components as varied and adapted to the different requirements of the plays, making important comparisons across the Sophoclean corpus.

Grene, David. *Reality and the Heroic Pattern: Last Plays of Ibsen, Shakespeare, and Sophocles*. Chicago: University of Chicago Press, 1967.
This volume is a comparative study of the three playwrights that examines the matured art of each through studies of his final plays. It does not dwell on philosophy or social and religious life but considers the works as performances and for their dramatic value. The volume is divided into thirds, and the Sophocles section contains analyses of the *Ajax*, *Philoctetes*, and *Oedipus at Colonus*. The Shakespeare section analyzes *Cymbeline*, *The Winter's Tale*, and *The Tempest*; the Ibsen plays considered are *The Master Builder*, *Little Eyolf*, *John Gabriel Borkman*, and *When We Dead Awaken*. The sections are themselves in reversed chronological order, with Ibsen's works analyzed first, Sophocles' last, allowing readers to see Ibsen's classicism as influenced by Shakespeare, Shakespeare's technique against Sophocles.

Haigh, A. E. "Sophocles." In his *The Tragic Drama of the Greeks*. Oxford, England: Clarendon Press, 1896. Reprint. New York: Dover, 1968, pp. 126-203.
This section of Haigh's handbook provides a life of Sophocles, discusses his innovations in tragic drama, his choruses, characters, language, religious and moral ideas, his use of irony, and his reputation in the ancient world. Haigh also provides plot summaries of Sophocles' extant plays.

Jaeger, Werner. "Sophocles and the Tragic Character." In his *Paideia: The Ideals of Greek Culture*, translated by Gilbert Highet, 2d ed., vol. 1. New York: Oxford University Press, 1949, pp. 268-285.
Examines the Sophoclean refinements of drama as a development of Aeschylean tragedy, considering that Sophocles' primary contribution is in the realism of his characters. Jaeger notes how Sophocles' characterizations complement the sophisticated art of Periclean Athens and logically extend those of Aeschylus.

Johansen, H. Fris. "Sophocles 1939-1959." *Lustrum* 7 (1962): 94-342.
An annotated bibliography of criticism, intended for teachers, scholars, and specialists and listing 844 items. It includes Greek texts and editions, criticism on grammar, style, and textual matters, and a broad survey of non-English criticism to 1959.

Kirkwood, G. M. *A Study in Sophoclean Drama. Cornell Studies in Classical Philology 31.* Ithaca, N.Y.: Cornell University Press, 1958. Reprint. New York: Johnson, 1967.

Kirkwood holds that suffering is the essential element of Sophocles' plays, that it unfolds around problems of morality and religion. He contrasts Sophocles' plays with parallel works of Aeschylus and Euripides, identifies the "diptych" construction of *Ajax*, *Trachinae*, and *Antigone*, the "linear" construction of *Oedipus Tyrannus* and *Electra*, the "triangular" form of *Philoctetes*. He treats Sophocles' use of restriction and suppression of background, introduction of oracles, scene building, and stage effects. Analysis of character portrayal appears in one whole unit of the book, with discrete essays on the protagonists of each play. Another section considers the role of the chorus, still others, diction and irony. A convenient index lists the lines of the plays discussed.

Kitto, H. D. F. *Sophocles, Dramatist and Philosopher: Three Lectures Delivered at King's College, New Castle-upon-Tyne.* Oxford, England: Oxford University Press, 1958. Reprint. Westport, Conn.: Greenwood Press, 1981.

Though acknowledged as a tragedian, Sophocles is not generally regarded as a profound thinker. These three lectures, written for a general audience by a distinguished classicist, consider how the plays show a deep philosophical concern with the human condition. Kitto illustrates how Sophocles, like Aeschylus and Shakespeare, repeatedly juxtaposes human elements (things that one can change) with divine elements (matters that admit no change). He makes frequent references to the plays of Aeschylus and Shakespeare but concentrates on the three Theban plays of Sophocles, most of all on the *Antigone*.

Knox, B. M. W. *The Heroic Temper: Studies in Sophoclean Tragedy.* Sather Classical Lectures 35. Berkeley: University of California Press, 1964.

Expanded versions of six lectures delivered as part of the Sather Classical Lectures at the University of California at Berkeley in 1963. The first two chapters analyze the nature of the Sophoclean hero. They note comparisons with Aeschylean heroes, how Sophocles' heroes correspond to Aristotelian definitions in the *Poetics*, and how Sophocles' heroes were viewed by fifth century Greek audiences. Two of the last four chapters treat the *Antigone* and its conception of heroism at considerable length. The final two chapters discretely analyze the *Philoctetes* and the *Oedipus at Colonus*.

Letters, F. J. H. *The Life and Work of Sophocles.* New York: Sheed and Ward, 1953.

This basic study introduces readers to Sophocles: his times, the man, the poet, and the dramatist. It concludes with interpretations and summaries of each play that are suitable for readers new to Sophocles' works. There are no special insights or distinctive interpretations, but the analyses may be helpful for those desiring information in handbook form.

Melchinger, Siegfried. *Sophocles*. Translated by David A. Scrase. New York: Frederick Ungar, 1974.

A companion volume to Melchinger's study on Euripides, cited above. Like that volume, it is a political reading of the plays that argues that the playwright used drama to transmit a series of messages that essentially challenged the accepted social norm. Melchinger's arguments are unusual when applied to Sophocles, whose political ideology is generally considered conservative and who is seldom viewed as thinker or philosopher; nevertheless, the study is valuable as an alternative, somewhat idiosyncratic view. It can be read profitably with this proviso in mind, especially against more traditional studies cited herein.

Mullahy, Patrick. *Oedipus: Myth and Complex: A Review of Psychoanalytic Theory*. New York: Hermitage Press, 1948.

Essentially a guide whose aim is to outline precisely Sigmund Freud's theory and to correct mistaken impressions about his ideas. It analyzes Sophocles' play only by way of Freud's own reading and is, therefore, valuable to readers who wish to know exactly what Freud believed rather than what those influenced by Freud's ideas have introduced. The review of psychoanalytic theory is appropriate for general readers and uses technical terminology only when essential. There is also a good introduction by Erich Fromm.

Musurillo, Herbert. *The Light and the Darkness: Studies in the Dramatic Poetry of Sophocles*. Leiden, Netherlands: E. J. Brill, 1967.

An excellent study of light and darkness imagery in the extant plays, viewing these images as indications of insight and ignorance and tracing their appearance in Sophocles' works. The volume is particularly insightful on the Oedipus plays. It is intended for undergraduate students of classics and comparative literature but can be read with profit by all who have a basic knowledge of the plays.

Nietzsche, Friedrich. "Sophoclean Tragedy." In *Sophocles: A Collection of Critical Essays*, edited by Thomas Woodard. Twentieth Century Views. Englewood Cliffs, N.J.: Prentice-Hall, 1966, pp. 16-28.

An extract from *The Birth of Tragedy* (1872), Nietzsche's theory of aesthetics. Sophoclean heroes have an impressive Apollonian directness, clarity, discipline, and order; yet, beneath this appearance, and indeed complementing it, is a dark, chaotic inner nature, the hero's Dionysian aspect. Nietzsche examines these aspects of Oedipus' personality in this context.

Reinhardt, Karl. *Sophocles*. Translated by Hazel Harvey and David Harvey. New York: Barnes and Noble Books, 1979.

Reinhardt's study examines Sophoclean tragedy in terms of a series of opposing tensions that vary with the individual plays but invariably cause the dramatic action to advance and yield a conclusion. The Theban plays, which Reinhardt examines in detail, present the tension of appearance and truth; the author understands these words in a philosophical sense of *doxa* (common opinion that appears true) and *aletheia* (the truth that has withstood scrutiny). The original version of this work appeared in 1933 with revised editions, all in German, in 1941 and 1947. This first English translation derives from the third edition of 1947.

Romilly, Jacqueline de, ed. *Sophocle: Sept exposés de discussions*. Geneva: Fondation Hardt, 1983.
This volume includes three essays in English, delivered originally as lectures. Responses and discussion appears following each presentation. Bernard Knox considers "Sophocles and the Polis," with special reference to how the city is treated in *Ajax*, *Philoctetes*, *Electra*, and *Antigone* and with contrasts to Aeschylus and Aristophanes. Oliver Taplin discusses "Sophocles in His Theatre," with concentration on the Oedipus plays. R. P. Winnington-Ingram examines "Sophocles and Women," concentrating on the characters of Electra and Antigone with contrasts to Euripides' plays.

Scodel, Ruth. *Sophocles*. Twayne's World Authors Series 731. Boston: Twayne, 1984.
Scodel follows the regular Twayne format, dealing first with what is known of Sophocles' life outlined against the social and historical circumstances of fifth century Athens. Sound, conservative analyses of the plays follow in individual chapters. There is a particularly good study of the *Ajax*, featuring a contrast with the Ajax of Homer's the *Iliad*, as well as a discussion of *hybris* (arrogant pride) and *sophrosyne* (prudence). Analysis of the *Women of Trachis* focuses on its bipartite structure and the roles of gods and oracles in the play. Discussion of the *Electra* makes good contrasts with Euripides' play of the same name and the *Choephoroi* of Aeschylus and offers comparisons with the style of the *Philoctetes*. The chapter on the *Philoctetes* contrasts the play with the myth as told in the post-Homeric *Little Iliad*. The most-read plays (*Oedipus Tyrannus*, *Oedipus at Colonus*, and *Antigone*) are treated in separate chapters. There is a final essay on Sophoclean drama, a short bibliography, an index, and a chronology of events that parallel Sophocles' life.

Seale, David. *Vision and Stagecraft in Sophocles*. Chicago: University of Chicago Press, 1982.
Intended for nonspecialists, particularly students of drama, but also for classicists who desire a good, basic interpretation of Sophoclean drama from the spectator's point of view, to visualize each play as it unfolds. The translations, based on those of Jebb, are Victorian, but there are good, discrete survey

interpretations, scene by scene, of the *Philoctetes, Electra, Antigone, Oedipus at Colonus, Ajax, Women of Trachis*, and *Oedipus the King*. There is also an introduction on Aristotelian principles and Sophoclean visual conventions and how these compare with the norms suggested in the *Poetics*.

Segal, Charles. *Tragedy and Civilization: An Interpretation of Sophocles*. Cambridge, Mass.: Harvard University Press, 1981.
A structuralist analysis of the seven extant plays intended to probe the meaning of Sophoclean tragedy. Three introductory chapters analyze what Segal calls the "civilizing power" of tragedy, the structuralist approach he intends to follow, and the relationship of language to the portrayal of kingship and ritual. The remaining chapters examine each of the plays with two chapters on the *Philoctetes*. Segal sees Sophocles as more an intellectual playwright than generally held and believes his plays represent timeless commentaries on the human condition. The selected bibliography is useful for its large number of articles on Sophocles.

Whitman, Cedric H. *Sophocles: A Study of Heroic Humanism*. Cambridge, Mass.: Harvard University Press, 1951.
This standard work, sometimes criticized for its thesis that Sophocles was a pioneer of Western humanism, remains an important work for general readers. Part 1 defines the classical understanding of tragic drama, primarily by using Aristotle's *Poetics* against Sophocles' works, discusses *hamartía* (tragic flaw) as a necessary element of characterization, and suggests a chronology for the extant plays. Part 2 discusses *areté* (virtue) as essential to the characterizations of Ajax and Antigone. Part 3 explores tragic knowledge in the *Trachiniae* and *Oedipus Tyrannus*; part 4 examines tragic endurance in the *Electra, Philoctetes*, and *Oedipus at Colonus*. A final section considers Sophocles in the context of fifth century Athens and outlines the "metaphysic" of Sophoclean humanism.

Winnington-Ingram, R. P. *Sophocles: An Interpretation*. Cambridge, England: Cambridge University Press, 1980.
This study derives from the author's lectures and treats aspects of all the extant plays. All Greek appears in translation, and the approach is suitable for general readers. There are good general analyses of the *Trachinae*, the *Electra*, the *Oedipus at Colonus*, and the *Philoctetes*. The volume features, however, interpretations of more restricted focus: the mind of Ajax and the burial of Ajax, irrationality and three choral odes in the *Antigone*, Creon and Antigone, fate in Sophocles, the fall of Oedipus, the Furies in Sophocles, and gods and heroes in Sophocles' plays.

Woodard, Thomas, ed. *Sophocles: A Collection of Critical Essays*. Twentieth Century Views. Englewood Cliffs, N.J.: Prentice-Hall, 1966.

This book, like other volumes of the series, contains a broad survey of interpretations by famous critics juxtaposed with those of contemporary scholars. Among the classic essays are Friedrich Nietzsche's "Sophoclean Tragedy" (from *The Birth of Tragedy*, 1872), Ostwald Spengler's "Tragedy: Classical vs. Western" (from *The Decline of the West*, 1926), Sigmund Freud's "Oedipus Rex" (from *The Interpretation of Dreams*, English trans. 1954) and Virginia Woolf's "On Sophocles' Electra" (from *The Common Reader*, 1925). Noteworthy among the contemporary selections are Charles Paul Segal on "Praise of Man and the Conflicts of the *Antigone*," Bernard M. W. Knox on "The *Ajax* of Sophocles," Seth Benardete on "Sophocles' *Oedipus Tyrannus*," Thomas Woodard on "The *Electra* of Sophocles," and Cedric H. Whitman on "Apocalypse: *Oedipus at Colonus*."

TERENCE

Recommended Translations and Commentaries

The Brothers (Adelphoe)
Gratwick, A. S., ed., trans. *Terence: The Brothers*. Wauconda, Ill.: Bolchazy-Carducci, 1987.

The excellent introductory material and a well-paced translation of Terence's play facing the Latin text broaden the appeal of this volume. There is a brief but comprehensive discussion of Terence's life and work with comparisons to Menander, a scene-by-scene summary of action, a discussion of the Roman context of *The Brothers* against the Greek original, an analysis of characters and stereotypes in Terence, and of the techniques of exposition followed by Terence and Menander. There are special references to Menander's original play, especially its middle and final scenes, and an excellent introduction to Terence's prosody. Metrical irregularities in the Latin text appear scanned for easy reading.

Martin, R. H., ed. *The "Adelphoe" of Terence*. New York: Cambridge University Press, 1976.

This edition of the Latin text includes an English commentary that elucidates matters of concern to all readers, specifically questions of scene division and discussion of the stock characters. There is also an introductory essay on Terence's life, a chronology, production history of the play, and its text transmission. The volume includes a selected bibliography of texts and editions that incorporates general and non-English criticism.

The Mother-in-Law (Hecyra)
Carney, T. F., ed. *Terence: Hecyra*. Salisbury, Rhodesia: Classical Association of Rhodesia and Nyasaland, 1963. Reprint. Cambridge, Mass.: Bristol Classical Press, 1988.

This excellent Latin with introduction and English commentary is readily available and suitable for school use as well as for those reading the play in translation. The introduction contains information about Terence's life, production history of the *Hecyra*, stage directions, and metrics. There are appendices on the theater, meter, and the role of slaves, as well as a chronology of Terence's life.

Phormio
Coury, Elaine, ed., trans. *Phormio: A Comedy by Terence*. Wauconda, Ill.: Bolchazy-Carducci, 1982.

A good translation facing the Latin text. The volume contains a commentary that is both linguistic and exegetical, so that it can be used by all readers. The introduction treats the life of Plautus, the plot of this play, its characters, and New Comedy.

The Self-Tormentor (Heautontimorumenos)
Brothers, A. J., ed., trans. *Terence: Self-Tormentor*. Wauconda, Ill.: Bolchazy-Carducci, 1982.
   The best-available edition of the play. It contains a translation facing the Latin text, a short apparatus, a commentary, and an excellent introduction that features a discussion of Terence's life, plot summary, character analyses, and general discussion of Old and New Comedy.

The Woman from Andros (Andria)
Shipp, G. P., ed. *P. Terenti Afri Andria*. Rev. ed. Melbourne: Melbourne University Press, 1960. Reprint. Salem, N.H.: Ayer, 1979.
   Shipp's commentary, originally produced in 1938, is designed for students as an introduction to the play. The revised edition, as reprinted here, includes references to postwar scholarship. The notes are both exegetical and textual, and the commentary can be used with a translation to elucidate stage action. Contains Latin text and introduction.

Complete Collections
Casson, Lionel, trans. *Masters of Ancient Comedy: Selections from Aristophanes, Menander, Plautus, Terence*. New York: Macmillan, 1960. Reprint. New York: Minerva Press, 1967.
   Contains translations of the *Phormio* and *The Brothers*, without notes. The volume concludes with an epilogue on the end of ancient comedy; this text is especially worthwhile for readers of Terence. See complete description of this volume under Menander collections, cited above.

Copley, Frank O., trans. *The Comedies of Terence: The Brothers, The Eunuch, The Mother-in-Law, Phormio, The Self-Tormentor, The Woman of Andros*. Library of Liberal Arts. Indianapolis: Bobbs-Merrill, 1967.
   This excellent translation of the extant plays remains in print. While the translations convey the idiom very well, the volume itself contains only the barest of introductions, and there are no notes or commentary on the text.

Harsh, Philip Whaley, ed. *An Anthology of Roman Drama*. New York: Holt, Rinehart and Winston, 1960.
   Includes translations of Terence's *Phormio* and *Rudens*. For complete contents and description, see entry under Plautus collections, above.

Radice, Betty, trans. *Terence: The Comedies*. New York: Penguin Books, 1976.
   Contains excellent translations of all the plays and a brief introduction to Terence and New Comedy.

Sargeaunt, J., trans. *Terence*. 2 vols. Loeb Classical Library. Cambridge, Mass.:
Harvard University Press, 1912.
These volumes, kept in print as part of the Loeb Classical Library, contain
satisfactory, though stiff, translations of all the extant plays on pages facing the
Latin text. The only advantage of this edition is the convenience of parallel
language texts. There is only a short introduction to Terence, and the translations appear without notes or commentary.

Recommended Criticism on Terence

The Brothers (Adelphoe)
Fantham, Elaine. "*Heautontimorumenos* and *Adelphoe*: A Study of Fatherhood in
Terence and Menander." *Latomus* 30 (1971): 970-998.
Notes the careful contrast·between Menedemus and Chremes and how the
problems the young men face find their real interest in the fact that they cause
a reversal in the old men's roles. Chremes' brutality, clearly illustrated in his
threat to disinherit Clitipho, comes close to repeating the error of Menedemus.
In his asking for advice, Chremes reveals his own hypocrisy and underscores
the humility of Menedemus. Fantham concludes with observations of Terence's
modifications of the Menandrian originals and on *contaminatio* (combining
two or more Greek originals in a single Latin text).

—————— . "Terence, Diphilus, and Menander: A Re-examination of Terence,
Adelphoe, Act II." *Philologus* 112 (1968): 196-216.
Examines portions of Terence's text, which parts he derived from Diphilus and
which from Menander, and the effect these alternate borrowings have on the
Latin version. It is likely that Aeschinus' carrying off of Bacchis had merely
been reported in Menander's *Adelphoe* B[1], though in Terence's play this happens onstage. The prologue of Terence's play mentions a play Diphilus had
written known as the *Synapothneskontes* (those dying together), which Plautus
had translated as the *Commorientes*, though with the abduction scene of that
play omitted (Terence claims) through carelessness. Terence claims to have
incorporated the scene from Diphilus word for word into his own *Adelphoe*
from Diphilus and asks the audience to judge whether he has turned Plautus'
mistake to the good.

Forehand, Walter E. "*The Brothers (Adelphoe)*." In his *Terence*. Twayne's World
Authors Series 745. Boston: Twayne, 1985, pp. 104-119.
An excellent general analysis. Forehand begins with a plot summary, discusses
the use of pairs as furthering the play's double plot, farcical elements and
broad humor, and the critical puzzlement regarding Demea's change in phi-

losophy of child-rearing. There is a brief discussion of each character and some concluding remarks on whether Terence favors Demea's conservative or Micio's liberal methods of raising sons.

Goldberg, Sander M. *"Contaminatio."* In his *Understanding Terence*. Princeton, N.J.: Princeton University Press, 1986, pp. 97-105.
The opening of act 2, from lines 155 to 196, in which Aeschinus insults the pimp Sannio and has him beaten, has been taken from another Greek original. Goldberg examines the interpolation and concludes that it is intended both to deepen the character of Aeschinus and to reinforce earlier doubts about Micio. This maneuver heightens the drama and strengthens its significance. Goldberg also provides shorter discussions on Terence's contrast of Demea and Micio (pp. 73-74), Demea's change of heart regarding the rearing of children (pp. 23-28), and comic reversal in the play (pp. 211-214).

Grant, John N. "The Beginning of Menander, *Adelphoi* B[1]." *Classical Quarterly* 30 (1980): 341-355.
Examines the first two sections of Terence's play against Menander's original. Grant takes these sections scene by scene, noting departures from Menander as indications of *contaminatio* (combining plots from at least two originals). Though scholarly, general readers can follow the argument with little difficulty, and the article is useful as an insight into the relationship of Latin and Greek New Comedy. Grant continues his study of the *Adelphoe* in the article cited below.

_____ . "The Ending of Terence's *Adelphoe* and the Menandrian Original." *American Journal of Philology* 96 (1975): 42-60.
Considers Demea's sudden renunciation of his principles of frugality and severity in the rearing of children and makes comparisons with Knemon's parallel *apologia* in Menander's *Dyskolos*. The dilemma is that if Demea is serious, his apparent victory over his liberal brother Micio at the play's conclusion becomes a punishment of Micio's leniency. If Demea is merely pretending to have changed his views, the ending of the play becomes a mere joke at Micio's expense. This article provides a close reading of the monologue against Menander's original. It suggests that the change in meter, to trochaic septinarii (the Latin equivalent of Menander's trochaic tetrameter catalectic), is an internal means of positing Terence's seriousness. Compare Grant's companion article on the play's beginning, cited above.

Greenberg, N. A. "Success and Failure in the *Adelphoe*." *Classical World* 73 (1979/1980): 221-236.
This article considers Terence's play as an amalgam of the serious and the

comic. It is written nontechnically and examines the character of Demea, as well as the comic reversal of the play's conclusion, at some length. Greenberg also summarizes traditional interpretations given the play: as a contest between conflicting methods of child-rearing; as an argument for permissiveness; as a criticism of permissive behavior.

Lord, C. "Aristotle, Menander, and the *Adelphoe* of Terence." *Transactions of the American Philological Association* 107 (1977): 183-202.
Though Aristotle's *Poetics* survives only as notes and in that portion that considers norms for tragic drama, it is clear that he is opposed to mixed plots and interpolations that affect unity. Because of its interpolation through *contaminatio*, the *Adelphoe* lacks unity by Aristotelian definition; nevertheless, Lord argues that its subplot provides an alternative to simple structural coherence.

Norwood, Gilbert. "*The Brothers (Adelphoe)*." In his *The Art of Terence*. New York: Russell and Russell, 1923, reprint 1965, pp. 106-130.
Begins with a plot summary, followed by an analysis that notes that this play is Terence's masterpiece. It has strong literary qualities and subordinates its characterizations of women to those of men. The play has a strong psychological interest in its portrayal of the brothers Aeschinus and Ctesipho and in the contrast of the two "fathers" (Micio and Demea).

The Eunuch (Eunuchus)
Earl, D. C. "Terence and Roman Politics." *Historia* 11 (1962): 469-485.
Begins with the premise that all literature is in some way rooted in its own time, yet observes that readers of Terence who hold this view are frustrated by the absence of references to living people in his plays. The *Eunuchus*, however, presents the prideful soldier Thraso. In his deploying of centuries and maniples before the house of Thais, he emulates the historical figure of Pyrrhus. Thraso's follower Sanga represents the stereotype of the Roman soldier in his considering force the primary virtue of a military commander. Earl notes that Terence avoids the more obvious political significance latent in words such as *gloria* (unbounded glory) or *virtus* (courage without limit) in favor of a more universally applicable subtlety. Earl's article, "Political Terminology in Plautus," in *Historia* 9 (1960): 234-243, takes precisely the opposite position in an examination of that playwright's works.

Forehand, Walter E. "*The Eunuch (Eunuchus)*." In his *Terence*. Twayne's World Authors Series 745. Boston: Twayne, 1985, pp. 68-80.
An analysis designed for readers new to the play. It begins with a basic plot summary, considers complications of plot structure and the Thraso-Gnatho

subplot, provides information on each of the characters as stock types, and labels its plot-type as *motoria* (active comedy, or a comedy of movement). Forehand notes the critical condescension of some regarding the play, specifically that of Norwood, cited below. The accusation of most who view the play unfavorably is that it is imitative of Plautus.

Gilmartin, K. "The Thraso-Gnatho Subplot in Terence's *Eunuchus*." *Classical World* 69 (1975): 263-267.
Discusses the effect of Thraso and Gnatho and considers that the scenes in which this bumbling soldier and parasite appear provide more than merely defective humor; indeed, their scenes comprise well over a quarter of the play, and they are onstage more than any of the other characters. Despite these facts, they are not essential to the plot. Even so, their exaggerated subservience, sustained throughout four scenes and in itself constituting a subplot, provides insight into similar qualities in the other characters. This parallelism is especially clear in the conclusion, where plot and subplot are reconciled. Compare Saylor's article, cited below.

Goldberg, Sander M. "*Contaminatio*." In his *Understanding Terence*. Princeton, N.J.: Princeton University Press, 1986, pp. 105-122.
Terence's *The Eunuch* derives from the lost *Eunuchos* of Menander with interpolations from Menander's *Kolax*. Because less than one hundred lines of the second Menander play survive, it is impossible to determine how much this play influenced Terence's plot. Goldberg argues that all the Thraso and Gnatho scenes represent interpolations and examines these passages.

Lowe, J. C. B. "The *Eunuchus*: Terence and Menander," *Classical Quarterly* 33 (1983): 428-444.
Discusses the effect of Terence's inclusion of interpolations from a lost play of Menander (*Eunouchos*) and Menander's *Kolax* (of which slightly more than one hundred lines remain extant). How closely Terence followed one or the other in certain instances directly affects the action of his play: the name of the soldier's parasite, the presence of two parasites, the events that derive from the love two men share for a pimp's courtesan. Lowe's presumption is that Terence used *contaminatio* (mixing together elements from different original plays) to improve the plot of his own play. He also considers the play's conventions, such as ridicule of the young man's surrender of reason to love.

Norwood, Gilbert. "*The Eunuch* (*Eunuchus*)." In his *The Art of Terence*. New York: Russell and Russell, 1923, reprint 1965, pp. 53-69.
Begins with a simple plot summary, followed by a rather mixed assessment of the play's worth. Norwood holds that this play marks a faltering in Terence's progress as a writer, that portions show evidence of the playwright's attempt to

imitate Plautine comedy. The play's strength is in its literary brilliance. Norwood considers that this play marks a transitional point in Terence's style, that seeking simplicity of plot he has sacrificed close-knit structure.

Saylor, C. "The Theme of Planlessness in Terence's *Eunuchus*." *Transactions of the American Philological Association* 105 (1975): 297-311.
   Most modern discussions of the *Eunuchus* focus on its seeming disorganization, the result of Terence's apparent insertion of the scenes involving Thraso the soldier and his parasite Gnatho. Saylor argues that this mixing of plot and subplot is intended as a means of defining and illustrating the primary characters of the play. Compare Gilmartin's article, cited above.

The Mother-in-Law (Hecyra)
Forehand, Walter E. "*The Mother-in-Law (Hecyra)*." In his *Terence*. Twayne's World Authors Series 745. Boston: Twayne, 1985, pp. 92-104.
   A straightforward analysis that begins with plot summary, then considers structure (especially the prologue question), the use of the protatic character Philotis to stimulate dialogue, and Parmeno's role of providing comic focus at key points in the play and offers brief portraits of the other characters. Forehand concludes by discussing Terence's use of irony in the play.

Gilula, D. "Who's Afraid of Rope-Walkers and Gladiators: Terence, *Hec*. 1-57." *Athenaeum* 59 (1981): 29-37.
   A discussion of the prologue of the *Hecyra*, appended for the third production of the play after its two previous failures. The earlier prologue is impersonally written and notes that the play's first presentation failed because the audience's attention was distracted by a ropewalker. The second prologue, written for the third revival, is personal, spoken by a producer given the name "Lucius Ambivius." The speaker pleads that the play has never enjoyed a silent hearing, that fighting in the audience, ladies talking, the claque (paid applauders), and the sudden announcement of a gladiatorial show drove the play from the boards. The appeal of the second prologue is distinctly Terence's own. The speaker here entreats audience appreciation of subtlety and asks that it not fall into the hands of those interested merely in spectacle. Compare the parallel study by Sandbach, cited below.

Goldberg, Sander M. "The Price of Simplicity." In his *Understanding Terence*. Princeton, N.J.: Princeton University Press, 1986, pp. 150-169.
   Menander's *The Arbitration (Epitrepontes)* ends with Charisios' admission of responsibility for his wife's dilemma, though Terence's version, the *Hecyra*, ends with the prospect of imminent reconciliation with Philumena, not with any general revelation of truth. Goldberg argues that Terence's play contrasts

young and old generations; the focus is on the two mothers-in-law and the dilemma that estrangement from Philumena creates for them.

Konstan, David. "*Hecyra*: Ironic Comedy." In his *Roman Comedy*. Ithaca, N.Y.: Cornell University Press, 1983, pp. 130-141.

Konstan's analysis illustrates that this much-criticized play remains within the formal conventions of New Comedy, yet challenges and confounds their customary meanings. He sees the *Hecyra* as an example of the ironic movement in New Comedy. Its most remarkable feature, which anticipates the comedies of Shakespeare, is that the blocking character is identical with the lover himself. Pamphilus thus becomes a more fully realized individual than is the rule for New Comedy.

Lowe, J. C. B. "Terentian Originality in the *Phormio* and *Hecyra*." *Hermes* 3 (1983): 431-452.

Considers the difficulties of reshaping the Menandrian originals into a form suitable for continuous performance. The absence of formal act divisions in Terence's version shortens the time an audience has to consider the interrelationship of the plays' elements. This study analyzes the techniques Terence employed to establish continuities quickly. Often these occur at transitional sections of the original where one act ends and the next begins.

McGarrity, T. "Reputation v. Reality in Terence's *Hecyra*." *Classical Journal* 76 (1980-1981): 149-156.

The *Hecyra* deals with Philumena's sudden return to her own family and Pamphilus' refusal to take her back as his wife. Pamphilus had been forced to give up Bacchis, the woman he first loved, in order to marry Philumena, though he had come to love Philumena. While Pamphilus was away from home, Philumena left her husband's home under mysterious circumstances. The reason is an untimely pregnancy that apparently could not have been caused by her husband. The reality, that Pamphilus had raped Philumela, emerges, though Pamphilus never makes the admission. Pamphilus steadfastly avoids this reality and thereby forfeits audience sympathy. McGarrity discusses Terence's plot as derived from an original by Apollodorus of Carystus and notes its affinities with Menander's *Epitrepontes*.

Norwood, Gilbert. "*The Mother-in-Law* (*Hecyra*)." In his *The Art of Terence*. New York: Russell and Russell, 1923, reprint 1965, pp. 85-105.

Following a plot summary, Norwood notes the two failed productions of the play and some negative modern criticism of the extant revised version. Norwood considers the play a perfect example of classical high comedy. He focuses on the play's maturity, reasonableness, and skill in its treatment of subject matter and cites examples of each of these aspects.

Sandbach, F. H. "How Terence's *Hecyra* Failed." *Classical Quarterly* 32 (1982): 134-135.

The prologue of the *Hecyra* recounts the three attempts Terence made to successfully produce this play. Sandbach discusses the sensitive subject matter that caused disturbances in the audience in its two previous productions, then notes that the producer, who speaks the prologue, is actually the playwright pleading his case for a hearing. Terence manages this unusual personal insertion despite his retention of certain conventions consistently found in comic prologues. Compare the parallel study by Gilula, cited above.

Sewart, D. "Exposition in the *Hekyra* of Apollodorus." *Hermes* 102 (1974): 247-260.

Argues that Terence omitted only Apollodorus' expository prologue, in which Parmeno reveals how unfounded the reasons for his self-importance really are. Parmeno's statements conflict with Bacchis' own account of her situation. A contrasting argument appears in McGarrity's article, cited above.

Phormio

Arnott, W. G. "*Phormio Parasitus*: A Study in Dramatic Methods of Characterization." *Greece and Rome* (1970): 32-57.

Arnott, having noted that Terence's *Phormio* is one of the least original of his plays, proceeds to show that it is paradoxically one of his most engaging plays. He bases these arguments on the play's ruthless amorality, and in a nontechnical analysis shows how Terence engages the audience through charming appeals to base instincts. A final section considers Apollodorus and Menander as Terence's sources.

Bohm, R. K. "Money Matters in *Phormio*." *Classical World* 70 (1976): 267-269.

Discusses the conversation between Davos and the crafty slave Geta to whom the protection of Antipho and Phaedria has been entrusted. Bohm sees this conversation as essential for outlining the play's theme and notes that the method of exposition corresponds to that which appears in the *Hecyra*. He cites the common influence of the Greek originals by Apollodorus.

Forehand, Walter E. "*Phormio*." In his *Terence*. Twayne's World Authors Series 745. Boston: Twayne, 1985, pp. 81-92.

Intended for those new to the play, this analysis begins with a basic plot summary, discusses the dual structure, the large number of references to law and court proceedings, compares what is known of Apollodorus' original as Terence's source, and lists and analyzes each of the characters. Forehand concludes by noting the role ethics occupies in the play as well as the theme of chance and fortunate accident.

Goldberg, Sander M. "The Well-Made Play." In his *Understanding Terence*. Princeton, N.J.: Princeton University Press, 1986, pp. 75-90.

A complete analysis of the play's structure that notes Terence's deliberate association of the clever parasite Phormio with Plautus' Curculio and the Plautine slaves Epidicus and Pseudolus. Goldberg focuses on the busy action of Terence's play, much of which centers around the character Geta.

Konstan, David. *"Phormio*: Citizen Disorder." In his *Roman Comedy*. Ithaca, N.Y.: Cornell University Press, 1983, pp. 115-129.
This chapter of Konstan's general study examines the conflicting demands of *pietas* (piety) and *amor* (love). In the *Epitrepontes* of Menander, Phamphile's dignity teaches Charisios that he himself must accept responsibility for his wife's moral attitudes. The Pamphilus of the *Hecyra* places himself at the mercy of others who would determine his fate, primarily because there is no confession in Terence's play; Pamphilus has become a victim of the opposing forces his *pietas* and *amor* create.

Lowe, J. C. B. "Terentian Originality in the *Phormio* and *Hecyra*." *Hermes* 3 (1983): 431-452.
Considers the difficulties of reshaping the Menandrian originals into a form which is suitable for continuous performance. The absence of formal act divisions in Terence's version shortens the time an audience has to consider the interrelationship of the plays' elements. This study analyzes the various techniques that Terence employed in order to establish continuities quickly. Often these occur at transitional sections of the original where one act ends and the next begins.

Norwood, Gilbert. *"Phormio (Phormio)."* In his *The Art of Terence*. New York: Russell and Russell, 1923, reprint 1965, pp. 70-84.
Following a plot summary, Norwood argues that this play has dramatic power missing in Terence's earlier works, also that there is an ease in character and plot development. Antipho's marriage, the intrigue of Phaedria, Chremes' bigamy, and Phormio's mastery of the entire action are all skillfully presented. Norwood also sees defects in imprecisely written dialogue and discusses these at the conclusion of his analysis.

Quinn, Kenneth. "Comedy as Plot: Terence's *Phormio*." In his *Texts and Contexts: The Roman Writers and Their Audience*. London: Routledge and Kegan Paul, 1979, pp. 100-111.
A straightforward discussion of the play's plot and characters as representative of Roman New Comedy in its most highly developed form. Quinn asserts that as a whole the plays show an elegant purism of style and that Terence's plays are generally duller than those of Plautus. He notes that fifteen years of Ennius' active career intervene between Plautus and Terence and that acquain-

tance with Ennius and the patronage of Scipio Aemilianus produced greater sophistication in Terence's comedies.

Segal, E., and C. Moulton. *"Contortor Legum*: The Hero of the *Phormio,"* *Rheinisches Museum* 121 (1978): 276-288.
A good discussion of the title character of the *Phormio*, whose attempts to twist the law constitute the plot of Terence's play. Though Phormio has been paid to annul the marriage of Antipho and Phanium, he has used the money to buy a music-girl for the son of Chremes. Phormio is spared the responsibility for his agreement when he learns that Phanium is Chremes' daughter and actually the bride intended for Antipho. Segal illustrates how Phormio concocts one illegal scheme after the next, yet wins the affection of the audience even as he wins absolute control of all the characters of the play.

The Self-Tormentor (Heautontimorumenos)
Brothers, A. J. "The Construction of Terence's *Heauton-timorumenos." Classical Quarterly* 30 (1980): 94-119.
Analyzes the relationship of Terence's play to the Greek original and includes evidence drawn from the Cairo codex of Menander. Brothers concentrates on evidence of *contaminatio* (combining of Greek originals) and notes that the possibility of *contaminatio* has been largely overlooked in previous examinations of the play. Firm evidence for manuscript contamination exists in the early parts of the play. The analysis is scholarly and detailed and considers as well how Terence might have altered irrelevant material in his originals; yet, even general readers will find plot comparisons among Menandrian originals and Terence's play interesting and worthwhile. For a parallel study on the *Adelphoe*, see Grant's article, cited above.

Fantham, Elaine. *"Heautontimorumenos* and *Adelphoe*: A Study of Fatherhood in Terence and Menander." *Latomus* 30 (1971): 970-998.
Notes the careful contrast between Memedemus and Chremes and how the problems the young men face find their real interest in the fact that they cause a reversal in the old men's roles. Chremes' brutality, clearly illustrated in his threat to disinherit Clitipho, comes close to repeating the error of menedemus. In his asking for advice, Chremes reveals his won hypocrisy and underscores the humility of Menedemus. Fantham concludes with observations of Terence's modications of the Menandrian originals and on *contaminatio* (combining two or more Greek originals in a single Latin text).

Forehand, Walter E. *"The Self-Tormentor (Heautontimorumenos)."* In his *Terence*. Twayne's World Authors Series 745. Boston: Twayne, 1985, pp. 54-68.
An excellent analysis for readers new to the play. It provides a simple plot summary, discussion of the claim Terence makes in the prologue to have

created a dual plot from a single Greek play and problems of structure (specifically, entrances and exits of Chremes, the incompleteness of Syrus' plans, and
the awkward discovery of Antiphila's identity). There are analyses of each
character and a discussion of the father-son theme.

Goldberg, Sander M. "The *duplex comoedia*." In his *Understanding Terence*.
Princeton, N.J.: Princeton University Press, 1986, pp. 135-148.
Terence calls his *The Self-Torturer* a fresh (*integra*) comedy from a fresh
source, a double plot made from a single one. Goldberg examines Terence's
plot and shows how the play that started out centered on Menedemus and
Clinia turns most of its focus upon Chremes and Clitipho.

Norwood, Gilbert. "*Self-Punishment (Heautontimorumenos)*." In his *The Art of
Terence*. New York: Russell and Russell, 1923, reprint 1965, pp. 37-52.
Begins with a simple plot summary. Notes Terence's ability to write clever lines
and phrases but holds that this play has no great comic impact. Norwood
describes the character-drawing as "nebulous," though he believes that some
dialogue, such as that of Bacchis and Antiphila, displays unstudied eloquence
in the characters. Norwood's chief objection is to the character and strategies
of Syrus, which he finds needlessly complicated. See Goldberg's study for a
more positive analysis of the play, cited above.

The Woman from Andros (Andria)
Forehand, Walter E. "*The Girl from Andros (Andria)*." In his *Terence*. Twayne's
World Authors Series 745. Boston: Twayne, 1985, pp. 38-54.
Begins with a simple plot summary followed by some observations on its
structure as traditionally the earliest of Terence's plays. It follows a rudimen-
tary form of the "duality method" by more or less pairing characters; however,
the second intrigue, centering on Charinus' frustrated love affair, never really
develops. Forehand then provides character analyses of Simo, Chremes, Pamphilus, Charinus, Davus, and the minor characters Byrria, Crito, and Mysis.
Finally, there is a discussion of the play's realistic treatment of love.

Garton, C. "*Andria*." In his *Personal Aspects of the Roman Theatre*. Toronto:
University of Toronto Press, 1972, pp. 41-139.
In the context of his larger study of the relationship between the Roman
playwrights and their Greek texts, Garton provides a valuable discussion of the
Andria. Terence introduces the play by means of arguments that resemble
those of a law court in their structure and vocabulary. Yet these arguments,
while vehement, are essentially cold and appear without the naming of the
rival to whom they refer. The ancient commentator Aelius Donatus (born c.
A.D. 333) claims this rival is Luscius Lanuvinus, though Donatus is vague

about the causes of this rival's dispute with Terence. Garton discusses what can be conjectured about Luscius and the nature of the quarrel.

Goldberg, Sander M. "The *duplex comoedia*." In his *Understanding Terence*. Princeton, N.J.: Princeton University Press, 1986, pp. 126-135.
Charinus and his slave Byrria were not in the Menandrian original of the *Andria*. Either they are Terence's own invention or borrowed from Menander's *Perinthia*; they serve the function of providing a second love interest and thus create a double plot. Goldberg examines this example of *contaminatio* (combining two or more Greek originals) and discusses the resulting complexity of plot.

McGarrity, T. "Thematic Unity in Terence's *Andria*." *Transactions of the American Philological Association* 108 (1978): 103-114.
Charinus and his slave Byrria were not characters in Menander's *Andria*; consequently, they are either original creations or borrowed from Menander's *Perinthia*. McGarrity considers how such *contaminatio* can add effective complexity and, paradoxically, greater unity to a plot.

Norwood, Gilbert. "*The Girl of Andros*." In his *The Art of Terence*. New York: Russell and Russell, 1923, reprint 1965, pp. 18-36.
Begins with a summary of each act and follows with a generally negative view of the play. Norwood considers that its faults of construction exceed its merits. Charinus and Byrria are dramatically useless; their action has no effect on plot, adds nothing, and leads nowhere. It is merely tied on to the main action. The part of Sosia is "a thoroughly amateurish device for helping to convey information to the audience." The whole part of Davus is "otiose." In short, Norwood criticizes the double plot and nearly every character. For a more positive view, see the Goldberg study, cited above.

General Criticism on Terence

Beare, W. "The Life of Terence." *Hermathena* 59 (1942): 20-29.
This study of Terence's life was adapted and amplified in Beare's book-length study on Roman drama cited above under "General Studies," above. Beare considers the alternative dates of birth and death and the arguments for these that appear in the ancient sources. He examines arguments for Carthaginian origin (based on the cognomen "Afer") and whether Terence was a slave or freeman at the time of his coming to Rome. Beare also notes that Terence's prologues yield no important biographical information. He accepts the tradition that Terence journeyed to the East and that this trip was probably to improve his Greek, though there is no ancient documentation on the reasons Terence undertook the voyage.

Clifford, H. R. "Dramatic Technique and the·Originality of Terence." *Classical Journal* (26) (1931): 605-618.

Discusses, in a way suitable for general readers, the degree to which Terence was influenced by the Greek originals he used. Clifford outlines the two generally held points of view: that Terence showed considerable independence from his sources; that his translations are closely tied to the originals. He then suggests that an important illustration of Terence's originality lay in staging: comic entrances, exits, and distant journeys planned followed by almost immediate reappearance of the character making them. The article also contains a good, simplified discussion with illustrations of the phenomenon of *contaminatio* (combining two or more sources in a single play). See Flickinger and Norwood below, both of whom also discuss *contaminatio* in Terence, though with differing conclusions about Terence's closeness to his sources.

Cupaiuolo, G. *Bibliografia terenziana (1470-1983). Studi i testi dell' antichità XVI.* Naples: University of Naples, 1984.

An exhaustive inventory of editions and scholarship of Terence, listings with indexed cross-references of materials that date from the inception of printing. This scholarly listing, though too detailed for the average reader, lists all printed editions and important scholarly criticism. It catalogues and collates but does not evaluate this material. The more concise survey of Goldberg, cited below, contains brief evaluations of materials most suitable for school use.

Flickinger, R. C. "Terence and Menander." *Classical Journal* 26 (1931): 676-694.

Argues against the position taken in Norwood's study, cited below, that the structure of Terence's plays is essentially his own. Flickinger cites ancient sources first, to show that the Roman world understood that Terence's relation to his Greek sources was close and that Terence's contemporaries saw him as an adaptor or imitator rather than an original playwright. The bulk of the article reads scenes from Terence's plays against similar scenes in Menander. Flickinger finds reason to praise Terence's graceful rendering of the Greek, his clever transitions, and the sophisticated Latin versions he created. See Clifford's article, cited above, for similar arguments.

Forehand, Walter E. *Terence.* Twayne's World Authors Series 745. Boston: Twayne, 1985.

This text is an enthusiastically written study for the beginning student, arranged according to the regular Twayne format. There are separate chapters on Terence's life (what is known and what has been conjectured, against the times in which he lived), his career as playwright and actor, the Roman theater at the time Terence was writing for it, the extant plays (with analysis of each), and a final chapter on Terence's influence. There are brief notes, a selected bibliography, briefly annotated, and a chronology of events that parallel Terence's life.

Forman, Robert J. "P. Terentius Afer." *Research Guide to Biography and Criticism: Dramatists Supplement*. Washington, D.C.: Research Publishing, 1986, pp. 622-625.
Contains a chronology and briefly annotated sections on major biographical sources, critical materials, and generally available commentaries. Though many of the entries appear in this volume, the article also lists and briefly evaluates major foreign criticism not covered herein.

Goldberg, Sander M. "Scholarship on Terence and the Fragments of Roman Comedy: 1959-1980." *Classical World* 75 (1981): 77-115.
One of the series of bibliographic surveys on various authors and topics that regularly appear in this publication. Its focus is on texts, editions, and commentaries suitable for high school and undergraduate classroom use. It also includes general works of criticism and peripheral works on drama and theater history, all works with brief evaluations and cited in continuous paragragraphs rather than as lists with annotations. Though intended for teachers, this survey is also useful for students seeking information on language texts in print and for readers who wish to consult criticism written in French, German, or Italian. It is both easier to find and includes less technical material than Cupaiuolo's survey, cited above. See also, the short survey that appears in Martin's edition of *The Brothers* (*Adelphoe*), cited above. Goldberg's survey continues the earlier work of H. Marti, *Lustrum* 6 (1961): 114-238; and 8 (1963): 5-101, 244-264.

——————. *Understanding Terence*. Princeton, N.J.: Princeton University Press, 1986.
This useful study includes an introductory chapter on the state of the Roman theater as Terence was beginning to produce his comedies, emphasizing at its conclusion the relationship of Terence and Plautus. Goldberg then examines the polemical nature of Terence's prologues, making contrasts both with Aristophanes (who often hides his argument within his plays) and with Plautus (who uses rhetorical devices such as the ascending tricolon and the indirect question to avoid tedium). There are ensuing separate chapters on "contamination" of Greek originals, complexities caused by two-tiered plots, simplicity, and moral lessons in Terence. A final chapter on the death of comedy is especially worthwhile. There is a short bibliography and close study of Terence's Latin, though Goldberg always translates extended passages, making this study accessible to generalists as well as specialists.

Gratwick, A. S. "Drama." In *The Cambridge History of Classical Literature: Volume II, Latin Literature*, edited by E. J. Kenney and W. V. Clausen. Cam-

bridge, England: Cambridge University Press, 1983, pp. 77-138.
A good essay on Terence, Plautus, and Roman drama, suitable for general readers. There are short biographies, a survey of titles, types of plots and characters, and brief discussions of the plays.

Jory, E. J. "Associations of Actors in Rome." *Hermes* 98 (1970): 224-253.
Discusses evidence for guilds among those who acted in Roman drama, concentrating on the theater of Terence. Jory notes existence of what were essentially fraternal associations of playwrights, leading and supporting actors and members of choruses, musicians, and even mimes. He notes an internal division of the guilds among those involved in creative, literary, and performance elements.

Norwood, Gilbert. *The Art of Terence*. New York: Russell and Russell, 1923, reprint 1965.
A basic and often-cited study that maintains, despite the implication of its title, a rather negative view of Terence's plays. Norwood examines the plays chronologically and is more positive on the later comedies but generally views conflation of originals as a negative rather than an improving feature. He inevitably notes what he perceives as their inferiority to the Greek originals. There are basic examinations of the extant plays and a general introduction. See above for Norwood's arguments on the individual works.

_____ . *Plautus and Terence*. Our Debt to Greece and Rome. New York: Cooper Square, 1931, reprint 1963.
This general study of these authors' influence includes basic information on their styles. Despite the implication of the title, it does not attempt any meaningful comparison of Plautus and Terence. Its Terence sections discuss moralizing style, characterization, plot structure, and basic thought. There are no extended discussions of the plays. See description of the Plautus sections of this volume, cited with general entries, above.

CLASSICAL
GREEK AND ROMAN
DRAMA

INDEX